Escape from
ALCATRAZ

Escape from
ALCATRAZ

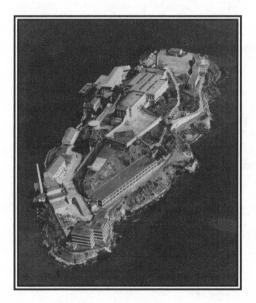

J. Campbell Bruce

TEN SPEED PRESS
Berkeley

Ten Speed Press and the Ten Speed Press colophon are registered
trademarks of Random House, Inc.

Originally published in the United States by McGraw-Hill, New York, in 1963.

Photographs in this book used with permission of the San Francisco History
Center, San Francisco Public Library. Photo from the movie *Escape from
Alcatraz* © Paramount Pictures; used with permission. Cover photo: National
Archives–Pacific Region (San Francisco).

Library of Congress Cataloging-in-Publication Data
Bruce, J. Campbell (John Campbell), 1906-
  Escape from Alcatraz / J. Campbell Bruce.
    p. cm.
  Reprint. Originally published: New York : McGraw-Hill, 1963.
  1. United States Penitentiary, Alcatraz Island, California. I. Title.
  HV9474.A4B7 2005
  365'.979461--dc22

                                   2005002738

ISBN-13: 978-1-58008-678-3

Printed in the United States of America

Text design by Chloe Rawlins
Cover design by Turner & Associates, San Francisco

14 13 12 11 10 9 8 7 6 5

First Ten Speed Press Edition

For Bianca,
who did time on this *rock.*

Above: Group posing in a fake prison cell labeled "Alcatraz," 1944.
Title page: Aerial view of Alcatraz Island, date unknown.

Contents

Foreword to the New Edition

THIS BOOK WAS FIRST PUBLISHED in 1963. Two weeks before the publication date the last prisoner was escorted off of America's Devil's Island and Alcatraz ceased to be a prison. In the ensuing years The Rock has taken on many guises. It was the locale of several Native American occupations and has become a thriving tourist destination administered by the National Park Service. It has been the subject of several movies, most notably the 1979 release *Escape from Alcatraz* starring Clint Eastwood, based on the J. Campbell Bruce book of the same name.

Both the book and the classic movie portray in spellbinding detail the daring escape attempt by Frank Morris and two accomplices. The movie was the first ever to be offered as a home-rental tape and has become a classic of the prison-film genre. It is considered by film historians to be a pivotal role in the remarkable career of Clint Eastwood.

The book is written in a terse but compelling narrative style and is easily discernable as the basis for the movie. However, there is more to the book than just Morris's dramatic escape. Woven between chapters on Morris's entrance, existence, and exit from this "inescapable" prison is a thorough chronicle of The Rock's transition from a Spanish fort into the maximum-security penitentiary that housed such infamous inmates as Robert Stroud, the Birdman of Alcatraz, and mobster exemplar, "Scarface" Al Capone.

This edition features a gallery of photographs including a scene from the movie. It invites the reader to discover the intriguing saga of Alcatraz, whose name is still synonymous with punitive isolation and deprivation where America's most violent and notorious prisoners resided in tortuous proximity to one of the world's favorite cities.

Kevin Bruce
August 2004

Acknowledgments

GRATEFUL THANKS GO TO Frances H. Buxton and Helen Willits, California Room, Oakland Public Library; Evelyn Gahtan and Miss Florence Marr, Berkeley Public Library, and the staffs of the University of California libraries and the Alameda Free Library, for their courtesies; to Sam H. Laub and Paul G. Morken, for technical advice; to Mrs. Jean V. Molleskog, U.S. Geological Survey, and Joan Bell, Carol Fisher, Kay Long, Betty Turner, Gordon Bergman, William Bronson, Ken Butler, Dale Champion, Dr. George L. Delagnes, Peter Delmas, Michael S. Gregory, Neil Hitt, Alvin D. Hyman, U.S. Deputy Marshal Alexander F. Koenig, Carl Latham, John Molinari, Robert O'Brien, Quentin Pack, John E. Peterson, Charles Raudebaugh, Dr. Robert L. Redfield, Augy Sairanen, Henry K. Thomas, William R. Whitener, and T. Robert Yamada for all their help, in many and varied ways; and to those who furnished so much, in confidence.

Chapter 1

JANUARY 14, 1960, A THURSDAY, broke dismal and drizzly over the San Francisco Bay region. The Weather Bureau had forecast a few showers in the morning, clearing in the afternoon. The showers would spill off the southern fringe of a disturbance centered in the Gulf of Alaska, spawning ground of winter storms along the Pacific Coast.

During the night the center had moved a bit southward and an hour or two after daybreak, as unexpectedly as an earthquake, the storm whiplashed the Bay Area. Gusty winds flung sheets of rain along the street, pelted hail at windshields, powdered the high peaks with snow. Commuter traffic crawled off the bridges and the Peninsula freeway, further choking the city's already clogged arteries.

The *Warden Johnston,* the boat to Alcatraz, grated against the landing at the Fort Mason dock as she rose and fell on the wind-stirred swells. She was a half hour late casting off for the nine o'clock trip to the island. The skipper glanced at the frothing whitecaps on the bay, then back at the gateway to the pier. He was waiting for an extra passenger, coming in from Georgia. The Southern Pacific's Lark, overnight train from Los Angeles, where it had made connection with the cross-country Sunset, had arrived on time, but the storm was now in full fury. At length, a black limousine rolled through the gate, the traveler came aboard, and the *Warden Johnston* pulled away.

The man from Georgia, of medium height and build, sat quietly in a cabin of the launch, staring at the rain-sloshed window. Drops of rainwater still dripped from his thick brown hair and coursed down his face, off his firm chin and strong-set jaws, but he appeared oblivious to any discomfort. His eyes, hazel eyes, held a bold, level gaze and, as any newcomer to the area, he seemed eager for his first glimpse of Alcatraz. Something about his face caught the attention: not just the good looks, not the manifest intelligence, nor even the solemnity. Something else . . . nothing, really, and therefore significant: this man, at the age of thirty-three, bore not the faintest hint of a smile line at the corners of his mouth, yet his lips had the fullness associated with an amiable nature.

A lawyer, perhaps, bound for The Rock to consult an inmate client? Looking again, lower: his hands are close together, gripped in handcuffs clamped to a padlocked chain around his waist. Looking still lower: his feet are close together, chained to leg irons.

Squalls buffeted the *Warden Johnston* as she plowed out into the bay, taking a wide loop to starboard to make a direct approach through the treacherous tide rips to the wharf on the southeastern end of the island. Seemingly, down by the bow, she plunged through the waves rather than over them, keeping the deck and the pilot-house windows awash. The grim outline of Alcatraz loomed up ahead, its massive bulk remarkably like an obsolete battleship riding at anchor, its prison and lighthouse on the crest like a superstructure and stack.

Below, the prisoner watched the formidable crag rise out of the spray and rain shroud—a granite keep at world's end—but only the curiosity of a sightseer marked his expression. His glance caught a sign on a cliff, its huge letters dimly discernible in the deluge: "KEEP OFF! Only Government Boats Permitted Within 200 Yards. Persons Entering Closer Without Authorization Do So At Their Own Risk."

The black plastic raincoat that had been thrown over his shoulders for the few steps from depot to limousine and, at the dock, for the fewer steps down to the landing float and onto the launch, now lay open. It became evident that his attire on the transcontinental trip—first-class Pullman accommodations—was the salt-and-pepper garb of a federal felon. The pants, a special pair issued at Atlanta for the journey to Alcatraz, were extra large and beltless. Thus, even though hobbled by ankle irons fettered together, should he try a dash for freedom the pants would drop and further impede flight. In addition, his shoes had been replaced at Atlanta by backless canvas slippers.

The *Warden Johnston* edged cautiously alongside the wharf and made fast. The doctor on his daily visit and other passengers debarked. Then the skipper performed a habitual security rite. He locked the wheel, went ashore, attached the key to a line and signaled the guard in a bulletproof gun tower. The guard came out to the tower rail and hauled up the key by pulley; he would keep it there until the next scheduled departure, and he would lower it then only if assured the *Warden Johnston*'s skipper was still in charge and *all* The Rock's convicts were accounted for.

The storm, worst in years, took a freakish turn as the prisoner, huddled under his black raincoat, now shuffled ashore. The *San Francisco Chronicle*'s weather story said that around 10 A.M.—just about the time the prisoner was stepping onto The Rock—lightning began to streak the sullen sky and thunder rolled like a cannonade, a phenomenon common to a humid eastern summer but rare at any season in this region.

A bolt struck the Point Bonita lighthouse on the north headland beyond the Golden Gate, disabling its radar and radio—the direct contact for Coast Guard help when a break occurs at Alcatraz. Lightning also hit a power line that blacked out communities along the Marin County shore to the north and nearby Angel Island.

The chink of the chains around his legs made a faintly musical note in the storm as the prisoner slowly climbed into a waiting bus. He glanced out at the dockyard where cargo is sifted and then passed through a metal detector—something like a doorframe with a humped sill, dubbed the Snitch Box by the convicts—before being carted to the crest. Another such detector, kept there for visitors, stood beneath a shelter at the far side. These "eyes," an Alcatraz innovation along with other advanced security devices, inspired an early inmate to characterize The Rock as "a scientific stir."

The bus labored up the narrow, tortuous road, its progress watched by the sentry in the higher tower. To return to the dockside the driver would descend by an equally twisting route carved into the southwest façade of The Rock. At the beige-colored prison on the crest a grim reception committee waited—guards in nickel-gray uniforms with maroon ties, rifles at the ready.

The prisoner, still hobbled by the leg irons, scuffled up a short flight of steps and through a granite archway to a grated door. To the right were the outer offices leading to the warden's headquarters. The turnkey, recognizing the party, opened the gate, and they stepped into a vestibule and turned left into the visitors' room. It had the cozy, inviting appearance of a windowless mezzanine lounge in a major hotel: a reddish brown rug; occasional chairs with lamps and stand-up ash trays, for visitors waiting their turn; walls tastefully done in tan and adorned with framed prints.

On this January morning only the prisoner from Atlanta and his guardians were in the room, as visiting hours were in the afternoon—the one o'clock boat over, the 3:20 back. No guard was armed now, except the sentry at the door, who carried a gasbilly, a combination metal club and tear-gas gun. The prisoner's manacles, midriff chain, and leg irons were removed, and he was ordered to strip to the skin for the ritual known as "dressing in." Just as a physician had done before his departure from Atlanta, a doctor now conducted an orifice search: ears, nose, mouth, rectum. He was probing for contraband—dope, a coded message, even a tiny tool useful in an attempt to escape.

"A convict once tried to smuggle in a watch spring in his ear," a guard remarked to a colleague. "Good to file through a bar, if you have plenty of time—and they got plenty of that here."

The prisoner, still naked, was led back into the vestibule. Directly opposite was the command post of the most important man, while on duty, in the prison—the Armorer. His station, the nerve center of The Rock, is accessible only from the exterior, and he alone can open the door. On this inner side he is sealed off by steel plate pierced with gun slots and a narrow vision panel of bulletproof glass.

The party with the prisoner in the vestibule began the complex progression into the cellhouse. They approached a barred gate, but the turnkey could not open it: a metal shield covered the lock on both sides. At a nod from the turnkey, the Armorer glanced into mirrors set at an angle and surveyed a chamber beyond the gate, then touched a button that released the shield. The turnkey opened the gate and, once they had all entered, closed it, the metal plate instantly sliding back into place.

They now confronted a solid steel door. The turnkey peered through an eye-level slit, scanned the interior, then opened the door. They passed through, and he relocked it.

They faced still a third door, barred and cross-barred, the last barrier to the cellhouse. The prisoner stared in surprise. With its high windows and skylights, and its triple-tiered cell blocks, the place vaguely resembled a vast aviary. His nostrils caught a distinctive odor, and a familiar one: the mingled scent of disinfectant, itself not unpleasant, and of men packed closely together. His surprise came in the splash of color, bright even in the murky daylight: the cell blocks were painted a shocking pink trimmed in barn red.

The naked newcomer scuffed his zori-like canvas slippers— "scooters" to the convicts—down an aisle between two cell blocks, a corridor called Broadway. His custodial guide directed him to turn right at the far end, along a lateral corridor to a stairway that took him to a basement room containing thirty-five showers. The officer on duty there noted the prisoner's tattoos: a devil's head on the upper right arm, a star on each knee, with a "7" above and an "11" below the star on the left knee. "Superstitious, eh? Any more?" The prisoner held up his left hand: a star at the base of the thumb, a "13" at the base of the index finger. The officer said, "Shower up."

The prisoner saw a single knob at each shower, indicating a single cold stream. He must have heard of this: stories of Alcatraz escapes usually mentioned how the convicts conditioned themselves with daily showers of frigid salt water pumped out of the bay. And, like most newcomers, he could well have fitted it into nebulous plans for an eventual getaway: a perfect conditioner to endure the icy waters, ranging from 51° to 60° Fahrenheit off Alcatraz, as he swam or paddled a makeshift raft. As others had, he braced himself under a shower head and turned it on full force for a quick drenching, to get the shock over with fast. He was shocked, but not by a chilling impact. The water was warm. It was premixed, the hot and the cold, by a guard at the end of the row.

After the shower he received a set of fresh clothes, including a pair of shoes. As he walked in the heavy square-tipped shoes along the lateral corridor toward Broadway again, he skidded on the cement, waxed and polished to the glossiness of a ballroom floor. He climbed a circular steel stairway at the west end of C Block to the middle tier and found his cell, the second, by the nameplate already on the door:

FRANK LEE MORRIS

The cell was in the quarantine section, and he would remain there for a week or two, until assigned a job.

Inmates delivered his regular issue: another set of clothing, from long cotton drawers to denim trousers and shirt, gray flecked with white; five more pairs of socks and a large handkerchief that looked as if it had been snipped out of a blue bed sheet; a safety-razor holder and shaving mug; a tin cup; a nailclip; a mirror; a face towel; toothbrush and dental powder; a mattress and cover, two sheets, one pillow case. An instant after the officer left with the inmates the cell door slid shut, locked. All cells were opened and closed, singly or in units up to fifteen, by guards at manual control boxes at either end of a block.

Frank Lee Morris, bank burglar and escape artist, stood at his cell front, staring down at the lustrous corridor floor. He was alone now, for the first time since he had left Atlanta to serve his remaining ten years at this super-maximum-security prison at Alcatraz. And super-maximum security is the word. From the moment he debarked at the wharf until he reached this cell, everywhere he turned there stood a guard. In all the institutions he had at one time or another called home, he had never seen so many custodial officers.

His open-faced manner gave the impression of casual interest, but whatever his glance fell upon, no matter how fleetingly, that object—man or thing—was instantly, expertly cased. He had a computer's ability to take in and store away detail, infinite detail.

Quiet, soft-spoken, Morris was essentially a loner, a recluse in a crowd. Yet on the surface he appeared personable, cooperative. At times he even seemed to make a shy overture of fellowship. These infrequent displays of camaraderie could be merely the patina of half a lifetime of enforced gregariousness in the lockstep of prison herds; or they could be the pathetic, smothered yearnings of a profound inner loneliness.

He turned away from his contemplation of mirror-bright Broadway and took stock of his new home, five feet wide by eight feet long. The rear wall was concrete, the side walls, sheets of steel. Only the barred front admitted light and air. He gripped one of the short, thick uprights between the stout crossbars. He did not know that these upright bars—cores of cable embedded in toughest alloy steel—supposedly could resist the most persistent saw or file, but he did not need to know: they had the feel of resistibility.

He considered the fixtures. A steel cot that could fold against the wall ran along the right side. At its foot—or its head, if the cellhouse lights bothered the inmate—was the toilet, without a lid or a seat. Bolted into the opposite wall were two steel folding shelves, at separate levels, for use as a seat and table top or desk. On the left rear wall was a washbowl with a single cold-water faucet; over it, at five- and six-foot heights, ran two wooden shelves for personal effects, and beneath them wooden pegs to hang clothes.

His roving eye caught an item near the base of the rear wall, to the right of the washbasin: a metal ventilator grille. Too small—about six by ten inches—to crawl through even if the grille could be pried loose, and a quick inspection revealed that it was tightly wedded to the concrete.

From the moment a convict sets foot on the Alcatraz wharf, he has, according to the guards, one consuming thought: how to get off. And the prison's physical complexity, the door after door blocking the intricate entrance passage, the multiplicity of guards, the solidity of walls and bars, the entombing security of the cell add up, for the new prisoner, to one despairing question: *How in the name of God can anyone possibly get out of here?*

Frank Lee Morris, the quiet, courteous young man with the handsome features, was to find an answer; no newspaper had reported his arrival, but he would leave in a blaze of front-page banner lines. And in so doing, he would call into question the very existence of the federal government's super-maximum-security prison at Alcatraz.

Chapter 2

THE SANDSTONE OUTCROPPING in San Francisco Bay that received Morris on that stormy January day in 1960 seems an island as dreary as the fog in which it is so often enveloped. But its history has been, if not edifying, certainly colorful. The island has been by turns a menace, an invitation, and a challenge to human beings ever since its discovery by Europeans in the late eighteenth century.

For almost two centuries after Sir Francis Drake first sailed up the West Coast in 1579, fog hid the Golden Gate from seafaring explorers. Alcatraz, facing the sea, was discovered by land. In the fall of 1769—the year a Scot, James Watt, invented the steam engine and revolutionized industry—Don Gaspar de Portolá, on an overland march from Mexico, scaled a peak and stared down at San Francisco Bay.

Not until 1775, about the time Paul Revere was galloping out of Boston, did the Golden Gate open in welcome to seafarers poking along the coast. On a clear afternoon that summer three Spanish vessels dropped anchor in a sheltering cove inside the heads. The next morning, August 5, seven weeks after the Battle of Bunker Hill, Don Juan Manuel de Ayala, in charge of a scouting party, maneuvered the first boat through the mile-wide passage. Directly ahead a bleak, barren mass of rock jutted out of the bay, covered as if frosted with white pelicans that stared curiously down their pouchy beaks at the intruders. Don Juan christened it *La Isla de los Alcatraces*. Later known as Bird Island and, from the snowy flocks, White Island, in time the Spanish singular for pelican, Alcatraz, took hold. (*Alcatraz* is a Spanish offshoot of an Arabic word ancient alchemists used to express the recovery of precious substances from a retort.) Don Juan turned to a neighboring isle that, by its verdant contrast, offered more hospitality. He named this *La Isla de Nuestra Señora de los Angeles*— the Island of Our Lady of the Angels—later Anglicized into the present Angel Island.

Alcatraz, lying three miles in from the headlands at the Pacific, passed through three hands—Spanish, Mexican, American—in the next seventy-five years before anyone ventured to set foot on its precipitous shores. And in the century since, fantasy, as well as fog, has frequently enveloped the island. Some years ago a web-spinner wove this colorful bit of fabric:

"Spanish authorities found an advantage in the island's inaccessibility. They tunneled the rock into dungeons and confined rebellious American settlers there, along with army deserters.

"Alcatraz was seized by the Americans in 1847 following the proclamation of the Bear Flag Republic. The settlers who had rebelled against the tyrannical Spanish rule were freed, and the dispossessed authorities placed in the cells in their stead."

Few, if any, Americans ever found their way to California when it was an outpost of the Spanish Empire. While the Americans were engaged in founding their own Republic, the brown-robed, benevolent Franciscan Padres trailblazed the celebrated El Camino Real in California. The briefer Mexican rule over California, remote from the troubled political scene of Mexico City, was memorable for its legendary fiestas at the haciendas of the vast ranchos, family domains held under Spanish crown grants.

For a time, after the Treaty of Guadalupe Hidalgo ceded California and New Mexico to the United States in 1848, another fog—that of title—hung over Alcatraz. One Julian Workman claimed that Pio Pico, Mexican governor of California, granted him the island in 1846 on condition that "he cause to be established as soon as possible a light which may give protection on dark nights to the ships which may pass there." Workman, after a closer look at Alcatraz, caused no light to be established; instead, he gave the pelican roost to a son-in-law who, equally dismayed by Pio Pico's conditional clause, conveyed it for $5,000 to General John C. Frémont, then military governor of

California and later first Republican Party candidate for President. The public-spirited Frémont took possession as an agent of the United States and President Millard Fillmore by executive order reserved Alcatraz for public purposes.

San Francisco had already embraced Alcatraz. The *ayuntamiento*—as, in happy remembrance of Mexican days, they still called the municipal government—had adopted a charter that extended the city limits over the bay one league from shore "including the islands of Yerba Buena, Los Angeles and Alcantraz[*sic*]." (Yerba Buena, linked to Treasure Island, is the island through which the Bay Bridge passes, by tunnel.)

The Gold Rush brought heavy maritime traffic, and by 1850 the bay was cluttered with sailing vessels that streamed through the Golden Gate bearing fortune-fevered passengers, and crews, bound for the fabulous Mother Lode. The need for a beacon on Alcatraz became urgent and that fall Congress authorized the fulfillment of Pio Pico's old dream. But from Act to action, then as now, a long interval stretched. The military decided the harbor itself needed safeguarding with batteries at the points at the Gate and, in the event a man-of-war might survive that gantlet of cross fire, a fortress on Alcatraz. The Army Engineers, surveying the task in 1854, found the island an irregular oblong running southeast to northwest, 450 feet across, 1,650 feet long, in all 11.9 acres. Its mesa top, 136 feet above mean tide, sloped off to precipices, some a sheer seventy-five-foot drop to the water. Soundings revealed a depth offshore varying from twenty to eighty feet, and something else: Alcatraz did not spread out to a broad base like a normal peak; centuries of tide rips, the turbulence of ebb and flood tides colliding beneath the surface, had eroded the underpart to the shape of a spindle. They also found the island destitute of soil and vegetation, but not of pelican guano.

By 1859, at a cost of about a million dollars, Fort Alcatraz and Alcatraz Light were a reality—the first American fortification and lighthouse on the West Coast. The latter, soaring 160 feet above the bay (then the tallest man-made structure west of Cape Hatteras), boasted a lantern visible twelve miles at sea, almost halfway to the

Farrallones, islands visible on a clear day to the lightkeeper. Cannon of immense caliber—something called columbiads, from the War of 1812—could hurl 120-pound shot through the Gate. In addition to these fearful five-ton muzzleloaders, just in case a sneaky foe slipped in under their dread snouts, close-range barbette batteries stood ready to hold the ramparts. And to prevent the landing of an assault force, the engineers blasted the only gentle slope, on the southeastern end, into a cliff. In the unlikely event that a party might storm ashore at any of the coves, a three-story citadel commanded the crest and from its parapets musketry fire could rake the cliff tops clear. The musketeers smiled down on the mighty columbiads.

Relics of that proud fortress remain. Ballast granite from China that buttressed the citadel's portal graces the entrance to the warden's office. The blue sandstone facing of the blockhouse that guarded the wharf forms part of a warehouse with the cornerstone inscription, "Alcatraces 1857." Some of the powder magazine, supply vaults, and 50,000-gallon cisterns bored in the solid rock serve as storage space for the prison.

No foe ever challenged Fort Alcatraz, and in less than a decade it was obsolete. The Civil War, as wars invariably do, produced radical changes in weaponry. The Army Engineers demolished the citadel, whose frowning parapets were now derided as "pretentious bastions," and built a new fortification with walls twelve feet thick and quarters underground for the garrison officers.

Even before this swift fate the majestic fortress, for want of a martial mission, had begun to assume a less noble aspect. In its very first year—a year of grandeur that had spectators gazing in wonder from the hills of San Francisco—Fort Alcatraz quartered a few prisoners from mainland posts, in a wooden shack in the shadow of the citadel. At that time Alcatraz, if not escape-proof, was awesome enough to discourage an attempt.

Civil War prisoners began to dribble in after 1861, and in the fall of 1867 a brick building replaced the shack. A year later the War Department, doubtful that the guns of Fort Alcatraz would ever bark in anger, designated the island as a prison for long-term military offenders and incorrigibles. And The Rock officially began its long career as a bastille.

That career was as checkered as that of any of the men confined there. In the 1870s Alcatraz took the "orneriness" out of intractable Indian chiefs from the Territories of Arizona and Alaska. During the Spanish-American War, The Rock assumed the added role of a health resort: soldiers returning from the Philippines with tropical diseases were taken there to convalesce, along with soldiers who had crossed the Pacific on the same boat, in the brig. The influx of culprits from that conflict so overtaxed Alcatraz that presidential pardons were handed down by the fistful to reduce the congestion. When San Francisco lost its jail in the 1906 catastrophe, the 176 inmates were removed, temporarily, to Alcatraz. (The earthquake broke the cable to the island but did no damage to The Rock itself.) During World War I still a new class of tenants arrived—enemy aliens and espionage agents.

In 1909 the prison building in use today was erected on the site of the old citadel, resting on the solid masonry of the cisterns, the supply vaults, and garrison quarters carved in the rock—a foundation that did double duty as the foundation for the legend of the Spanish dungeons. It was built by the prisoners, at a cost of $250,000, plus the cost of their labor, $191,498.20.

By an Act of Congress in 1907 Alcatraz became the Pacific Branch of the United States Military Prison. That impressive status, along with the disturbing effect of the huge new cellhouse, kindled agitation to remove this penal stronghold from San Francisco's aquatic front yard, an agitation that erupts perennially, always for the same reasons: economic and esthetic. Congress, fretting over its high cost, in 1914 debated turning Alcatraz into a West Coast Ellis Island on the assumption that the opening of the Panama Canal would bring "a large stream of European immigrants" direct to San Francisco.

San Francisco, espousing the esthetic view, once found a surprising ally in the Army's Judge Advocate General, whose concern however was based on a military, rather than civic, pride. In a report to Congress in 1913 he deplored the infamous nature of Alcatraz as a tourist attraction: "It's more the subject of inquiry than any other object in the harbor. The answer they receive, that it is a prison for confinement of our military offenders, gives an impression of the character of our enlisted personnel and of the discipline of our army, which is unfair and unjust to the service."

Congress, impressed, pondered the matter for several years, then denatured Alcatraz by converting it into the Pacific Branch, United States Disciplinary Barracks. This was more than a mere euphemism. With serious offenders packed off to a federal penitentiary, the milder species of malefactor left on The Rock joined disciplinary companies, doing the work of soldiers, not convicts. The aim: reformation. If a commanding officer felt a man wanted to make good, he was restored to Army duty. While civilian prisons were racked by riots, The Rock hummed with industry. As an example of their efficiency, the soldier-prisoners in the late twenties built a Class-A, concrete, three-story structure—in use until recently as the Model Shop Building—at a cost of $150,000. An astonishing record was achieved: 89 percent of the men returned to active service made good, a credit to their regiment. The key was the certainty of discipline, without malice or favoritism. Penologists the world over came to the island, went away singing encomiums. Alcatraz was enjoying the finest reputation of its penal history.

Chapter 3

IN THE EARLY THIRTIES shock waves of panic swept the country. The gangster era, spawn of Prohibition, was in full blaze. No one minded much when a beer baron sieved a rival and dumped him coffined in cement into a river. It helped to decimate the underworld and made good newspaper copy.

But the evil spread beyond the bootleg traffic and the rackets. A new hoodlum element strapped on guns and strode forth. The Dillingers, the Baby Face Nelsons, and the Machine Gun Kellys. Rock-hard, ruthless. Outlaws of the Old West incarnate. Their stock in trade: bank holdups, kidnapings. Their tommyguns beat a rat-tat-tat of slaughter that echoed in big black type, and their outsized egos gorged on the scare banner lines.

They barged into homes and packed off adults, reaping fortunes in ransom. They made hit-run forays: an Illinois bank in the morning, an Indiana bank in the afternoon. Local authorities were helpless; the FBI, lacking jurisdiction, was stymied. Terror seized the people: where would a gang strike next? . . . in what town? . . . what home? Citizens of one Midwest community organized a vigilante group, loaded their hunting rifles, manned a concrete blockhouse across the street from the bank.

Congress acted. And on the scene came the now legendary G-men. Many fell in pitched battles, but in a remarkably short time they brought the gangster to his knees. Everyone rejoiced, except wardens. The gangster, an animal caged, proved too tough for his keeper to handle. The FBI had shifted the problem from the helpless constable to the helpless jailer.

A superbastille seemed the only solution; a special lockup to quarantine these mad dogs, as they were branded; something along the line of a Devil's Island. This would permit wardens elsewhere to pursue their work of rehabilitating the redeemable, unhampered by these disturbers and the long-termers bent on escape. The Justice Department began searching for a site. Penologists voiced misgivings, but their warnings were whispers in a canyon: unheard, or unheeded.

The hunt for a perfect site for a super-lockup ended when the War Department announced in 1933 it was abandoning its Disciplinary Barracks on Alcatraz. The Justice Department took over, and Attorney General Homer S. Cummings asked James A. Johnston of San Francisco to set it up and take charge. Johnston seemed an odd choice as ruler of The Rock. Gentle-voiced and mild of manner, bespectacled, white-haired, he had more the look of a Latin professor, emeritus. This scholarly air contrasted incongruously the self-assurance he expressed: "I believe I know precisely what the Federal Government expects of me and that I can live up to the government's expectations." He was a banker and civic leader, twice president of the Commonwealth Club of California, but he had an earlier background to support his confidence. As a young department store clerk, he had studied law at night, entered politics, and won a seat on San Francisco's Board of Supervisors. He was catapulted into the field of penology in 1912 when the governor picked him to clean up Folsom, the state's prison for hardened criminals and scene of reported barbaric practices. Johnston's work in pulling Folsom out of the Middle Ages earned him a reputation as a humanitarian. The next year he became warden of San Quentin, retiring in 1925 to practice law and banking in San Francisco.

The Rock became largely Johnston's creation. He replaced the soft iron bars on most of the cells and the cellhouse windows with tool-proof steel. He installed automatic locking devices and tear-gas outlets, gun galleries at either end of the cellhouse, and an outside gunwalk along the south windows of the mess hall. He put steel doors on the utility alleys between the banks of each cell block and sealed off the tops of the blocks to the convicts. He erected gun towers, set other towers on roofs, and gun boxes on the yard wall, and connected them with catwalks. He set gates with electric locks, controlled by tower guards, in the roads to the shops. He enclosed the entire prison area with a cyclone fence topped by barbed wire. He put bars on the sewers. And he established a 200-yard keep-out zone around The Rock, marked by orange-hued tank buoys. It all added up, beyond doubt, to an escapeproof, super-maximum-security prison. It was he who scattered metal detectors about so that a convict would have to pass through them at least eight times a day. And it was he who devised the Armorer system of control over the interior of the prison.

The Armorer, in his vault sealed on the inner side, accessible only from outside the prison, enjoys virtual omniscience about what is going on in the cell blocks. Microphones hidden about the prison relay sounds to him day and night. If a phone is off a hook for more than fifteen seconds a bulb lights on his board, and he dispatches an officer to investigate. He receives for the record twelve official counts a day of the inmate population (there are some thirty additional, special counts), and if a count reveals a prisoner missing he radios the Coast Guard and the San Francisco police. In the event of a riot or break, he hits the siren button to summon off-duty personnel and distributes weapons from an arsenal in his vault—rifles, pistols, submachine guns, gas grenades, ammunition.

The complicated array of gadgets through which a turnkey leads a new convict into the prison are even more complicated in the procedure of getting out.

In the reverse steps, the turnkey leads the way through the barred gate and the solid steel door into the middle chamber. Then he must buzz the Armorer, who scans the situation through his mirrors. If he sees a lone prisoner—or a prisoner standing suspiciously behind the officer—the Armorer lets the shield remain over the keyhole and throws a switch that clangs shut an emergency door of solid steel. The chamber becomes a trap.

To keep Alcatraz escapeproof, and to keep its desperate charges in line, called for exceptional custodial personnel. Guards were handpicked from the staffs at other federal penitentiaries—men selected for efficiency, intelligence, incorruptibility. Crack shots, they were trained in a military style to combat readiness; trained in the art of judo, then further trained in ways to cope with unruly troublemakers, to match wits with plotters. The Rock required one guard to every three inmates, compared to a one-to-ten ratio in other prisons. Johnston, pleased with the custodial force he gathered together, used what was purported to be an anonymous convict's censored letter to indicate the quality of the officers—a strange letter that, if typical, seemed further to indicate that Alcatraz was not the dread Devil's Island it was reputed to be, and that its inmates were well above the level of mad dogs: "Another thing of which I approve highly is that the guards and the prisoners are not allowed to fraternize together. This does away with having to meet one another socially . . . and does away with a great deal of friction with which most other prisons must contend. The guards, too, have affected me favorably. I expected to meet a group of martinets that cracked the whip instead of using their brains. So far they have been extremely polite and have used patience and instructions instead of the orders and growls one would expect."[1]

The Rock's scheme of discipline conceived by Johnston, with its emphasis on certainty, rather than severity, of punishment without favoritism, was reminiscent of the predecessor Disciplinary Barracks, but the similarity ended there. Alcatraz held to the principle of punishment, not reformation, with nothing to be gained by obedience to rules, everything to lose by their violation. The rules fixed perhaps the most relentlessly rigid routine of any American prison in this century. Most talked about the rule of silence. No one could speak, unless absolutely necessary: to request a tool in the shop, or the salt at a meal. Chitchat meant the dungeon.

The food was good, and any man might heap his plate to match a Gargantuan appetite, but woe unto him who left so much as a sizable crumb. First offense, he skipped the next meal; a repeat offense, ten days in the dungeon on bread and water.

---

[1] This letter was quoted by Warden Johnston in his book, *Alcatraz and the Men Who Live There*, published in 1949, after his retirement. (New York: Charles Scribner's Sons).

Even the garb had a punitive quality: coveralls, apparel the men resented almost as much as the silence. There was no commissary, no candy bars; the one concession here was a sack of tobacco once a week, except in solitary where smoking was forbidden, but not as a safety measure. There were no trusties, no bonaroo jobs as elsewhere. There was no honor system as an incentive to good conduct, no inmate council to consult with the administration on such matters as library purchases or educational activities. The men were confined in single cells, to enforce silence and discourage homosexuality. In the evening they could read censored literature, write letters, or study University of California Extension courses, in the eerie quiet of a school for deaf mutes. During a recreation period in the yard on Sunday afternoon, closely supervised to prevent fraternizing, the men could sit on concrete steps, or stand, or walk, or play softball, a game also closely watched to stifle competitive instincts as part of the overall design to deflate the criminal ego. If a convict could afford an instrument, and preferred the solace of music to the outdoors, he could spend his weekly recreation period practicing harmony, or discord, in a basement room.

Everyone from felon's mother to the attorney general must undergo an electronic frisking in the metal detector at the dockyard. He first steps into an adjacent office to register in a big ledger, along with the exact time of arrival, and to empty his pockets of all coins, keys, fountain pens. If he wears glasses, they come off. He then goes out to the shelter, walks through the frame and back again. Inside, an officer watches an oscilloscope for a dancing green line and listens for a raucous buzzer—signals that somewhere on or in the visitor's body a metallic object still resides.

At the cellhouse, the visitors' room is pleasant enough, but there is no mistaking the nature of the institution. Along the prison side runs a low, wide shelf with a half-dozen armchairs spaced about a foot apart, and there relatives talk to inmates and lawyers confer with clients. At each place, set off by wedges of plate glass, is an intercom box, and above it, deeply niched into the thick wall, a small window with a bulletproof pane, through which the caller beholds the convict and a monitoring guard. In the early days a visitor spoke through two perforated strips of steel set in the base of the window, the tiny holes offset to prevent passage of contraband. A metallic diaphragm transmitted only firm voices so that no whispered message got past the eavesdropping guards.

This necessarily strict routine could sometimes be disconcerting. Al Capone's mother once paid a call. As she stepped through the metal detector the green line danced and the buzzer sounded. The officer took her purse and directed her to try it again. The reaction was just as frantically telltale. He summoned the associate warden's wife, who escorted Mrs. Capone to a room where it was discovered she was wearing corsets with metal stays. She removed them, and the electronic eye let her pass. Bewildered, she rode up to the prison where she seemed even more confused by the guard standing over her, urging her to speak louder—and in English only. She never came back.

The process of ego deflation that reached into sports began with the "dressing in" ritual upon a prisoner's arrival, as related by Johnston: "I never saw a naked man yet who could maintain any sort of dignity. There is very little egotism left in a man when you parade him before other men in his birthday suit."

In his memoirs, Warden Johnston wrote of the Federal Government's expectations of him: "They wanted everything tight, firm, strict, but they wanted to make sure that we could at the same time be just, decent and humane in our treatment of inmates. What it boiled down to in essence was that Alcatraz would be a prison of maximum-security custody with minimum privileges."

Three years after The Rock's founding, Johnston, perhaps in a delayed response to the critics of this penal concept, told a reporter in a rare interview: "Alcatraz as a civil prison is an experiment which may have its effect on prison systems throughout the world. We get only the most perplexing problems—problems for the most part which cannot be solved in other prisons."

The dungeon—in convict jargon the Dark Hole—was one solution to these problems at Alcatraz. Johnston wrote that the brick walls of these rough-floored basement cells "were often damp," due to their proximity to the old water cisterns. "They were dungeons," he said, "but they were not Spanish, though they were bad enough and I did not like them. They were badly located, poorly constructed and unsafe, because they were easy to dig out of and in the few instances when we did use them we had to chain the men to keep them from breaking out and running amuck."

Even though the men had to be chained to the cold, damp walls of the dungeon—painted black to deepen the inkiness—there remained what the warden termed "a decent regard for the humanities." No man was kept in a dungeon cell for more than nineteen days at a stretch. At the end of that period, he was removed for a day, to break the monotony, and to get a shower, before resuming his solitary confinement.

The Rock, then, was created as a laboratory for an experiment in penology: to reduce to the size of ordinary people the era's arch-desperadoes, felons labeled by the old *Literary Digest* as "the most incorrigible incorrigibles." Johnston felt the experiment was a success from the start, as he related in the three-years-afterward interview: "We have some tough customers, but I believe we have whittled them down to their proper size. We have brought all of them to the realization that they are not as big as they thought they were." A random sampling of the whittling would seem to bear him out:

Harvey Bailey, who drew life with Machine Gun Kelly for the Urschel kidnaping, boasted: "Everything's okay, just as long as they didn't crack my neck. No prison will ever hold me." Alcatraz did.

Al Capone came defiant from Atlanta, where he had fattened on special foods and smoked his favorite cigars, enjoyed a radio and conferred with his underworld henchmen. He left a babbling idiot.

Alvin (Old Creepy) Karpis, of the Midwest's Barker-Karpis kidnap gang, bragged he could break his way out of bars anywhere. After a quarter century on The Rock, he went to McNeil Island Penitentiary near Tacoma, a reward for good behavior.

Getting The Rock and its custodians ready for the remnants of the gangster era was an arduous task, but at length inaugural day came, August 18, 1934. On that sunny morning Attorney General

Cummings and Warden Johnston co-hosted an open house for the press—a limited hospitality before Alcatraz was closed to public scrutiny. (No newspaperman was permitted on the island again until a late Saturday night twelve years later, at the end of the Battle of Alcatraz.) At a brief ceremony on the steps to the entrance of the prison, Johnston, as newsreel cameras whirred, said to Cummings, "Mr. Attorney General, Alcatraz is ready."

Cummings told the reporters: "Alcatraz is a necessary part of the government's campaign against predatory crime. Certain types of prisoners are a constant menace. They create an atmosphere of tension and unrest whenever they are confined. They break down the morale of the more promising inmates and are constantly plotting violence, sabotage, riot, or escape." And, in prophesy or in reply to the penologists, he said: "This prison is one of our pet projects . . . a vital part of our work of segregating prisoners. We are looking forward to great things from Alcatraz."

Newsmen were impressed with what they saw. One account ran: "Alcatraz, at last transformed into the impregnable fortress it always had appeared to be, is Uncle Sam's most potent answer to the crime wave. This new and astonishing prison is designed to subjugate a new type of criminal. . . . It was made clear that the prisoners, the most vicious and desperate in the country, will not escape from Alcatraz."

Chapter 4

THE FIRST SHIPMENT of convicts to Alcatraz packed all the drama inherent in any hush-hush operation. Newsmen at the island that August day when Warden Johnston pronounced The Rock ready could elicit no hint as to when the new tenants might be expected, their identity, or from what prison they would be drawn.

That same midnight, on the other side of the continent, a special train backed into the yard of the federal penitentiary at Atlanta. It was a short train: a baggage car, diner, Pullman, club car, two coaches with barred windows. One at a time, the chosen convicts were routed out of their cells, hustled into the visitors' room, stripped, searched orifically from ears to rectum, garbed in loose-fitting outfits that included beltless trousers and backless slippers, manacled to a chain girdle, fettered in leg irons, then prodded aboard the coaches. In all, fifty-three. The train pulled out of the Atlanta yard before dawn on its long, secret journey. Guards patrolled the aisles; others manned machine guns at the vestibules. The convict train roared past stations. To change crews, or take on fuel and water, it rolled into a yard well away from any depot. Even then guards patrolled both sides to keep the curious, attracted by the window bars, at a distance of twenty yards.

Warden Johnston said these elaborate precautions were amply justified. Many of the passengers had escape records, even to leaping from trains. Fresh in memory were the exploits of Roy Gardner, the mail bandit, who on two occasions, while being escorted with another felon to McNeil Island, managed to swap roles with the deputy marshals and jump from the Pullman compartment, leaving his dismayed guardians in manacles and Oregon boots.

More compelling, Johnston said, were rumors that mobster pals of the Rock-bound convicts planned to ambush the train. Only ten months earlier gunmen tried to free gangster Frank Nash at Kansas City's Union Station, slaying four federal agents and Nash. Harvey Bailey, implicated in the massacre, had as a federal prisoner broken out of the Dallas jail with a saw and pistol smuggled in to him. Bailey was aboard the next special.

At Benicia, on the Carquinez Straits, the train swung onto a seldom-used branch line to Tiburon, north of Alcatraz. There the two coaches were shunted onto a railroad barge and towed under Coast Guard convoy to The Rock in what became known as a "store door" delivery. The convicts trudged up the winding road to the prison, some on bare feet too swollen for the loose slippers. They arrived, as Johnston put it, "hot, dirty, weary, unshaved, depressed, desperate, showing plainly that they felt they were at the end of the trail." And when the last of the batch had been locked into a cell, Johnston shot off a cryptic wire to Attorney General Cummings: FIFTY-THREE CRATES FURNITURE FROM ATLANTA RECEIVED IN GOOD CONDITION, INSTALLED, NO BREAKAGE.

Several weeks later the special train came in from mid-continent, and Johnston's coded wire announced: ONE HUNDRED THREE CRATES FURNITURE RECEIVED FROM LEAVENWORTH IN GOOD CONDITION, NO BREAKAGE, ALL INSTALLED.

Alcatraz was in business, to test a penal theory the French were already considering a failure at Devil's Island.

Among the convicts who broke in The Rock were names once emblazoned across front pages—Al Capone, Machine Gun Kelly, Roy Gardner, Bugs Moran, John Paul Chase. Despite the elaborate precautions to assure secrecy, press boats hovered as near as Coast Guard cutters permitted that morning the group arrived from Atlanta. News services had spotted the train roaring through Texas and had reported Capone aboard: his well-publicized face had been recognized, grinning, at a barred window. Queried about the Chicago mobster, Attorney General Cummings had said: "That's one point on which all the newspapers are wrong. Capone is not headed for

Alcatraz. That's all I can say at this time, since we never discuss such matters."

Roy Gardner, mail-train bandit, made The Rock not because he was vicious, a troublemaker, or a long-termer, but as a tribute to his escape artistry. A stocky, muscular man seemingly without nerves, Gardner, for all his headlined notoriety, had a surprisingly gentle nature. Even in his train robberies, among the more spectacular of criminal pursuits, he backed the railway postal clerks into a corner with a revolver that held imitation, pinewood slugs. Between prison terms Gardner plied his mechanic's trade, a model family man, until seized by an impulse to rob a train, aberrations attributed to a piece of shrapnel that pierced his skull in France during World War I. When shipped to Alcatraz, Gardner had less than three years still to serve. He was perhaps the one inmate most respected by other convicts.

Gardner in all likelihood was the only convict who ever helped tighten the security setup of The Rock. He invented a receiving cage in the vegetable room below the kitchen that made escape from the basement impossible. Vegetables and other supplies came down a chute from the outside. Gardner rigged up a device like a crab trap that allowed things to come down but nothing, including a convict, to go up.

In a sense, Alcatraz was a homecoming for John Paul Chase. On clear Sunday afternoons in the yard he could gaze to the Marin shore at hilly Sausalito, whose streets he roamed as a boy. A product of Prohibition, he grew up with a feeling for adventure. He went to the mountains to work in a state fish hatchery near the hamlet of Mt. Shasta, but found nursing baby trout too tame for a restless nature. Returning to the Bay Area, he became a rumrunner, an exciting and, in the warped thinking of that extremely wet Dry Era, a romantic calling. Then came the gangsters and Chase jumped into the big time as Baby Face Nelson's lieutenant, the restlessness of youth now an arrogant swagger. Two G-men died breaking up that gang at the Battle of Barrington, a Chicago suburb, in November 1934. Nelson was slain. Chase, a Public Enemy, his fingertips burned by acid to mar prints, slipped through a massive dragnet, hitchhiked west by the northern route and reached Mt. Shasta the day after Christmas—as Mr. Elmer Rockwood, tourist. A small lapse tripped him up. He went out to the hatchery to borrow twenty dollars from an old coworker. The foreman spotted him, tipped off the police chief.

A federal court jury in Chicago convicted him of murder on the night of March 26, 1935. Sentenced to life imprisonment, he was whisked away, destination a secret. Newspapers hinted he had gone to Leavenworth for "seasoning" before removal to Alcatraz. This was the announced policy of the Federal Bureau of Prisons, as restated by Warden Johnston to an interviewer in May 1937: "No prisoner is ever sentenced directly to Alcatraz. All have been transferred from other institutions as incorrigible or to break up prison gangs." Chase had apparently slipped his mind: four days after his sentencing Chase was on The Rock.

A year later, still untamed, Chase was a leader in the first revolt of The Rock. Many sojourns in solitary, and long years of the exacting Alcatraz routine, went into the deflation of the Chase ego. And then one day in 1951, in a San Francisco department store, his boyhood Sausalito friends saw evidence of a remarkable change in John Paul Chase. On exhibit were art works offered for sale as a contribution to the American Cancer Society, and a particularly arresting self-portrait captivated patrons—arresting because of the unconventional pose: an artist awkwardly painting in handcuffs and wearing, not the traditional smock, but a gray shirt with a number. The signature, J. P. Chase. John Paul Chase, Public Enemy, had become J. P. Chase, artist, donating his handiwork to the cause of cancer research—five canvases that netted about $300.

Art as therapy was clearly discernible in the development of Chase as an artist. At the outset he leaned bitterly toward prison scenes, unrelenting in their harsh lines; as his skill grew he lifted his vision beyond his bleak environment. He captured on canvas all that his eyes could behold: a series of thirty-five oils that formed a continuous panorama of the San Francisco Bay Area, as seen from Alcatraz Island.

Machine Gun Kelly, for all the hard ring of the name, settled quietly into the routine of The Rock. He and Harvey Bailey strode one summer evening in 1933 onto the porch of an Oklahoma City home where Charles Urschel, an oilman, and his wife were playing bridge with friends. The gunmen abducted both men, freeing the guest when they made certain which was Urschel. Handcuffed and blindfolded, the millionaire rode all night on the floor of a car to a hideout, where he was held until payment of a $200,000 ransom nine days later. Here too a small detail led to capture. Urschel had noted the time of day a mail plane flew overhead, twice daily, and that it had skipped a trip. FBI agents, checking which plane had flown off course that day, tracked down the hideout, a farm near Dallas.

Kelly, a college man, became a cobbler on The Rock, later a shop bookkeeper. "He was tall, well built, a little gray when I knew him, and he walked very erect, a distinguished air about him, like a banker," says a former guard. "I got a kick out of him poring over his ledger. Once he came up three cents short, spent hours going over the figures and we had to drag him off to his cell. Next day he was at it again. Found the three cents, by God."

In those days, The Rock's most notorious tenant was Alphonse Capone, dethroned czar of the Chicago underworld. For years Scarface Capone had gotten away with murders, but not until he stopped off in Philadelphia one day en route from his winter palace in Florida did he see the inside of a jail. He drew a year, for a rap that had him bewildered: carrying a gun. This was a tool of his trade, like a plumber carrying a wrench. Equally bewildering was the ten-year federal rap as a tax dodger. He pouted, entering Atlanta, "This is a funny kind of justice."

For Capone, the move to Alcatraz was like checking out of the Waldorf into a cave. No Corona Coronas; only roll-your-own, and he had fat thumbs. No old cronies to visit him; only Mae, his blonde wife, once a month for forty minutes, the time limit then; and she would squeeze in two visits on each trip from Florida, by arriving in San Francisco toward the end of a month. None of those niceties that $20,000,000 could buy. Sanford Bates, then federal prison director, called Warden Johnston one day: what was this he heard on the radio?—Capone ordering silk underwear from a London haberdasher.

"That's funny," said Johnston. "I just left Capone and I distinctly remember he was wearing regulation long johns because they were held up with a safety pin."

The food was all right, but not what *he* would order, none of the gourmet dishes he sent for at Atlanta. And the job, a real laugh. Dry cleaning and laundry. He'd got his start in the Chicago rackets by organizing the dry-cleaning industry—*his* way. Alcatraz did that work for military posts in the area and soldiers began bragging in letters home how Al Capone was doing their laundry. The warden, who knew that any detail relating to his charges was grist for columnists and strove to keep their activities a secret as part of the ego-deflating process, heard about that. He promptly reassigned Capone to mopping up the shower room and toilets.

The thing about Alcatraz that bugged Capone most was the enforced silence. He had been a compulsive talker, a big, expansive talker, around a cigar. At the outset, walking into the mess hall, he began jabbering over his shoulder to the convict behind him. Ten days in the dungeon. He began talking about that experience when he got out. Ten more days. This time he kept quiet for almost a week before spouting off. Ten days. He shut up, for a long time. And then, missing the radio he had at Atlanta, he talked again, but to a guard. He offered a bribe for a bit of news of the great outside. The guard informed the warden. Nineteen days in the dungeon. Three years later the bribe attempt leaked out to the San Francisco papers. The *Chronicle* reported: "And ironically enough the information sought by Capone was not information from any of his underworld playmates. The dreaded silence rule had merely incited a gnawing passion for news from a world of which he was no longer a part. All he wanted was to be brought up to date on current events."

Capone's illicit millions were as valueless here as stage money. At the beginning, when he dared to join the population in the yard on Sunday afternoons, he was disturbed at seeing softball outfielders bumping into trotting exercisers. Later he told Johnston, "Warden, that yard ain't half big enough," and liberally offered to have it enlarged. The warden said Uncle Sam would take care of the prison's building needs.

His bootleg wealth did enable him to acquire several items that lent him distinction among the convicts. Gifts were verboten, but a request that his wife bring him a new pair of glasses seemed reasonable. She did—a pair with gold rims. Equally reasonable seemed a request for a musical instrument, which convicts were permitted to buy. She brought a $1,500, gaudily bejeweled banjo. Thereafter, during the Sunday recreation period, he joined an orchestra, of sorts, in an abandoned shower room in the basement. A robber, identity long since lost, banged a battered upright piano as if it were a custodial officer; Harmon Waley, lanky, pale kidnaper who had a quick smile and eyes that gleamed with mischief, played a saxophone; Frankie Vasconcellas, a melancholy kidnaper, picked at a mandolin; Machine Gun Kelly, erect, looking everywhere but at the instrument at his knee, beat a rat-tat-tat on a drum; Scarface, gold specs imparting an odd dignity to the flabby features, twanged his $1,500 banjo. Capone, not entirely pleased with what he heard, went to the warden and offered to buy new instruments all around, including a grand piano. The warden shook his head, firmly.

Hatred of Capone grew. Bugs Moran, erstwhile boss of Chicago's North Side rumrunners, and a few of the defunct Tuohy gang, all doing long stretches, begrudged Capone his easy ten years on a tax rap. Others had a special gripe: their pals had been rubbed out by Al's boys. He was a suspect as a stoolie for not joining strikes against the rules. He was hated for his wealth. The orchestra was an escape; he dared not mingle with the men outdoors, for fear of getting a shiv in his ribs. He was given solitary jobs, mopping the latrines, toting books and magazines from the library to cells, sweeping the cellhouse and the yard. A convict at that time could subscribe to nine of a list of one hundred magazines, from which stories of crime and Alcatraz inmates were excised, but he had to keep them to himself. In a rare concession, Capone was allowed to order the full list and donate them to the library, in a bid for good will. If anything, the gesture heightened the ill will. There was even talk of hustling him off to McNeil before they had to summon the coroner. Arthur D. Wood, chief federal parole officer, queried about that, told newsmen: "Capone has been one of the best prisoners on Alcatraz, and he has earned the consideration of the government on the question of transfer."

For a man who did his best to keep out of trouble, Capone was always up to his fat neck in it. Before placed on solo jobs, he was feeding a machine in the laundry with a bank robber named Bill Collier on the other end. "Crisake, slow down!" Collier ordered. Capone, not accustomed to taking orders, speeded up. Collier flung a role of wet wash in his face. Fists flew; both got ten days in the dungeon.

One Sunday in the music room the playful Waley kept his sax almost smack against Capone's head until the mobster turned in a rage and shouted, "You dirty, goddam babysnatcher!" Waley, a six-footer who towered over Scarface, said nothing. The band played on. At the proper moment, Waley took a baseball bat grip on his sax and whacked Capone across the back of the head, knocking him off his stool, the $1,500 banjo banging on the cement floor. Fists flew; once again the dungeon.

A more serious demonstration occurred in the laundry room. J. P. Chase, the Nelson henchman who later turned artist, had been out of the dungeon for just one day. He was furious with Capone for refusing to take part in a revolt some while before, and easily persuaded a confederate to attract the guard's attention while he worked his revenge. If the gentle Roy Gardner had not happened to be present, Capone would almost certainly have been killed; but just as Chase hurled an iron sash-weight at Capone's head, Gardner glanced up, made a flying tackle, and knocked Capone backwards. The missile struck the mobster on the arm, and the plot to kill him misfired. Chase went back to the Deep Hole. It is a tribute to Gardner that the convicts held him in such respect that neither Chase nor his friends ever sought revenge for his interference in their plot. And it is also a tribute to him that he dared to befriend the friendless Capone.

Capone's money, ill-begotten, became an ironic source of trouble. Convicts, in clandestine whispers, told of hardships back home and Capone directed his wife to see that the families were cared for. A guard monitoring one of these conversations reported the matter and Warden Johnston, fearing a mob in the making, ordered the largesse stopped. One day scrappy James (Tex) Lucas sidled up to Capone and said he had a good thing going in the courts—a life term awaiting him down in Texas for the same bank holdup that landed him on The Rock—and how about the dough to see it through? Capone related what the warden had said: lay off, or else. Lucas, thinking it was a stall, stalked off seething. A week later Lucas was walking into the barber shop, then in the basement, when he saw Capone emerge from a room down the corridor. He grabbed up a pair of shears, deftly separated the blades, wrapped one in his handkerchief and, as Capone passed by, stepped out. Capone sensed something, whirled just as Lucas was about to strike. Fast as a boxer, Capone went into a clinch, and the blade plunged into his back. He grunted, pushed Lucas away. Lucas lunged again. Capone raised his arm to fend off the blow. The blade sliced into his left thumb and broke in the middle. Capone shot a short right to Lucas's jaw and laid him out cold, then went to the hospital upstairs for a week. Lucas was tried in The Rock's own court—prison officials doubling in brass as judge, jury, prosecutor, with no defense counsel—and confined to the dungeon for a series of nineteen days.

Alcatraz being a world apart, all these incidents leaked out weeks, months, even years later. The story of the stabbing broke out of Washington, far from the scene, secondhand, and garbled. The account in the *San Francisco Chronicle* said:

"In line with the strict secrecy maintained concerning happenings on Alcatraz, first reports of the outburst reached here in dispatches from Washington, with the announcement coming from the Department of Justice. . . .

"Instead of a trial for Lucas, the prison authorities dealt out punishment. It is against the prison policy, it was announced, to let prisoners have even the dubious freedom of leaving the island under guard for court appearances."

Capone's attempt to bribe the guard remained a secret for three years. When the Chase sash-weight-hurling episode came to public attention, Warden Johnston denied it happened. As for the scrap in the music room, Johnston told newsmen: "I first heard the story from you newspaper boys. There wasn't anything I could find to verify it. In fact, I think I can say that Capone doesn't even know what Waley looks like." (The press was not aware, of course, that Capone and Waley were fellow musicians.)

The badgering and veiled threats by the other convicts, the attacks and fights, the spells in the pitch-black dungeon began to take their toll. Capone sought solace in religion, sang in the choir on Sunday mornings. It was too late. There were now days he kept to his cell and when the guards tried to coax him out for a meal, he backed into a corner, staring in terror. Other days he was a child at play, making and remaking his bed, prattling to himself. Or again, he would stand at his cell front and lustily sing "O Sole Mio." At length, he was locked in an isolation ward—bug cage, to the convicts—in the hospital upstairs. His wife read about it, a month later, and rushed out to San Francisco. She was forced to wait until he had one of his lucid days, when he could be brought down to the prisoners' side of the visitors' room to stare through the bulletproof pane recessed in the three-foot-thick wall.

Rumors began flying off The Rock early in January of 1938 that Capone was insane. Attempts to reach prison authorities were unavailing, but the reports had enough substance to make headlines. And then, in February, the Department of Justice in Washington broke official silence, announcing simply that Capone was in the prison hospital and that no insanity hearing was contemplated. Warden Johnston now talked to the press by phone: "I don't propose to issue hourly bulletins on Capone's temperature and pulse. He is being given the usual care and there is no intention to remove him. We have just as good a hospital here as the U.S. Medical Center at Springfield, Missouri." He admitted that Capone's wife had not been informed: "But she must know of his illness. The papers have been full of it."

Two weeks later the Justice Department issued a bulletin: Capone was suffering from "mental disturbances. . . . His condition is in no wise due to his confinement, but grows out of conditions originating prior to his incarceration." There were vague hints of paresis, resulting from syphilis contracted in his youth. The Justice Department lapsed into another silence that endured until December, when it began employing paresis as though it were a diagnostic fact. Dispatches said Justice officials were debating whether to keep Capone at Alcatraz "for his own good, so he can continue under treatment there for paresis." He was scheduled for release the following month, January 1939.

One night early in January Capone was taken secretly off The Rock with six weights on each leg and escorted by three armed guards to the new Federal Correctional Institution on Terminal Island in Los Angeles Harbor, there to serve out the extra year he was originally sentenced to serve in the Cook County jail in Chicago for contempt of court. Warden Johnston wrote long afterward that Capone had spent his final year at Alcatraz in the prison hospital, and that upon his departure the psychiatrist then heading The Rock's medical staff reported he was "in good physical condition, in good spirits, that he appeared to understand his difficulty, and that his speech was entirely relevant and adequate."

(Certain factors, in medical opinion, suggest paresis was perhaps a convenient coverup. Capone's quick recovery, permitting removal to a minimum-security facility, contradicts the diagnosis: in those days before penicillin there was no reliable cure for syphilis or paresis. And if indeed paretic, he would have been sent to the Springfield Medical Center for the drastic treatment then employed, along with arsenicals: an induced malarial fever to burn out the syphilis—and no more than 20 to 30 percent ever showed any improvement.)

In 1940 he was taken to a rendezvous in the Midwest and released to his wife, who took him to their walled hideaway in Florida. Here in 1947, at the age of forty-eight, he died of a complication of heart attack, stroke, and pneumonia. Scarface Al Capone, who in his hoodlum heyday had lavished $25,000 funerals on underlings slain in the Chicago gang wars, was given a simple burial.

Only a few years earlier, the one Alcatraz inmate who had befriended him, Roy Gardner, had also regained his freedom. Early in 1937, headlines reported Gardner's departure from The Rock. His time served, he was released through Leavenworth. Alcatraz by now had become an island of mystery, and Gardner drew the veil aside with "Hellcatraz," as told to James G. Chesnutt, in the *San Francisco Call-Bulletin*. It was a grim portrayal that, as such exposés often do, soon faded. He sold his life story to the movies (*I Stole a Million* starring George Raft) and for a time lectured to women's clubs. At the 1939 World's Fair on Treasure Island he ran a concession, admission ten cents, on the theme: Crime Doesn't Pay. Neither did the concession. He stopped by a mortuary, selected and paid for a coffin. He hung a sign on the hall door at the hotel to warn the maid: Danger, Stay Out, Call Police. Then, mixing the same ingredients used at San Quentin, he transformed the bathroom into a lethal gas chamber . . . his last headline.

Chapter 5

T HE COUNTRY'S MOST VICIOUS and desperate criminals share The Rock with children of all ages, infants to teenagers. Most of the custodial and clerical staff commute from San Francisco, but about a third, bachelors and fifty-seven families, dwell below the prison heights on four acres terraced into the island's southeastern tip—the slope blasted by the Army Engineers in the 1850s to provide a protective cliff on that side. Theirs is a strange sort of village life, in the shadow of gun towers, under the brow of a brooding prison that once did, and might again at any moment, explode into murderous mutiny. Ever present is the menace of being taken hostage by armed escapees; but they live a normal life, just as other San Franciscans go about their daily affairs without a neurotic fear that the San Andreas Fault underfoot might at any moment slip a bit and shake the city's cornices loose.

In some respects, the Rock dwellers can boast the choicest residential site in the Bay Area, as picturesque as any isle in the Mediterranean. To awe-struck tourists, purchasing an intimate glimpse at rows of binoculars on Telegraph Hill and the end of a pier near Fisherman's Wharf, the island, much of the year a vivid splash of ice-plant pink, bears the deceptive appearance of a precipitous Capri minus castellated villas and bikinis. Weathered, red-roofed cottages set in flower gardens line one edge of this terrace or middle level; and on the south side two modern apartment houses with picture windows and balconies stand above the rocky shore, not so magnificent as the apartment towers along Rio's Copacabana but offering an unsurpassed panoramic vista: the Golden Gate span and its after-dark strands of sodium-vapor lights, the serrated skyline of San Francisco, the Bay Bridge and Treasure Island, the landmark Campanile of the University of California and the cities crawling up the surrounding hills, the verdant mass of nearby Angel Island. Only a section of the Marin County coast to the north is invisible, blocked off by the prison crest.

A path leads down through a grove of eucalyptus trees to an esplanade along the leeward shore, a few feet above the surf, with benches to enjoy the flat marine view or wait for a striped bass to strike. Color abounds on all sides: the greens of a few hardy scrub pines on the windward, and the eucalypti on the leeward; the rosy blossoms of the creeping ice plant; the bright yellow flowers of oxalis, related to the sour grass family; even the dull red faces of the arid cliffs. Many succulents, such as the century plant, border footpaths. These trees, shrubs, and flowers—planted in soil brought over from the mainland—thrive on the moisture of the summer fogs. Water is barged over by Army tugs, 170,000 gallons at a time, two or three loads a week.

Some of the seventy-five children were born here, knowing no other home than The Rock. Daughter of the guards grow up to be wives of guards. The island once had a kindergarten class; now all the children go to public or private schools in the city. Pupils caught up by a favorite television program at night catch up on their homework on the twelve-minute ride to the mainland on the prison launch, the *Warden Johnston.* Before dashing down to the wharf, one lad delivers the morning papers. Occasionally, on the return trip after school, there may be a convict aboard, but he is shackled and out of sight in a sealed-off cabin.

The youngsters of Alcatraz lead a life very much like that of their urban classmates, even to a curfew that sends them home at nine o'clock week nights, eleven o'clock Saturday and Sunday. They play ball beneath the frowning prison cliff, fish off the shore, shoot billiards or bowl at the Officers' Club, where teenagers gather at a replica of a drugstore fountain.

Only in one regard is a boy's life different on Alcatraz: he cannot own a rifle to hunt or sieve tin cans on a fence post. Nor a cap pistol.

Nor a rubber knife. When they play cops-and-robbers, forefingers serve as revolvers and lusty "Bang! Bang!" for shots. And they must never step outside the fenced-in limits of the family acres.

Humor resides here with grimness, and the personnel christened the new staff dining room up at the prison The Top o' The Rock. The Officers' Club down below is the social and cultural center of the civilian colony: here old-fashioned square dances make The Rock sing on Saturday night; here the Alcatraz Women's Club holds meetings, bridge parties, an annual Yule bazaar; here too the Alcatraz Ballet—girls four to fourteen, taught by a guard's wife who had been reared on the island—stages performances.

Alcatraz was once the setting for nuptials, when a light-keeper's daughter married a classmate at Utah Agricultural College. The Coast Guard still operates the light, a new light mounted on an octagonal column towering 214 feet above sea level, with a flashing beacon visible twenty-one miles at sea. While on duty the Coast Guardsmen—a married man and a bachelor, who occupy two of the three apartments in the lighthouse—are under the control of the prison authorities.

Rock families enjoy all the freedoms of the mainland. They can have guests at any hour of the day or night, and parties till dawn, subject to the same rules as party-givers anywhere: if they get too rowdy, they are told to pipe down. Residents are responsible for what their guests carry onto the island.

"We hope they're sensible enough not to bring any firearms," says Warden Olin D. Blackwell. "We're particularly anxious about ammunition. The inmates can make guns, but it's harder to make cartridges."

Blackwell, fourth and current warden of The Rock, is a rangy, amiable, middle-aged, onetime Texas rancher who still wears an imprint of the open range: a western Stetson; on occasion, a bolo or cowpoke's string tie; a tooled leather belt with an outsized buckle of Navajo Indian silver, turquoise adorned; a Navajo open bracelet on the left wrist, silver inlaid with turquoise stones. He feels that The Rock is an ideal place to live: "We have more privacy than people in the city. A lot safer at night, too. We never lock our doors."

Like the islanders, guests need not pass through the metal detector. They reach the four-acre settlement by a private stairway to a footbridge over the dock area, then through a gate controlled by the tower guard. On departing, they stand at the gate until the guard opens it—after prison visitors are aboard the boat, after the five convicts on the dock detail line up in his sight, and after he has been assured that all the other prisoners are accounted for.

When the doorbell rings, an Alcatraz wife knows for a certainty it will not be a salesman, for this is one territory even the Fuller Brush man cannot penetrate. Rock wives do their shopping at their own "co-op" on the island or at markets in the city, either in person or by phone. They are no farther from downtown San Francisco department stores than women in residential areas such as the ocean-fronting Sunset district—perhaps closer, with no traffic lights on the bay segment of their trip to town. Normally, it's a twelve-minute run from the island to the Fort Mason dock, where the Alcatraz wife takes either a bus downtown or the family car, parked in the huge pier shed. Rock residents can have a jolly night in town and catch a late, or early, boat back. The boat makes twenty-two trips a day, the first at 5 A.M., the last at 2 A.M.

Although the children share this tiny island with about 260 convicts, they seldom see any at close range except those who collect the garbage or tend the gardens and the sharp-spiked century plants along the paths. The older children ignore the inmates, but the tots sometimes grow curious, such as the preschool child who once asked her mother why a playmate's daddy (a guard) watched over the gardeners so closely. After a moment's perplexity, the mother answered: "They're bad men—they're being punished for not eating their spinach." Later the child hop-skipped up to a domesticated gunman kneeling at a shrub and scolded, "Shame on you! Aren't you sorry now you didn't eat your spinach?"

The penal concept that created Alcatraz ruled out the trusty, the model prisoner trusted to perform duties outside the walls. Associate Warden Lawrence Delmore once explained: "Trusties get the idea they are privileged characters and expect the run of the place. Besides, guards are apt to turn their backs on them because they think they are safe. You can't do that here."

Warden Blackwell, who occupies a three-story, eighteen-room house on the edge of the bluff a few steps from the prison building, voiced a regret on that score: "It's hard to find a prisoner to work in the house because if they can be trusted to do that, they don't belong on the island."

During the regime of Warden Johnston, in a day when the felons were regarded as far less trustworthy, a dinner guest at the mansion, aware of the reasoning that gangsters made unreliable trusties, was astonished to discover the butler was a convict. He was even more astonished to learn the chef was an armed robber.

"We'll soon be losing our cook," the warden said. "He's coming up for parole."

Barbara, the warden's eighteen-year-old daughter, protested: "Oh, Daddy, you can't let him out—he's the only cook we ever had who could make *Bar de Luc!*"

Chapter 6

A RAUCOUS BLAST, THE CELLHOUSE alarm clock, jars you awake at 6 A.M. Twenty minutes till the head count. You wash up at the cold-water tap, comb your hair, brush your teeth. (If sensitive, you might vary the routine by brushing your teeth first, or putting on your right shoe first, but as you wear into the set ways of an automaton you skip these small variations.)

You get into the gray shirt, the gray trousers, the sturdy shoes. You make your bed, tidy up your cubicle, then take your position at the bars of your cell front. After the stand-up count, you hear the lieutenant call: "Ring in outside B!" A dozen cell doors slide open. You step out, march along the tier gallery, descend the circular steel stairway. As you approach the mess hall you remember and quickly button your collar. (This becomes automatic, for an open collar at mess lands you in solitary.) You file past the steam table with a compartmented tray, picking up your breakfast—rolls, dry cereal and milk, coffee, and you know the day is Tuesday: menus are your calendar.

Twenty minutes to eat. A whistle, you stand up; a whistle, you turn; a whistle, you check in your flatware and march out, up the winding stairway, along the tier, into your cell. Another count, then the command: "Ring out B!" Cells open, you march along the tier, down the circular stairs, through a metal detector into the yard. You stand on a yellow line until all convict workers come out. Then, "Brush shop!" You are checked off as you go through a gate, down a flight of steps in the cliffside to a landing, through another Snitch Box, down another flight, along a road to the shops.

At 11:20, you come back up the road, back up the flights, back through the yard, back up the steel stairway, back along the tier, back into your cell. A head count, the lieutenant's command. You go along the tier, down the stairs, into the mess hall, eat, obey the three whistles, march back to your cell. Another count. You walk along the tier, descend the stairs, go into the yard, stand on the painted line, file through the gate, down the flights, along the road to the shops.

At 4:30, you come back up the road, back up the flights, back through the yard, back up the stairway, back along the tier, back into your cell. A head count, the lieutenant's command. You go along the tier, down the stairs, into the mess hall, eat, stand, turn, march back to your cell. The door clangs shut, stays shut for thirteen hours. At 9:30, your cell light winks out.

At 6 A.M., a raucous blast. . . .

In the timelessness of The Rock, an hour thins out into a day, a day lengthens into a stretch, and even a term with a fixed end seems endless. You pass through day after day after day with the feeling that somewhere in the past life came to a stop. Only Sunday offers a rupture in the routine, and after a time Sunday takes on a routine within routine: an hour at chapel in the morning, two hours in the yard in the afternoon (one hour, if you went to chapel). For this gift of Sunday you pay extra in solitude: lockup comes earlier. Twice a year you get an extra Sunday, Christmas and New Year's, unless they fall on a Sunday; but there is no yuletide. All other holidays are routine days.

This was the way it was in the early years of Alcatraz, a brooding and grimly forbidding island prison in the bay, shrouded in fog and secrecy. And then came rumblings that this pet project of the Department of Justice was not an original experiment in penology after all, but an idea borrowed from the Middle Ages, a horror chamber Torquemada might have dreamed up. Bryan Conway, a released convict, reported: "Men slowly go insane under the exquisite torture of routine." Al (Sailor) Loomis, counterfeiter and onetime boxer, set free in February 1936 after sixteen months on The Rock, told the United Press that a suicide watch was even maintained while a man shaved. A guard twice a week handed a convict a dull blade, gave him two minutes to shave, then stood by to prevent any attempt at self-destruction. Loomis said: "Many almost succeeded by slashing legs and arms. It's hell there. Life gets so monotonous you feel like bucking the rules to break the monotony. That's it—the monotony. It's driving the men screwy." He said the one-man cells were maddeningly simple: "The walls were the barest things I ever saw. No pictures. Nothing. If a con tried to put up the photograph of his mother he was headed for the hole." Loomis summed up life on The Rock: fog, sand fleas everywhere, unceasing scrutiny, censored mail, utter lack of hope, no amusement, no relief from boredom. "They never give a guy a break."

Conway, writing in the *Saturday Evening Post* ("20 Months in Alcatraz," February 19, 1938), reported that in his last year on The Rock fourteen prisoners went "violently insane" and "any number of others" were isolated as stir crazy. In a period of three years thirty-five inmates reportedly were packed off in straitjackets to the Federal Prison Bureau's asylum at Springfield, Missouri.

The Department of Justice ignored these reports with a loftiness that indicated they were the mere ravings of ex-convicts. However, in 1938 the physician in charge of the medical staff (the prison hospital was then staffed and accredited, but no longer is) was abruptly replaced, without explanation, by a psychiatrist, Dr. Romney Ritchey.

It was about then that Roy Gardner, the train bandit, came off the island to report Capone a madman: "Al's mind is gone. His enemies and the hell nights did it." He described hell nights as the nights made sleepless for a convict by anxiety over family affairs, or a long term awaiting him in some state prison when he leaves The Rock, or enemies on the outside waiting to fill him full of slugs; or by the screaming wind and blasting foghorns. Almost nightly the wind funneling through the Golden Gate shrieks down the ventilator shafts of the cellhouse. On foggy nights, and it's more often foggy than clear, the horns at each end of the island set up a strident reverberation, one every twenty seconds, the other every thirty seconds.

The evidence seemed clear that hell nights alone had not deranged Capone. The "exquisite torture of routine" played a part, and the minor infractions, such as talking, that put him so often in the dread dungeon. What apparently tipped the scales, a convict later testified, was a medieval display of punishment in which Capone was forced to squat for days in a cage three feet high.

Other stories, some shockingly grisly, of inmates being driven to suicide or self-mutilation by the rigors of The Rock began coming to light, either through coroner's inquests or tips to newspapers long after they had happened. There was the suicide-by-flight of husky, forty-year-old Joe Bowers, described by Warden Johnston as a man of more brawn than brains. He was serving a twenty-five-year term for the $16.63 robbery of a store in the mountain hamlet of Isaiah in the Feather River country of the High Sierras—a federal offense because the post office was in the store.

Joe Bowers worked alone at the incinerator on a lower level of the island's west side facing the Golden Gate, next to the cyclone fence. He burned trash and mashed tin cans and sent them rattling into the bay down a chute through the fence, a chute too small for use as a slide. The fence bordered a cliff with a sheer drop of sixty feet to jagged rocks.

His job came under the surveillance of the south gun tower. On duty that bright April morning of 1936 was Guard E. F. Chandler, whose keen custodial eye pivoted from incinerator to the yard, to the steps from the yard, to the vehicles on the winding road from the shops to the wharf, on around to the bay where a boat might venture within the buoyed boundary and need a warning shot. When he heard the 11:20 whistle, the signal for all workers to return to their cells for the pre-lunch count, Chandler glanced down to watch Bowers head up the road. He was astonished to see the convict dash to the fence and start climbing.

Chandler grabbed up his megaphone and shouted, "Joe! Get down out of there! Joe! Stop . . . ! Get back down, Joe!" Bowers kept climbing. What happened in the next few seconds, Chandler described to a coroner's jury:

"I picked up Mary Ann and fired a couple of low ones, thinking I might get him in the leg. When he kept on going and went over the fence I leveled Mary Ann and let him have it. I knew if he got to the bay, God knew where he'd go next. He might be robbing banks in

San Francisco. I had my orders and I followed them. That's what I'm there for.

"Bowers was over the deadline. He knew what he was doing, and I couldn't get him without wings."

Bowers was at the top, picking his way over the barbed wire, when Chandler leveled Mary Ann and let him have it. A single bullet sped from the tower, on target. Bowers leaped convulsively, plunged to the rocks. The prison launch recovered the body. He had been shot through the lungs.

The general belief among the inmate population was that Bowers, growing stir simple and bent on ending it all, had taken this means to circumvent the canon against self-destruction.

John Stadig, counterfeiter isolated in a bug cage upstairs when he began acting a bit wacky, exhibited a gruesome cunning. A guard handed in lunch one day and then, instead of standing watch, let Stadig alone behind the locked, solid door. Stadig bent a prong of the fork and jabbed it in his wrist, worked it under the big vein and pried the vein out into the open. Then he bit it in two. He was prying the vein out of the other wrist when the guard returned for the luncheon tray. Besides his wrist, Stadig punctured a hole in the concept of Alcatraz as a super-lockup for troublemakers: too much of a trouble on The Rock, he was shipped back to Leavenworth. The day he arrived there, safely locked away in a cell, he broke a lens of his eyeglasses, took a jagged piece and sliced his jugular vein. He had at last found release.

One night in 1937 the *San Francisco Chronicle,* a morning paper, received a tip of an incident on the island and, unable to get verification, ran a vague account of "a prisoner, last name of Percival," that read, in part: "A story of horror, almost unbelievable, came out of the prison fortress, Alcatraz, last night. It rivaled in grimness some of the tales of Poe and, although shrouded in a close veil of secrecy, it remained undenied . . . Warden Johnston would neither deny nor confirm the story."

Washington conformed it the next day. The episode had occurred *a month earlier.* The convict who played the Poe protagonist was one Rufe Persful, Arkansas robber. He was working with the dock gang.

He laid his left hand on a block and chopped off the fingers with a hatchet, one after the other, like a butcher cleaving chops off a pork loin. He then offered the hatchet to a gaping convict, laid his right hand on the block and said, "Chop them off, too!" The convict flung the hatchet aside and ran shouting to the guard.

A question naturally arises: How many other incidents of men driven to appalling self-mutilation by The Rock's refined system of medieval torture have been successfully covered up?

For three years the grim rule of silence gave The Rock the strange aspect of a prison for the dumb, convicts untutored in sign language. Warden Johnston contended the rule was not so severe as it sounded, that the men could talk in the shops during a three-minute rest period in the morning and for three minutes in the afternoon; that, at meals, one might say, "Pass the sugar"; that they could chat in the yard on Sunday afternoons, except that the guards zealously kept the men separated to prevent the hatching of plots. In 1937 Johnston announced to the press he had rescinded the rule as a step in easing the rigidity of discipline. The action was commended as a humanitarian gesture.

Convicts who were there at the time offer another version. Johnston, dubbed Salt Water for a reputed practice of hosing down unruly inmates, had a habit of coming into the mess hall at lunchtime to sample the fare. He would then stand near the door as the prisoners filed out. The dining room had the subdued, almost sedate atmosphere of a gentlemen's club, the polite requests for salt or pepper arising like the murmur of cultured conversation. Suddenly, above the murmurous quiet sounded a clear, strong talking voice, distinctly not saying, "Sugar, please?" The effect produced was that of a rattle of gunfire. The warden glanced in surprise at the captain. A guard headed for the culprit. A voice broke forth in response to the speaker, then a convict piped up at another table, then another. Within moments the place range like a boilermakers' banquet. The guards were helpless. There wasn't room in the eight dungeon cells to hold everybody. The rule of silence on The Rock had come to an end, by the simple expedient of talking.

Years afterward a sartorial change was effected by a similarly spontaneous, but much more dramatic, action. One evening a convict flung his coveralls out onto Broadway and shouted to the officer on the floor, "You can shove 'em!" Soon the hated garments were flying from all the tiers. Artists shook out bottles of turpentine, then a convict threw a flaming roll of toilet paper from a top-tier cell. Broadway blazed merrily, bright as its namesake. And the men were measured for trousers.

Weapons at their disposal to protest conditions, when verbal pleas fail, are cellhouse rackets and strikes, a refusal to work or to eat. Publicized hunger strikes imply dissatisfaction with food, which is sometimes the case but not always; more often, these are merely a means to an end. Even an industrial strike takes on a hunger aspect: the men are locked up and kept on bread and water, a no-work, no-eat management countermeasure that invariably proves effective. In a hunger strike pure and simple, the men refuse to leave their cells for the mess hall.

In 1940 the strangest strike of all occurred at Alcatraz. No violence of any kind, no shouting, no banging on the cell bars at night. By choice they invoked silence. They did their work in the shops without a word. They filed mutely into the mess hall and on past the steam tables without touching the hot food. They sat down and silently dined on a slice of bread and coffee. Word of the novel action leaked out and the papers, enchanted by the passive, Gandhi-like behavior of the nation's toughest criminals, played up the story as the Mystery of The Rock.

Warden Johnston felt impelled to comment, and his words were in tone with the bizarre quality of the affair: "It's the reaction of frustrated men. You lock a man up in a hotel for sixty, seventy, even ninety-nine years, and every so often he will seek to gain the attention of the world outside." The silent strike lasted a week, ending as abruptly as it had begun; to the press still a big mystery. Actually, the men *were* seeking to gain attention, but not so much the attention of the world outside as the attention of the federal jurists in San Francisco. Convicts there at the time report that petitions were not getting off the island and the strike, its purpose no mystery to the officials, was called to protest that denial of access to the courts.

Monotony dominated life on The Rock, but there were moments of relief. Work offered physical activity and a companionship of sorts: you were in a room with others; and in the three-minute conversation breaks in the forenoon and afternoon, you could hear your own voice in natural talk. Religious services—Saturday, for Jewish inmates; one Sunday for Catholics, the next for Protestants—provided both spiritual solace and a break in the grinding monotony. So bent was the warden on punishing that equal time was deducted from recreation—surely the only place in America where prayer drew a penalty. The warden theorized that, without such an option, all the convicts would want to attend chapel simply to get out of their cells for an hour. (It could be argued that long exposure, even on this basis, to the teachings of the chaplains might well prove beneficial.) This theory was disproved years later when, at the insistence of a priest, the penalty for church attendance was removed. The convicts did not all suddenly get religion. Chapel attendance continued as it had been, and as it has been through the years: an average of 10 percent of the inmate population.

Convicts devised their own ways to ease the lonely solitude of their monastic cell life. They made pets of mice that crept timidly into their cells. (Rats also skulked the tiers at night, but they were less attractive as cellmates.) The prisoners made nests in their bathrobe pockets for the mice, even took them on journeys to the basement on shower days. They fed the pets bread snitched at meals at the risk of solitary confinement, some daring to take them along, under their shirts, to the dining room and feed them furtively at table. Once a guard-foreman of a shop saw a convict catch a fly and slip it in his pocket, then another fly, and another. Curious, he kept an eye on the convict as they went along the road after quitting time, saw him step lightly on a beetle, then pocket it. Later, he slipped up to the convict's cell and saw him feeding the beetle and flies to a pet lizard. The guard, a sympathetic sort, quietly retreated, smiling.

As in all prisons, the convicts of Alcatraz managed in the ingenious ways of imprisoned men to brew alcoholic beverages. In the federal penitentiaries intoxicants, whatever their nature, go by the generic name of pruno. The most exotic concoction of The Rock in the early days was a pruno cocktail: milk and gasoline. (Mention of this drink was made during a federal court trial, but its effects not discussed.) On occasion, whisky was smuggled in by kind-hearted guards, but generally the convicts had to make their own booze, and the best place for such an illicit operation was the bakery in the basement beneath the kitchen. Here the yeasty aroma of a fermenting brew was so akin to that of rising dough that the making of pruno went undetected for a long time. Until a couple of drunks spoiled things, the bake shop was perhaps the one spot on the island where the inmates were really happy at their work. The recipe was simple: put raisins and other dried fruit to soak in a crock, add yeast to speed up the fermentation, and cover the crock with flour sacks. The bakers, realizing they had a good thing going, drank in moderation, an aperitif before meals. One afternoon a couple of bakers dipped into the crock too early, and too often. They became spiflicated and, as drunks anywhere, fell to boasting, then to arguing, then to fighting. The guard on duty in the basement heard the commotion, came running, moved in to break it up. He seized the convict he thought was the aggressor—and then saw, too late, that the other had a knife. The guard held his breath as the other convict started to lunge. Luckily, the convict recognized the uniform in time to divert the blade. He meekly handed the knife over to the guard, one of the most respected officers of The Rock. Thereafter, bakers confined their art to bread, rolls, and pastries.

The bakery was not the only place where brew-making went on. One day the foreman of the furniture shop reached into a barrel of grommets, used to make wooden mats for the Navy. His fingers struck something solid, and he pulled forth a gallon jug of raisin pruno. He dug into other barrels, found another jug of fermenting grog. The men had brought the raisins down in their pockets a few at a time, slipped to them by a pal in the kitchen crew as they moved along the mess hall steam table.

Reading a letter was a more frequent diversion than writing one, for a convict could send out only two a week but receive seven.

Writing was restricted to one side of the paper, and correspondents were warned not to refer to any person by nickname or initials, nor to make any cryptic remarks. At the beginning, a convict could correspond only with an immediate member of his family, the restriction later eased to include a fiancée or old friend—but not an ex-convict nor an inmate at another prison. Mail privileges began three months after the convict arrived on The Rock, to provide time for an FBI check on the listed pen pals. These investigations still occasionally turn up an old acquaintance who backs off upon hearing the letters will bear an Alcatraz postmark (although the island lies within the city limits of San Francisco).

All mail, outgoing and incoming, is censored. This prevents the hatching of plots but also tends to dampen a convict's ardor to a girlfriend when he knows his protestations will first be read by the mail officer. Suspect portions of a letter to a convict are not snipped out with scissors; the missive itself is typed, and a carbon copy given the inmate, for a special reason: the original might be saturated with dope—a letter both to mull over and chew on.

The limitation on correspondents is sometimes misunderstood by the public. During the regime of The Rock's second warden, Edwin B. Swope, a special-delivery letter came for Robert Stroud, the celebrated authority on bird diseases, from a woman in Southern California, seeking advice regarding her sick canary. It was returned with a notation that regulations prevented its delivery to the prisoner. Not long afterward the warden received a package by express marked "Personal." It contained a tiny coffin, and in the coffin the canary. He gave the bird a burial.

The chief diversion of the convicts in the early years of The Rock was the two-hour recreation period outdoors, if the weather permitted. Blustery weather was a thing to dread, for it meant confinement to a cell with little to do from 5 P.M. Saturday until 6:30 A.M. Monday, a stretch of monotony broken only by treks to the mess hall and the hour in the chapel for the churchgoers. Those who prayed prayed often for a clear Sunday and a period in the yard, an area roughly the size of a football field, extending from the angle of the T-shaped prison looking toward San Francisco and the Golden Gate. Twelve concrete steps, serving as bleachers, rise against the mess hall, the stem of the T, and from the high steps the view can be spectacular, especially if rains or high winds whipping through the Gate during the night have swept the atmosphere clean. To the west the convict sees the majestic sweep of the Golden Gate Bridge, its towers orange-red against the azure sky, Sunday motorists streaming along its deck. A fresh breeze comes off the Pacific, just spanking enough to gratify the weekend skippers, their small craft, white sails full, skimming along the blue surface of the bay. Beyond rises the green patch of the Presidio of San Francisco. Pull the gaze to the left and San Francisco, dazzling in the cleansed air, seems unreal, a scene in a stereoscope. The apartment skyscrapers on Russian Hill, the streets like rows in a hillside vineyard, Coit Tower on Telegraph Hill, the spatulate-fingered piers spreading out from the Embarcadero—all so startlingly close. A cable car is clearly visible clambering up the Hyde Street hill. A mile and a half away? Why, you could ricochet a flat stone to the San Francisco shore!

And then the convict looks near at hand, to the yard enclosing him. Along the top of its twenty-foot wall runs a gunway with parapet, and at the three corners squat gun boxes. A catwalk links the wall to the south gun tower, and another catwalk, like something built with an Erector set, extends to the gun tower atop the shop building. The convict looks again at the life teeming just beyond—on the bay, on the Gate span, on the hills of San Francisco—and the truth of the Rock saying jolts home: It take ten minutes to come over from San Francisco, ten years to get back.

The wail of the wind in the ventilators at night may disturb the convicts' sleep, but it gave many a military prisoner in the Army days the shudders. For there was a superstition then that the prison was haunted, a superstition that had a tragic basis. Back in the nineties, an apartment upstairs where the chapel now is located was occupied by an Army doctor, his pretty young wife, and their baby. One morning their Chinese houseboy found the baby sitting up in the crib, playing, and in the bedroom the wife murdered, the doctor a suicide, the pistol in his hand. No one knew why; they had been a devoted couple.

There is no evidence that the Spanish explorers ever set foot on The Rock, nor the Mexicans after them. Certainly the Indians, before either of them, did not. But the Indians had a special reason to shun the island. They considered it a dwelling place of evil spirits.

Chapter 7

A FEW YEARS AGO a marshal escorted an Alcatraz convict to the Federal Prison Bureau's hospital asylum at Springfield, Missouri. Word had spread, and a score of guards gathered to stare at the prisoner—a man from The Rock. It was striking evidence that guards as well as convicts at other penal institutions hold Alcatraz in awe.

You are a rookie guard at Alcatraz, a place *Time* once described as "the human zoo of the 'world's most dangerous men.'" You had been aware of its reputation for years, and your very training for the job had heightened that awareness. And now for the first time you walk into the cellhouse, unarmed. The muscles around your stomach knot up. You walk down Broadway outwardly cool and unconcerned, but inwardly keyed to a high pitch, every nerve alive.

A former guard says: "I never lost that feeling. In time I got to know the convicts and as individuals many of them were pretty good guys. Really surprising, a lot of them, after what I'd heard: polite, intelligent, no trouble, like fellows you might run into anywhere. But there was that wall between you, an invisible wall; you could sense it in their courtesy, in the way they addressed you, always as Mister. Something uncanny about it. This feeling could bug you if you let it, for wherever you were—the cellhouse, the mess hall, the yard, the shops—you knew that eyes were on you, watching, speculating. And every morning as I walked into the cellhouse, my stomach muscles tightened up. I always had the thought: maybe today's the day it's going to happen."

Another former guard says: "I got a kick out of the men. They were like kids, in a way, up to some prank or a bit of mischief, and real clever about it. Such experts at casing, if you moved something two inches, next time they came through they knew it. My shop had a partition with a window so I could keep an eye on the men in the next room. One day Tex Lucas winked at Machine Gun Kelly, then slipped up and laid a shiny green wrapper off a typewriter ribbon on the window sill. Kelly tipped me off, and we watched out of the corner of our eye. Pretty soon a prisoner in the other room hurried by the window, did a double take, moseyed back, shot a glance around to see no one was looking, then peered over his shoulder at the green wrapper. He started on, came back again, glanced carefully around, then peered closer. He went across the room. A moment later one of the other men comes over as if he's got important business, but as he passes the window he slows down and, making sure nobody's looking, takes a quick gander at the wrapper. He goes back. A third man saunters across, as if he hasn't got a thing on his mind, but as he gets near he glances around, then sidles up and peers, shoots another quick look my way, then peers down close. That thing really bugged them—some sort of signal sure as hell, maybe for a break. They were a kick, all right, but you had to keep your wits just the same, always a jump ahead of them. I'd look at a man and think: 'Now, if I were him, just what would I be plotting?' It was no place to be caught napping."

That's the way it was with the guards: perhaps amusing moments, yet a constant vigilance against a constant danger. At any moment of the day, or night, anything could happen—and often did. It happened one day at the noon meal, a sudden and savage attack, not by a big-name gangster but a studious young inmate.

Trouble had been long brewing. For a year and a half the convicts had endured the crushing grind of relentless routine, and then on January 22, 1936, they revolted against the rigid rules, the rule of silence in particular. It was the first known disturbance on The Rock and the participants, about half the population of 250, were put on bread and water. Warden Johnston described the affair, a strike, as a "test of strength between the prisoners and the Department of Justice as to who is going to run the prison." The Department of Justice won. At the strike's end, after three days of the spare diet, the warden announced that the rules remained "exactly the same."

Tex Lucas, the strapping Texas Badman who did thirty days in the dungeon as a leader of that affair, spent three months the following year, 1937, organizing a second strike. His lieutenant was Burton (Whitey) Phillips, twenty-five-year-old Kansan doing life for bank robbery and kidnaping. One autumn morning Lucas gave the signal in the machine shop, and the men dropped their tools and began shouting, "We want to talk! We want newspapers! We want radios!" Soon the cries rang through all the shops. Notified by phone, Warden Johnston said: "Give them a half hour to get back to work."

Jeers and curses greeted this ultimatum, and the warden issued an edict: no work, no eat. They were locked up, and placed on bread and water. For days the cellhouse reverberated with shouts, tin cups banging on bars, steel table tops slammed against steel walls, iron beds dropped on concrete. By the end of a week most of the convicts, tiring of the skimpy diet, returned to their jobs. Lucas, Phillips, and a dozen other suspected leaders made the dungeon. A guard inquired daily if the holdouts were ready to work. On the fifth day Whitey Phillips meekly gave in. He seemed thoroughly repentant as he ate lunch, stood up with his tier group at the first whistle, turned at the second, and at the third filed past the steam table to check in his flatware.

Warden Johnston chatted with the captain near the door, his back to the convicts. Guards stood idly at their scattered posts. The armed guard on the gun balcony outside kept a wary eye on the room. All was quiet, except for the shuffle of heavy shoes and a muffled clatter in the kitchen. As he approached the door, Phillips bolted from the line and crashed a fist behind the warden's right ear. The warden dropped unconscious, as if struck by a mallet. Phillips kicked his face, then straddled him and rained trip-hammer blows. The guard on the catwalk rammed a machine-gun barrel through a port but dared not fire. It took five guards to drag Phillips off the warden and subdue him.

Johnston spent a week in the Marine Hospital in San Francisco.

A prison official told the press Phillips was hospitalized on The Rock but declined to state the "nature of his ailment." In the rescue of their warden, and aroused to a cold fury by the viciousness of the attack, the guards had requited blow with blow in generous measure. P. F. Reed, a counterfeiter who witnessed the scene, described it after his release in a series of articles, "Alcatraz is Hell," in the *San Francisco Examiner* in October 1938. He related that Phillips was floored with a gasbilly and then two guards took turns playing croquet on his head with their metal clubs, driving him, inches at a whack, halfway across the dining room.

The impression gained at the time was that Phillips's wild attack was motivated by anger over the warden's action in starving out the strikers. James Martin MacInnis, San Francisco lawyer who later conferred with Phillips on a writ, said the convict revealed a deeper motivation.

"Phillips was a victim of the hysteria of the early thirties," says MacInnis. "He was a young fellow who got in with bad company and joined in robbing a small-town bank in Kansas. They took the manager as hostage, drove down a country road and let him out, unharmed. This was Phillips's first offense, but he drew a life term. Driving down that back road they happened to cross a state line, and he was the first to be tried under the new Lindbergh Law, making it a federal offense to take a kidnap victim across a state line.

"A bright, sensitive kid, Phillips took a philosophical view of Alcatraz, became interested in the people and started writing a book about life on The Rock. He heard the warden had published a book and requested an interview. He asked the warden if he would look over his manuscript and perhaps offer his criticism. The warden agreed, and Phillips handed it to a guard. Weeks went by. He saw the warden again and asked, hopefully, 'What did you think of my book?' The warden replied, 'I read that manuscript and decided it's not the kind of material you should have, so I confiscated it.' That changed Phillips's whole outlook, and he began to brood."

A violent incident such as Phillips's attack serves to widen the gap between inmate and keeper at a place like Alcatraz, designed primarily to punish, not reform. And when punishment is the aim of incarceration, any further punitive action taken against a few wins the sympathy of all. The culinary crew struck when their work was abruptly reclassified as a nonpaying household chore. They were slapped in D Block, an isolation section the prison command euphemistically calls the Treatment Unit, where convicts are treated for misbehavior. The grapevine carried the news. That night a muted howl, like the mournful cry of a coyote on a far ridge, drifted out of the concrete-walled D Block, then answering howls. A signal from TU, as the prisoners call the unit. Convicts in the outside bank of C Block, across from TU, picked it up, began howling. In a short time the whole cellhouse was a bedlam as the inmates shouted, chanted, banged tin cups, beat their beds down in a sympathy demonstration.

The next day woodworkers in one of the shops gave a warmer demonstration of their sympathy. They lit a stub of a candle behind crates of desk trays ready for shipment, then went artlessly about their work. In time, the candle burned down, and the flame ran along a trail of paint thinner to a rubber glove filled with the inflammable fluid—whoosh!, and the crates and freshly shellacked trays were soon ablaze.

An Alcatraz guard, aware of the infinite cunning of the inmates, knows the need for steady vigilance. "They had another little fire trick that worked now and then," says a former officer. "This was a gadget with rubber bands on a small cylinder timed to run down in half an hour and explode a bunch of matchheads. They'd set it going when they knocked off work in the afternoon, and they'd be sitting in the dining room when a fire'd break out in some shop. They were always figuring angles. When the men were passing through the Snitch Box from the shops, for instance, I'd never let a whole batch go through free. They'd think the thing wasn't working and next time they'd be carrying up half the shop tools. Every so often I'd hit the buzzer button and yell, 'Hey, come back!' just to keep them leery. They were always suspicious of one another too and when we 'shot' a man—that is, reported him for some infraction—he had to make the hole for his own safety; otherwise, the others would peg him for a stoolie."

Sometimes several prisoners will stage a phony fight in a section of the yard or mess hall to distract the guards from real trouble, such as a stabbing, in another part. A routine check turned up a pair of screw-drivers and a brace and bit fashioned out of half-inch pipe fittings. Although not found in his cell, they were linked to Teddy Green, the convict who once led an uprising in the Massachusetts State Prison.[1] Green went to TU, and the guards went to work on the cellhouse, giving it a fine-tooth shaking down. In many of the cells they found cleverly contrived secret hiding places in the hollow bases of the toilets. With great pains the convicts had cut out small holes, just big enough to reach in a hand and hide a gun or a knife or other contraband. They covered the holes with paper, stuck on with white glue snitched from the brush shop, and painted the paper white to blend with the white toilet base.

Hide a *gun* in a cell cache? A gun stolen or smuggled in? A gun manufactured right in the cell. To a "free-world man," as the prisoners term a person on the outside, the very tightness of The Rock's security system would seem to preclude such a possibility. Bill Mahan, alias Bill Dainard, an accomplice in the Weyerhaeuser kidnaping in the lawless era of the thirties, proved that the impossible was possible on The Rock. He made *two* guns, not as fancy as the Colt models but no doubt as effective. They were muzzle-loaders, with copper tubing for barrels and rubber bands for triggers. He even made ammunition: matchheads for powder and little pellets of lead. Warden Johnston found the guns and supply of ammunition stashed under a mattress in an empty cell next to Mahan, after another convict had snitched. This was not proof they belonged to Mahan, but a search of his mattress disclosed a hole big enough to receive the guns. Still only circumstantial evidence, but there was a clincher: with the weapons were instructions—in Mahan's own handwriting.

For some custodians of The Rock in the early days alertness had a strange companion, tedium. A duty that called for proximity to the prisoners—in the cellhouse, the mess hall, the yard, the shops, on

---

[1] Teddy Green led the desperate but futile Massachusetts Prison revolt in January 1955. The convicts surrendered to a seven-man civilian committee headed by Erwin D. Canham, distinguished editor of the *Christian Science Monitor*, in the hope the group could help obtain prison reforms.

the dock detail—generated wakefulness. But a guntower was a lonely watch, a perch loftily removed from contact with inmates, and this remoteness gave convicts the impersonality of ground squirrels or gophers. A guard going on duty picked up a key from the Armorer, climbed the tower, opened the trapdoor, then turned the key over to the guard going off duty, who locked in his relief and delivered the key to the Armorer. In a sense, the guard was akin to a convict: he was a prisoner of the tower for eight hours. Tedium set in, the hours dragging as monotonously for him as for a convict in solitary. As a result, a onetime guard reports, they were subject to a peculiar occupational affliction: they became "tower happy." To while away the time, some took to scribbling doggerel on the walls, along the line of "The sky is blue beyond the Gate/The life of a guard is a helluva fate." The former custodial officer reveals how boredom can spur a natural desire for action in a robust man: "I was on a catwalk passing the time of day with a tower guard and after a while he yawns and stretches and says, 'I wish to hell one of them bastards would stick his head up so I could take a pot shot at him.' I could understand how he felt. Eight hours up there gets you sort of on edge." Later, the tower guards achieved a bit more freedom of movement. They locked themselves in, could stroll along a catwalk for exercise.

Their lookout post was an important one in the security scheme of The Rock. They kept a wary eye on virtually every inch of the island, kept the convicts under surveillance when they moved to and from the shops or the dock area. With their binoculars they brought under close scrutiny suspicious objects drifting by on the tide. They were armed with a pistol and a high-powered rifle to warn with a near miss, if a megaphoned warning went unheeded, any boat that strayed within the buoy-marked boundary—and to pick off any convict fleeing to a cliff's edge or swimming away from shore.

But all the stress that made the life of a guard "a helluva fate" seemed, in those early years, worthwhile, for none of the big-time criminals and escape artists the prison housed succeeded in getting away. On April 1, 1936, a calendar date cherished by children as April Fool's Day, Congressman Wright Patman of Texas, in a speech

Chapter 8

RALPH ROE AND TED COLE were from Oklahoma, as their easy, drawling speech suggested. Roe, thirty-two, a lanky, friendly sort, serving ninety-nine years for bank robberies, once escaped from McAlester Prison in Oklahoma by riding out on a truck hidden in a crate. Cole, seven years younger, runt-sized but hard and crafty, was a murderer at seventeen, saved from execution by his mother's eloquent appeal. He later killed a cellmate at McAlester, then managed an escape as uncomplicated as Roe's from that prison, in a laundry bag. Picked up on a federal kidnap rap and awaiting trial, he fled the county jail in a garbage can. He was easily recaptured, but continued to saw cell bars and, on trips to court, to wriggle out of leg irons. When he landed on The Rock, to do fifty years, he boasted, "Don't think I'll like it here. Doubt I'll stay long."

On December 16, 1937, a tulle fog, a motionless mist, clung to the bay. Roe and Cole worked in the ground-floor mat shop on the north tip of the island, making rubber mats for the Navy out of used tires. The guard counted in the crew at one o'clock, then went to the adjacent machine shop. Roe and Cole ran to a window where they had already cut two bars, concealing their handiwork with a smear. They now bent the bars, broke two panes (the sound apparently drowned by the noise in the machine shop), sawed a sash, and slipped out, taking along a Stilson wrench. They moved through the fog, invisible to the tower guards; smashed a gate lock in the cyclone fence and tossed the wrench aside; groped to the edge of a cliff and jumped twenty feet onto a mound of discarded casings from the mat shop. They plunged on into the bay.

At one thirty the guard returned to the mat shop for the half-hour count, found Roe and Cole missing, discovered the smashed window, phoned the Armorer. For the first time since Alcatraz became a super-bastille, the warden heard the rising wail of the siren. It was a signal to herd the prisoners back to their cells; a summons to off-duty guards to grab a rifle from the armory and get with it; a call to the skipper of the launch to cast off and warily circle the island.

Throughout the afternoon and night the cellhouse rang with a great clamor as the convicts celebrated. Roe and Cole had proved that the unbeatable Rock could be beaten. An escape was such an unthinkable occurrence it seemed to baffle the warden, who ran from tower to tower with binoculars, trying to scan the bay through the woolly fog. First inkling to the press was a tip that the warden had requested aid from the Coast Guard, whose spokesman, apparently in the dark himself, could only say, "Yes, we sent some patrol boats over there." Late editions banner-lined trouble at Alcatraz, vaguely hinting at a possible escape. The hint justified extras: the mystery of Alcatraz, the uncommunicative warden, the call for Coast Guard help on a densely foggy day all added up to sensational news.

Not until that night was official word of the escape released— from the other side of the continent, by James V. Bennett, director of the Federal Bureau of Prisons in Washington. Not until then were law enforcement agencies of the Bay Area notified, and roadblocks set up. San Francisco police prowled the shoreline opposite the island. Coast Guard cutters halted and boarded all small craft.

The fog lifted the next day. San Franciscans, alerted by press and radio, were understandably tense. An escape from Alcatraz! The phrase had a fearful ring—Alcatraz felons at large. Bank managers were alerted for a possible holdup. Police stopped all cars with Oklahoma license plates. FBI agents swarmed over Fisherman's Wharf crab boats. Alcatraz guards poked cautiously into water-line caves that honeycomb the cliffs on the windward side. Patrol boats searched for bodies or clues.

As always, tips kept authorities hopping. Anyone who saw two men in an auto phoned police. Enough phantom yachts were reported to hold a ghostly regatta. For weeks every stickup man in California fit the description of Cole or Roe. They kept materializing as hitchhikers throughout the West. Two boys found a skull on a lonely seashore and pried loose two gold teeth. Roe or Cole? Neither had gold teeth. Four years afterward the *San Francisco Chronicle* carried an exclusive story that the fugitives were luxuriating in South America, a story that to this day remains exclusive.

Did they survive? At the time they struck out, an ebb tide was racing past Alcatraz and out the Golden Gate at seven knots, about eight miles an hour. "Small boats could not have bucked that current," said Lloyd C. Whaley, a San Francisco city engineer. "A strong swimmer starting at Alcatraz would have found himself going out the Gate in the fog before he had expended sufficient energy to reach shore in still water."

Thus the first breach of The Rock's security stirred its hour of intense excitement. It shook the prison people, but their dismay quickly turned to new determination. Bennett, the top man, announced: "We intend to make Alcatraz as nearly impregnable as the mind of man can conceive." This assurance served both to shore up his own, and Warden Johnston's, shattered faith in Alcatraz and to allay the revived fears of San Francisco that it might expect an invasion of cutthroats any night. San Francisco women's clubs had raised a shocked outcry when the Department of Justice first disclosed that it was going to crowd the nation's toughest killers, robbers, and rapists onto the little island. No need for anxiety, the Department replied in effect; nature itself had supplied perfect security: no man could conquer the vicious rip tides that swirl around The Rock.

The women's clubs came up with a dramatic answer. A teenage girl swam over to the island in forty-seven minutes. Just to drive the point home, another girl in her teens swam over, circled Alcatraz, then swam on back to San Francisco, looking as if she had taken a turn around a swimming pool. For years there was a midwinter swim contest across the Golden Gate, a much more arduous course, with its strong currents, to negotiate. And then there's the San Francisco swimming club whose members, getting permission to start in close at Alcatraz, make a sport of streaking over to Angel Island, a mile-and-a-half swim, in about twenty minutes. Convincing support for the women's side came a few years ago when a physical culturist swam from Alcatraz to San Francisco handcuffed. It should be pointed out, however, that all these swimmers were experts, in prime condition. Still, some insist, an escaping Alcatraz convict has one big factor in his favor: incentive.

The very fact that men are imprisoned under any circumstances implies that some will try to escape. Even when Alcatraz was a military prison and then a disciplinary barracks, its inmates lavished great energy, ingenuity, and courage on attempts to get off the island. The first recorded escape from Alcatraz took place during the Civil War when three Confederate prisoners rowed away in a boat, but the record fails to state how far they got.

Ingenuity once served as a deterrent, in the fall of 1926, when the disciplinary barracks held about five hundred prisoners. For days the grapevine hummed of a bold plot for a wholesale break. At a signal, every prisoner would quit work, make a wild dash for the cliffs, leap into the bay like a horde of lemmings, and head out in all directions—for San Francisco, the East Bay, past Angel Island to Marin County—to confuse the gunning guards and hamper the hunt by boat.

The ringleader estimated their chances bluntly: "Some of us will drown, some will be shot, some will be recaptured—but *some* will make it." An attractive gamble, and these were soldiers disciplined to the gamble of war itself: each felt *he* would be the lucky one. It also held the enormous appeal of a venture that would go down in penal history as the most daring, most dramatic mass break of all time. Reckless excitement infected the men.

The grapevine whispers came to Colonel G. Maury Crallé, who had recently taken over as commandant of Alcatraz. He was a handsome, scholarly man who wore a pince-nez. For some time he paced his office, then summoned his aide. He ordered the prisoners assembled on the parade grounds—guarded by only a handful of officers and men, bearing no arms. After a deliberate delay to heighten the prisoners' bewilderment, Colonel Crallé strode forth, an imposing figure. He looked over the assembled plotters, adjusted his pince-nez, then delivered a farewell address:

"I know what you men are up to. It's a damn-fool idea—a lot of you will drown. But I'd like to see it settled, one way or the other, right now. If you're determined to go, we won't stand in your way. There will be no pursuit, and no notification of the police." He gestured toward San Francisco. "Go ahead, swim!"

He turned on his heel and strode back to his headquarters. The men glanced at one another, with a vague misgiving, then glanced at the bay, with a distinct qualm. The water, frosted with whitecaps, suddenly took on a chill aspect. They, as the commandant had, turned on their heels and marched smartly back to their jobs.

Not all the plotters were fortunate enough to have a Colonel Crallé as commandant. In 1918, while the barracks celebrated Thanksgiving, four inmates slipped past the sentries, crept down to a beach, lashed planks together for a raft and shoved off for San Francisco. They vanished as completely as the later Roe and Cole. Three others tied driftwood together and paddled off one night. They rode out the Gate on the current, back in on a flood tide. By dawn, chilled and seasick, they were on their knees praying for rescue. A ferryboat crew picked them up. Another trio tried a new tack—they headed northward for the Marin shore. They too welcomed a rescue party. Their raft had come apart, and they were clinging to pieces, one of them unconscious.

Other escapes were marked by greater artistry and less risk. One prisoner who did clerical work vanished but did not, as Roe and Cole presumably did, go out the Gate on a swift ebb tide. On a day when the commandant was off the island, he simply wrote out an order for his own release, forged the commandant's signature, put on his cap, trotted down to the wharf, presented it to the sentry, boarded the boat, rode over to Fort Mason, walked down the gangplank, presented the order to that sentry, caught a streetcar downtown.

On another occasion, an officer on the commandant's staff died, and the widow ordered a mourning outfit from the city. Not long after it arrived, the widow, weeping behind the heavy black veil, appeared at the wharf. The sentry, reluctant to ask her to produce her pass, considerately helped her onto the boat. The dock sentry at Fort Mason, equally sympathetic, helped her off and on her way. Hours later the commandant's office received an inquiry from the widow—about her mourning outfit.

In all the escapes, and escape attempts, during the Army days on Alcatraz, none led to violence, none to bloodshed, for these inmates were essentially a different breed. The men who came to The Rock as federal prisoners were classed as professional criminals. They made custodial care a far more risky business. Warden Johnston once put it: "The first thing a prisoner does is case the joint. They watch everything, every guard. They look and look for a weak point."

Such men were Tex Lucas and two other long-term bank bandits, Rufus Franklin and Thomas R. Limerick. They had looked, and looked, and found a weak point. It was Guard Royal C. Cline's habit of going into his office after counting the crew into the furniture factory on the third floor of the old Model Shop Building. He did this as usual after lunch on May 23, 1938. Franklin and Limerick slipped into an adjacent saw-filing room to prepare a window that opened horizontally, while Lucas sawed a two-by-four brace. A moment later, in an unlucky departure from routine, Cline walked into the smaller workshop. They cracked his skull, fatally, with a hammer.

Lucas came in with the slab of wood. They filled their pockets with short pieces of pipe and bolts, then braced the window open with the two-by-four. Lucas, pliers in hand, stepped out. His foot crashed through two panes, making a noise that apparently no guards heard. Lucas hesitated and Franklin gave him a nudge. He reached up with his pliers, cut the barbed wire edging the roof, then clambered up. The others followed.

They spread out and stormed a gun tower, hurling iron missiles. Guard Harold P. Stites fired his .45 automatic, caught Limerick above the right eye. Limerick looked startled, smiled, and fell. Franklin came at the tower with a raised hammer. Stites, pistol empty, fired his rifle.

The slug slammed into Franklin's right shoulder, and he stumbled backward across the barbed wire, the hammer dropping to the ground. Guard Clifford Stewart, patrolling the far side of the roof, came on the run, saw Lucas trying to force the tower door. Stewart raised his shotgun and shouted, "Hold it!" Lucas flung himself under a catwalk.

Lucas told the FBI: "We planned to grab the tower guard's guns and make our way to the dock and grab the launch and escape. It was a crazy scheme and I now realize how nutty we were."

Lucas, already serving fifty years, drew life for the guard's murder, and Franklin had now achieved perhaps a record: thirty years, plus two life terms. While a lifer in Alabama, he was given a temporary release upon the death of his mother and picked up a thirty-year federal rap by robbing a bank on his way to the funeral.

So far, the two who made a clean break—if being swept to sea can be considered a successful escape—and the bloody break attempt on the rooftop breached the security of the area outside the walls. Soupy fog made the one possible, a guard's regularity of routine set off the other. The Rock's cellhouse was something else: all the scientific devices, the intricate locking systems, the toolproof bars, the endless counts and cell checks, the constant shakedowns, the vigilance of the guards—it was inconceivable that any man could best such a formidable array and break out. Yet, as a convict once said, what seems impossible to someone on the outside looks possible to the inmate plotting in his cell, completely surrounded by steel and concrete. Even at Alcatraz, one January morning in 1939 the impossible became the possible—an escape not just from the cellhouse but, more incredible, from solitary. It happened on a Friday the Thirteenth. . . .

About 3:45 A.M. Guard Tom Pritchard, on outside patrol, groped along the road above the cliffs, his flashlight poking a ragged hole in the cottony fog. The foghorn behind him at the southeastern tip vibrated mournfully; the one at the north end answered, then distantly the horns at the Bay Bridge and the Golden Gate, like croaking frogs around a lake. In one of the seconds-brief intervals of silence,

Pritchard heard a distinct call, "Hey!" He stopped, turning his head like a radar antenna. A foghorn blasted the quiet. He hurried onto a blurry patch of light, the south gun tower, flashed a signal beam and shouted, "Just heard a voice. That you calling?"

"No," replied the towerman. "I heard voices too, coming from the cove. Something going on down there."

"I'll go see," said Pritchard.

"Stay right there, where I can see you."

About then the cellhouse guard walked into D Block. All had been well at the 3 A.M. count. He glanced into the cell of Arthur (Doc) Barker, notorious kidnaper and life-termer. He peered closer. The cell was empty. He phoned the Armorer. He checked the cell next to Barker's. Empty. Then the next, and the next, and the next. Five in a row, all vacant.

Down in the cove below the south gun tower five gray figures worked desperately in the chill fog: Doc Barker; Dale Stamphill, also doing life for kidnaping; Rufus McCain, ninety-nine years for bank robbery, kidnaping; William Martin, twenty-five years, postal robbery; Henri Young, twenty years, bank robbery.

McCain had horned in on the escape by a ruse. He had the job of delivering meals to convicts in solitary on a table with rollers and had intercepted a note from Young to Doc Barker regarding the plot. He then made a dagger, and in the yard on the following Saturday he feigned a fight with a prisoner. As he had foreseen, they slapped him in D Block and, better luck, in a cell next to the conspirators.

And now they were all on the beach, working feverishly, the sound of the siren goading them on. McCain and Young were stripped to their long drawers, and the five were using their other garments to bind driftwood into a raft.

"Shhh!" warned Doc.

The prison launch burp-burped by. Its searchlight, like the mobile searchlights hauled to the cliff above, only whitened the mist, failing to penetrate it. Guards with submachine guns were inching down toward the shore.

Moments later Doc again cautioned, "Shhh!"

A Coast Guard patrol boat came along. Its powerful beam spotlighted a tableau of raft makers. The convicts scattered.

"Halt!"

A fusillade ripped into the flight. Stamphill stopped, slugs in both legs. Doc Barker dropped, a slug in the thigh, another in the neck that came out near the right eye. He died an hour later. Martin stood stock-still, hands high. They found the near-naked McCain, cold-blue, around a jutting cliff, on his knees begging for mercy. A few feet away stood Young in his drawers.

Doc Barker was the youngest of the clan that Kate (Ma) Barker led out of the Ozarks. One, a small-time hoodlum, fell in a hail of police bullets. Another went to Leavenworth for life. Ma, Fred, and Doc, now joined by Alvin (Old Creepy) Karpis, blazed a career that culminated in the $200,000 abduction of Edward G. Bremer, St. Paul banker, in 1934. They took him to a hideout in Illinois and there kept him captive for twenty-one days. Later G-men traveled the route time and again; on one trip they found empty gasoline cans by the roadside, and off a can came a set of fingerprints—Doc's. This linked the kidnaping to the Barker-Karpis gang. Doc was captured in Chicago, and ten days later G-men fought a pitched battle with Ma and Fred in Florida. She died lying behind a silenced machine gun, he beside an automatic rifle. Doc drew life. Karpis, caught soon afterward, also drew life, and on the morning Doc broke out into the fog to his death, Karpis watched him go from a cell down the row.

At the Fort Mason pier, as Doc's body was borne on a blood-stained stretcher from the launch to an ambulance, a guard remarked: "Well, he's a lot better off now where he is than where he was." Doc was buried in a plotter's field, the brief services attended only by the prison chaplain, a prison clerk, and four paid pallbearers from an undertaking parlor.

The multiple break from the isolation block of the escapeproof cellhouse brought Director Bennett of the Prison Bureau flying out from Washington for a personal investigation. He then explained to the press how it had happened: The quintet cut through the bottom of a bar in each cell—not with saws, which he felt could not have passed the metal detector, but possibly with a banjo string or piano wire or watch spring or any thin strip of metal, along with an abrasive such as a valve-grinding compound. They then spread the bars of a window, its sill about waist high, with something heavier than a crowbar, presumably a jack. They dropped eight feet to the ground, made their way to the beach and tossed the tools into the bay—again presumably, inasmuch as none were uncovered in the subsequent search.

"Alcatraz," Bennett said, "houses the country's most cunning and nervy escape artists, who have plenty of time to think up ways of getting out. And when they go through our first line of defenses, we have to rebuild them. That is what we are doing. We have found nothing to lose any confidence in the prison personnel. . . ."

At the inquest Associate Warden E. J. Miller, the sole witness, offered this sworn testimony: Smuggling of tools into the cellhouse was possible because the metal detector worked only about 60 percent of the time. The convicts had sawed away for a long period, undiscovered, despite periodic bar examinations by officers experienced in the ways of escape artists. No saws had been found, no trace of filings, no smear used to conceal the progress of their work on the bars. They had wrenched apart the toolproof window bars in spite of constant vigilance. No searchlight on the island was strong enough to pierce fog, but two guards patrolled the north and south halves of the island through the night, passing any given point once every half hour, shoving driftwood into the bay to prevent raft-making. The prison was well manned.

"How many guards were on duty at the time in the cellhouse?" asked the coroner, Dr. T. B. W. Leland.

"Two in the gun galleries, one on the floor," Miller replied.

"Were they asleep?"

"Possibly," said Miller. "They definitely were not alert."

Said the jury: "From the evidence at hand, we believe this escape was made possible by the failure of the system for guarding prisoners now in use at Alcatraz and we recommend a drastic improvement.

Further, we recommend . . . that the citizens of San Francisco unite in an effort to have a more suitable location chosen for the imprisonment of the type of desperadoes at present housed at Alcatraz."

Said Dr. Leland, closing the case: "The citizens of San Francisco resent Alcatraz. However, as long as it is here, and not a beautiful park as I'd like to have it, we can but hope it will be open for inspection by the public."

This was January 24, 1939, and Coroner Leland's hope proved forlorn. The veil remained over Alcatraz, parted briefly for second-hand inspection only when a killing required an inquest or a riot a trial. Associate Warden Miller's candor seemed to contradict Director Bennett's earlier comment that he had found nothing to lose any confidence in the prison personnel. Further contradiction came in the firing of a guard, an item withheld from the press.

The jury partly got its wish: the system of containing the desperadoes in solitary was improved, not so much a drastic step as a simple modernization, for the "first line of defenses" was actually a relic of the old Army days. This was the prison's old D Block, and a year after the flight of the quintet a new isolation quarter, featuring toolproof bars and electrically controlled locks on the dark cells, was built with a WPA appropriation.

In a way, the secrecy of Alcatraz worked to the advantage of the prison administration, for it served as an effective cover on the real story of that break—a story that reveals both the brazenness of the convicts and an incredible custodial laxness. Unlike the new D Block, isolated behind concrete walls in the southwest corner of the cellhouse, the old block had a grate partition. The cell bars were the antiquated, flat, soft-iron. Although Bennett's investigation indicated that no saw was used, the convicts did use a saw, a two-inch piece of a hacksaw blade. It took them, as Miller testified, a long time to cut through (they had only the one bit of blade for the five bars), but they did not rely on the protection of nighttime for this phase of their project. They chose to work days. Their chief problem was the guard in the west gun gallery, whose patrol took him periodically into D Block. However, a window in the cellhouse run of the gallery overlooked the mess hall, and the guard was stationed at the window during meals. And so the convict in possession of the blade at the moment sawed safely away through breakfast, lunch, and dinner. He flushed each session's filings down the toilet, smeared soap over the cut, then rubbed burnt matches over the soap to complete the camouflage.

Even though the work was concealed in this way, normal checks would have detected the escape plot, considering the time required to sever a bar in each of five cells. In a check, a guard taps a bar with a rubber mallet. Tampering produces a distinctive sound.

The window operation called for night work: they had to leave their cells. The bars were toolproof: tough alloy steel surrounding a loose rod. Cut the outer part, and that's it: the inner core simply turns with the saw, or guitar string. The core is brittle. Nightly, like gray-clad brownies, the convicts bent their severed cell bars, crawled out, took turns hacking while one stood watch, crawled back in, straightened the bars. They placed an order on the grapevine for a bar spreader, and when they were ready (the window bar cut full circumference) it was ready, a device of remarkable simplicity: two bolts, with left- and right-handed threads, screwed into the same outsized nut. They set the bolts between two bars and turned the nut. The bolts unscrewed, the cut bar spread, the inner core cracked, and out they went.

(Such toolproof bars are already obsolete. Convicts found they could even get by without a spreader. Cut the outer part as a woodsman fells a tree, at a slant; insert a wedge to hold the core tight; go to the other side and saw right through. Toolproof bars are now more toolproof: a half-dozen hard thin bars set in a steel tube, then steel poured in. Too tough to spread or crack, take forever to saw.)

Plotters fear other inmates more than guards, and the fewer in the know the safer. There's always the snitcher currying favor, and one tried it on the quintet. He snitched to a guard, "A bunch of cons keep runnin' past my cell all night." The guard gave him the eye, then led him to Miller, the associate warden. Convicts loose at night in D Block? The associate warden gave him the eye, then they both led him upstairs and locked him in a bug cage. Three nights later the quintet decamped.

All these episodes, many marked by violence and bloodshed—the Roe-Cole escape and the several other escape attempts, the amazing break out of solitary, the attack on the warden, the incidence of insanity and suicides—suggested a flaw in the conceptual structure of The Rock. Warden Johnston simplified the problem in one comment to the press: "It's not possible sometimes for men contemplating seventy-five years on Alcatraz to face such a prospect with perfect equanimity. Life is pretty monotonous here. We feed the men well and treat them well, but they just don't like their surroundings."

One feature of their surroundings the men abhorred was target practice. In the evenings, after lockup, the cellhouse echoed the rattle of gunfire as guards on the yard wall outside emptied pistols, rifles, machine guns. Sometimes an inmate's nerves cracked, and his screams of "Stop it! Goddammit, stop it!" heightened the macabre effect. In the morning, when the convicts marched out to the lineup on the way to the shops, they encountered a sight that made some queasy. Strewn about the yard, like bullet-riddled corpses, were dummies in convict garb. Even this grim object lesson failed to deter plotters, intensifying instead the desire to get away, and in time it was stopped.

Johnston tried color psychology to relieve the dull, depressing reality of steel and concrete. He felt it would help those men who had fewer than seventy-five years of contemplation in prospect in return to society with a happier outlook. Color schemes varied: cell ceiling white, walls pale and dark greens; cellhouse walls green, gray, and white (later a startling pink with barn-red trim, still later a deep tan); pink and ivory in the mess hall; other combinations in other areas, including the shops. This brightened up the place, but not noticeably the men; they still did not seem to enjoy their surroundings.

The starvation diet imposed on strikers and other miscreants in solitary was improved. At the time of the early strikes against the severe rules prison officials denied that the warden had issued a no-work, no-eat edict and indicated the men were fed as usual. Much later, the warden offered his own views on dungeons and diets, and the punitive merit of hunger: "People get the wrong idea when you talk of dungeons. We have the dungeons and we sometimes use them. But it is not always necessary to use dungeons to punish a prisoner. You'd be surprised how much enforced absence from a meal or two will do to change the attitude of a recalcitrant prisoner."[1]

The new diet in solitary called for a minimum of 2,100 calories a day (3,600 in the mess hall), but it did not specify in what form. An ex-guard recalls: "We called it the monotony diet: bread and water in the morning, and in the evening plain boiled spaghetti, no seasoning or sauce of any kind. To make their breakfast more palatable, we'd slap a little mustard on the bread."

Still trouble brewed on the island, periodically erupted. Johnston attributed it to the inability of some long-termers to embrace a stoic attitude, insisting that the food and treatment were all any incarcerated man might desire. He decried the brutality of a solitary confinement, said it was seldom inflicted. Only when a prisoner became obstreperous was he sent down to the dungeon to cool off. He told a reporter that strong-arm methods were not actually needed on Alcatraz because the "everyday safeguards instill a feeling of helplessness." Even if the safeguards failed, the regular guards never resorted to bullying or beating to pacify an unruly convict: "Like noncommissioned officers in the Army, they use only moral suasion."

---

[1] Warden Johnston's views on dungeons and diets were told to Alfred P. Reck, North American Newspaper Alliance writer and later city editor of the *Oakland Tribune*.

Chapter 9

IN THE SPRING OF 1941 a murder trial took place in the United States District Court of San Francisco that became celebrated as the Trial of Alcatraz. It began routinely as the trial of Henri Young for the slaying of Rufus McCain, but midway The Rock itself superseded Young as a defendant *in absentia*.

Young had engineered the break out of solitary two years earlier, and McCain was in on it. Both landed in the Dark Hole. McCain emerged first and spread word that when Young got out there would, in short time, be only one of them left on the island—McCain. His verbal sniping included what the newspapers referred to as "a revolting remark" about Young's mother. He flew into a rage when informed his hour of freedom, shivering on the beach in his long cotton drawers, had cost him 11,880 days of good time off, a third of his ninety-nine-year term. He blamed Young for the failure of the escape and branded him "a yellow punk bastard."

Young attributed McCain's hostility to various causes. He was chagrined at being found out a coward, on his knees pleading for mercy at the time of the capture. He was sore because Young wouldn't go along with his desperate plan, once the jig was up, to snatch a couple of wives as hostages. Their feud predated the break: McCain had long harbored a resentment at Young's response to a homosexual advance with a sock on the jaw.

McCain's threats to kill him came to Young in solitary by the grapevine. They began to bug him. Everywhere he looked—and everywhere, in the Dark Hole, was midnight—McCain was giving him the evil eye. One morning, not long after his release from solitary,

Young slipped out of a third-floor shop, down an outside stairway, into the tailor shop on the second floor. A canvas holster on his belt held a steel blade with a rounded butt. In his hand at his side he gripped a seven-inch, bronze stiletto with a tape handle, honed to razor keenness. He walked up to McCain and rammed the stiletto into his stomach. McCain fell like a sack. Young stood staring at him. Guards relieved Young of the knives, and as they led him away he muttered, "I hope I killed the bastard." He had, and it looked like the gas chamber at San Quentin for Young.

These details came out at the trial. . . .

Almost seven years had passed since The Rock became a Devil's Island, and its mystery-nurtured reputation was such that spectators gasped when the twenty-nine-year-old Henri Young walked into Federal Judge Michael J. Roche's court for arraignment that April morning in 1941. Alongside the husky guards, he had a gentle, amiable look, the groomed appearance of a shoe clerk in his gray suit, white shirt, and blue tie, dark hair slicked in a meticulous part.

Asked if he desired counsel, the accused slayer, in his fifth year of a twenty-year bank robbery term when he abbreviated Rufus McCain's ninety-nine-year stretch, put on an act that patently astonished the venerable jurist. He strode to and fro before the bench, like a veteran trial lawyer, as he addressed the court: "May I have two attorneys, Your Honor? Categorically speaking, I have a preference among attorneys. I would like to have for my counsel two young attorneys with no established reputations either for verdicts or hung juries."

"Rather an unusual request," commented the judge.

"I want the two most youthful attorneys I can get," Young said. He grinned. "They probably won't do any good for me, but maybe they can use the experience."

On his next trip to court, for plea, Young beamed at the sight of his counsel. Both had a fresh-off-the-campus aura: James Martin MacInnis, in his middle twenties and four years out of Stanford Law School, sporting a derby and double-breasted overcoat; Sol A. Abrams, thirtyish, pink-cheeked, cherub-faced. Young was not aware that MacInnis already had a wide Hall of Justice experience, and that Abrams was a former assistant U.S. attorney. Judge Roche had been deluged with pleas from young barristers clutching law degrees but, for the prisoner's own welfare, preferred counsel with trial practice.

They came up with a unique defense: Alcatraz, not Henri Young, killed Rufus McCain. Alcatraz had put Young into a "psychological coma" and rendered him "legally unconscious" at the moment of the slaying. Questioning veniremen, they delved into the misty realm of the subconscious, of dual personality, of irresistible impulse, sleep-walking, dissociation of ideas. At length, a jury of six men and six housewives sat in the box, their foreman a cultural leader of San Francisco, Paul Verdier, president of the City of Paris, a pioneer department store.

"Henry Young was only eleven days out of the dungeon, where he had spent three years and two months, when he killed Rufus McCain," MacInnis told the jurors. "The mental torture he suffered during those years robbed him of his senses. Thirty-two men have gone insane and have been taken off the island in straitjackets and placed in asylums since Young entered Alcatraz in 1935. Alcatraz, not Young, is responsible for the murder of McCain."

Prosecutor Frank Hennessy called for the extreme penalty, invoking the simple law of the land in homicide, a law that ignores moral insanity, a law rooted in the old British Macnaughten Rule, recognizing insanity only if a man does not know the nature of his act or does not know that the act is wrong.

Warden Johnston took the stand, the image of mildness in anti-quated steel-rimmed spectacles. And the page-one story in the *Chron-icle* next morning started off: "Out of the mist-shrouded walls of Alcatraz Prison has come for the first time the inside story of life upon the most dreaded island in the United States."

In his memoirs, Johnston described the treatment of prisoners at Alcatraz: "Privileges are limited, supervision is strict, routine is exacting, discipline is firm, but there is no cruelty or undue harsh-ness, and we insist upon a decent regard for the humanities."

Under cross-examination, Warden Johnston said the cells lining two walls of an underground area, relic of the old fortress citadel, were abolished as a dungeon in 1938, four years after Alcatraz became The Rock.

"Is it dark there?" asked MacInnis.

"Well, persons confined in the cells had no light."

"Any sanitation facilities?"

"No."

The warden admitted men were sometimes lodged in the pitch-black dungeon cells for months with only a single blanket and no bed, sleeping on a concrete floor. Young had been in such absolute darkness for nineteen days at a time without a bath. When the dungeon was abandoned, he was confined in a narrow cell with a solid steel door in the isolation block and, the warden said, was removed once for a period of "thirty to thirty-five minutes" in a year.

"Can any light get in these cells?"

"Some light can creep in," said the warden. "And creep is the word."

He said that men in solitary received one meal in three days, with bread and water in between; that straitjackets were never used as punishment, only when prescribed by a doctor.

"Was Floyd Hill in a straitjacket for forty days?"

"By the doctor's orders," said the warden.

"Is brew-making an ordinary hazard at Alcatraz?"

"It's not frequent."

MacInnis spoke of a maize brew and the exotic drink made of milk and gasoline, then asked: "Was Young ever supplied with such concoctions?"

"It is unknown to me," the warden said.

They reviewed Young's record. He had been placed in the dungeon or solitary, and deprived of 2,400 days of good behavior time, for such infractions as not eating all his food, giving a Bronx cheer, having two extra pairs of socks in his cell, agitating a strike, insolence, a fist fight over an umpire's decision in a ball game in the yard, loud talking, raving in his cell.

"Once," said the warden, "Young was put in the dungeon for banging his pillow on the concrete floor."

MacInnis, momentarily taken aback, inquired: "How much noise can such an offense create?"

The warden replied, "Strangely, quite a racket can be made by banging a pillow on the concrete floor."

A defense request for writs of habeas corpus testificandum to bring over a dozen of The Rock's most notorious inmates made the headlines and drew even greater throngs. The bailiff posted a "No Standing Room" sign. Spectators had to identify themselves before they could enter the courtroom. Persons in the overflow that filled the long corridor had to produce identification. A score of Alcatraz guards and deputy marshals stood sentry at the doors and mingled with the audience and the crowd outside. Convict witnesses arrived from the island in pairs, manacled and shackled. When called, each was relieved of these restraints, hurried swiftly through a rear door, and the door relocked. The witness then passed by the press table; behind the counsel table at which Young sat; behind the prosecution table at which Warden Johnston and Associate Warden Miller sat; past the front of the jury box to the stand. At either end of the jury box stood a guard.

For days a parade of robbers, kidnapers, murderers took this route to recite chilling tales of Alcatraz. The spectators, and the jurors, sat enthralled.

First came William Dunnock, thirty-four, doing fifteen years for a Baltimore bank holdup. He seemed nervous in his civilian garb, looked tired, had an ashen pallor, coughed frequently. At the outset he waited while objections were made, and sustained, to counsel's questions, such as: Was he struck across the nose in the hospital with a blackjack, so hard that the nose was broken, and *then* did Associate Warden Miller punch him in the nose? After he had kept silent through a series of questions, Dunnock began snapping out answers before the prosecutor could utter an objection.

"Did Miller tear off your clothes, strike you, and shove you into a dungeon cell without bedding?"

"Yes."

"Do you expect to be physically punished for testifying here?"

"Yes."

"Were you in a pitch-black cell for long periods—nineteen days or more—without a bath, without soap, without tooth powder?"

"Yes."

The court repeatedly admonished the witness to wait for prosecution objections and instructed the jury to disregard these rapid responses. Nonetheless, MacInnis managed to get before the jury by this back-door route the fact that his colleague, Abrams, on his first trip to Alcatraz to consult prospective witnesses had been refused permission to see Dunnock in his isolation cell, where the convict said he was nursing wounds inflicted by a guard with a gasbilly. Abrams had to obtain a court order to interview Dunnock and saw him on the second visit, but the prisoner said he had been hastily removed to an open-front cell "that had a bed."

To a prosecution protest that such testimony was irrelevant, Abrams replied: "We are putting Alcatraz on trial, but we can't help that. We must show it in its true light."

Ray Stevenson, forty-one, Michigan bank robber doing twenty-five years, tall with a good bearing, spoke calmly but with an apparent effort. He corroborated Dunnock's testimony.

Had he heard Dunnock groaning as he lay beaten on the floor, pleading for mercy, yelling "Stop twisting my leg, for God's sake!"

Yes.

Long intervals elapsed between pairs of witnesses. Only when the convicts who had testified were safely back in their Rock cells were the next two escorted over. During these breaks Associate Warden Miller was recalled to the stand for rebuttal. He denied ever laying a hand on Dunnock or ever beating an inmate before lodging him in solitary. He admitted that prisoners were not always provided with a blanket in their damp, dark dungeon cells during the day. He admitted too that men were stripped naked before placed in these cells, but he said their clothes were tossed in to them later.

Next came Sam Berlin of Baltimore, doing three to fifteen years for robbing a brewery in the District of Columbia, a first offense. He was forty—a tall, thin, balding man with an eager face and wispy voice.

The word about prosecution objections apparently had sped along the Rock grapevine: Berlin, and others to follow, spat out answers.

Was he aware that a convict, Whitey Lewis, had his skull cracked by guards, was later sent to an insane asylum? Yes. Did he recall that a convict named Wutke was driven to suicide by unbearable treatment? The jury saw him nod as an objection was sustained.

Ed Wutke was thirty-six, doing a stretch for murder on the high seas, when he became The Rock's first suicide. A guard stood over a convict in those days while he shaved, to see that the razor blade was used for the purpose intended. Wutke discovered another means. He extracted the tiny blade from a pencil sharpener and after lights-out one night he climbed into bed and slit his throat. The deed was not discovered until the next morning when he failed to appear at his cell front for the standup count and the guard went in to rouse him.

Abruptly, the prosecutor began allowing the convict witnesses more latitude by raising fewer objections. Thus, when asked if Walter Bearden, an inmate with tuberculosis, had been confined to a solitary cell with him for twelve days, Sam Berlin could reply with more than a fast affirmative or a nod: "Yes, he fainted and slumped to the floor of his cell, but wasn't given any medical treatment. He was spitting up blood and begged to be sent up to the hospital. He died a month later." He said Bearden was pushed into the cell stripped naked. His clothes, except for shoes, were later tossed in.

Berlin said it was general knowledge among convicts that Joe Bowers, slain climbing the fence at the incinerator, was daffy. He testified an inmate named Vito Giacaloni, sick in his cell, was so viciously beaten by guards that he died en route to the hospital asylum in Missouri.

Berlin reported a conversation with Young regarding Giacaloni: "I told him that they just beat him (Giacaloni) over the skull and locked him up in isolation. He could not read or write or talk the American language, he is ignorant of what is going on all around him."

He said that an inmate, Jack Allen, was in agony one night and rattled a cup on his cell bars to attract the guard, who came with the lieutenant and warned Allen they would put him in the hole if he didn't quiet down. "He kept hollering for a doctor and they put him in the hole and he died fifty-two hours later."

He described the dungeon cells as damp from water seepage, and drafty. He depicted life in the dungeon darkness: inmates, deprived of shoes, walked the cold concrete floor in stocking feet; they received a cup of water twice a day, a slice of bread once; the bucket substitute for a toilet was not emptied or cleaned in nine days; occasionally a doctor would "peek into the cells."

"What was he looking for?" asked MacInnis.

"To see if we were dead, I guess. A lot of men have died there."

Newsmen questioned Berlin as he waited in the marshal's cage for the return trip to the island. This was in itself a rarity as Bennett, the prison director, forbids the interviewing of any federal prisoner.

Berlin told them: "I've been over there six years. I'm going crazy. They talk about that being a prison for hardened criminals. Lot of young kids over there, for minor offenses, and they're going crazy like I am. Since I've been there I've seen thirty prisoners go crazy, be put in a straitjacket and get shipped off to some government hospital. There are few visitors. Most of the inmates are from poor families, whose relatives can't afford to travel this far to see them."

During a wait for another brace of witnesses, Associate Warden Miller resumed the stand. He said the dungeon toilet buckets were emptied two to four times a day, and inmates had a bowl of water at all times.

Abrams stepped forth, asked a question that focused the eyes of every juror on the prison keeper: Had he, on the night of July 9, 1939, inflicted upon the defendant, Henri Young, brutality of the most savage sort?

Miller said he had never touched Young, nor any other prisoner; that he had never ordered a guard to strike a prisoner; that he had never seen a guard mistreat a prisoner.

Abrams produced prison records. They showed that on the date in question Young was sent to solitary for banging his pillow on the floor and leading the convicts in a song. Were they singing a ballad in reference to him? "They'll hang old Meathead from a sour apple tree."

The associate warden replied in a low voice: "They may have."

In retaliation for that chant, did Miller himself drag Young from his cell, throw him down a circular steel stairway, then jump on his face with both feet, knocking out several teeth? Thereupon, did he look on while two guards beat Young mercilessly with saps, and two stood by in reserve to take over when the first pair wearied? And then did they dump him, unconscious, in a dark cell?

The heavy-set associate warden denied the entire episode, with one exception: he did order Young into an isolation cell. He then volunteered a custodial viewpoint of solitary: some prisoners thrived on such confinement, gained weight, emerged spiritually benefited, with "a better outlook on life."

Others present a different portrait of Miller. An old-time gangster, who admittedly had been chained more than once to a wall of The Rock's dungeon says: "Miller was all right. He might beat the hell out of you one day, but the next day you ask him a favor and he did it. He was a good guy."

A former colleague recalls: "Lefty Egan, one of Capone's torpedomen, was up near the roof painting with his left hand when the end of the scaffold slips. He grabs at the rope with his crippled right hand but it's no good. The guard's an older fellow with a bad heart— he can't help. Just then Miller comes by. He runs up and catches Lefty. It knocks the wind out of him and he staggers and goes down, Lefty on top. Lefty told me later if Miller hadn't risked his own neck, he'd've been a goner, sure as hell."

The parade of horror-bearers kept up.

Harmon Waley, thirty, doing forty-five years for his role in the Weyerhaeuser kidnaping, related how he made the dungeon while sick. He had asked for medicine, was told it would be sent to his cell later. He asked for aspirin, again was told he would get his medicine later. "So," he recounted, with a retrospective grin, "I told the doctor what to do with his aspirin and was thrown in the dungeon. I got sicker, then raving, and they put me in a straitjacket."

Carl Hood, twenty-nine, a Texan who had stabbed an inmate at Leavenworth, recalled that he and Young, in whispered conversations in the dungeon, had "wondered why the people of the United States let a prison like Alcatraz stand." He told of an insane convict dying after a blackjack clubbing by guards. He said a male nurse had cruelly wielded a metal pan on a helpless hospital patient, "paralyzed from the hips down."

Harry C. Kelly, forty-one, a San Francisco mail robber, testified: "Young came to Alcatraz a well-educated, sane young fellow, but after those years in solitary he was about crazy, mentally unbalanced. One morning he started to the dining room without his trousers. I had to help him. I told him he couldn't go to eat that way. One Sunday we happened to have steak for dinner. He walked right by the steam table and sat down without any food. He didn't seem to know he was in the dining room. I had to share my food with him."

To support the claim that an "irresistible impulse," induced by conditions on The Rock, had driven Young to slay McCain, the defense summoned Dr. Ritchey, Alcatraz psychiatrist. He testified that Young was "emotionally unstable" and had acted under "tension."

Prosecutor Hennessy produced a report by Dr. Ritchey on Young, eliciting testimony that Young was "rational" and knew what he was doing on December 3, the morning he killed McCain.

"When did you make a report on Young's condition, Doctor?" asked MacInnis.

"A few days after December 3," said Dr. Ritchey.

MacInnis then offered evidence that the report was dated April 10, 1941, "a few days before this trial began."

"Why," counsel asked, "did you leave out your conclusions that Young was emotionally unstable, that he was acting under tension?"

"I thought it was self-evident," said the doctor.

Henri Young took the stand. The jury, and the audience, sat rapt as he gave a vivid portrayal of the dungeon on The Rock.

"The cell was all black, the walls painted black. It was nine by five by seven feet high. I was placed in there nude. After my clothes had been searched for particles of tobacco, they were thrown in to me. But not my shoes. I had no tobacco, no soap, no toothbrush. Because of the stink, it was like stepping into a sewer, nauseating."

Abrams asked about furnishings, food.

"I had no towel. Two blankets were thrown in to me at 5 P.M. There was no bed, no mattress, no furniture. During the thirteen days I was in there the first time, I had two full meals. In between was bread, three or four slices of bread in the morning. When you get a meal you literally gorge it. It all tastes the same."

Abrams asked, "Did the winds of the Golden Gate sweep in?"

"The cell I was in is called the ice box. There is an old-type ventilator in the wall. It was open. I shivered all the time. I was in my stocking feet on concrete. At times I would get in a corner and put my coveralls around my head to keep warm. When you walk in the black cell, you have to keep one hand on a wall so you won't hurt yourself. Often you get dizzy spells. I'd sit in one position until my legs went to sleep, then I'd move. Then I'd lie on the floor. It was cold concrete and damp. You never have a bath in solitary. All the time I was there I saw only one man get a bath. He had a bucket of cold water thrown on him. You hardly ever sleep, only cat naps. You wake up shivering, hardly able to move. You ache. Men were beaten into unconsciousness. I could hear their yells and screams. One boy was beaten after he hadn't eaten for fifteen days. I could hear Miller cursing and raging like a madman. I was scared to death. Sometimes I got to raving. It was impossible to be calm."

Abrams asked, "What do you think about?"

"You can only think about your own problems. You wonder how human beings could do that to human beings. It was a pretty heavy penalty to pay for refusing to do some laundry work. . . . You can't talk to Warden Johnston, you have to talk to Miller. If you do get to Johnston, he is a master of equivocation. They don't follow the federal penal laws at Alcatraz. We had a congressional pamphlet showing the rules. We took it to Miller and showed him we had not violated regulations in several respects.

"Miller said to me, 'You don't run Alcatraz. I run it. And Alcatraz is not a penitentiary. Alcatraz is Alcatraz.'"

Dr. Joseph Catton, noted alienist with wide experience in homicide cases, a witness for the defense, told the court: "Men should not be beaten for their natural reactions to corporal punishment, which should be termed corporal control. After it has served its purpose for subduing a prisoner, it becomes a torture. Prison produces a mental condition not unlike the 'shell shock' of war." As for the Black Hole of solitary:" "God and nature gave us eyes to appreciate masses and forms. We're supposed to get messages from the things we see. Being alone for weeks in lightless cells works havoc. Man is selfish, sexual, and social."

Prosecutor Hennessy, in his closing argument to the jury, said: "They brought a lot of those lost men over here from Alcatraz. In the catalogue, they pass as men, but they are reckless in everything they do or say. They are at war with society."

MacInnis summed up for the defense: "Alcatraz is on trial here. It was Alcatraz that killed McCain. It was the cold, sadistic logic that some men call penology that killed him."

The six men and six women of the jury agreed with the defense. They found Henri Young guilty of involuntary manslaughter, adding a maximum of three years to his term. And then, in an unprecedented action, they convicted Alcatraz of a far graver offense—crimes against humanity. They issued a statement to the press and wired copies to the Department of Justice and Congress.

The gist of their indictment: "That conditions as concern treatment of prisoners at Alcatraz are unbelievably brutal and inhuman, and it is our respectful hope and our earnest petition that a proper and speedy investigation of Alcatraz be made so that justice and humanity may be served."

As he left the bench at trial's end, the judge beckoned to a reporter to come into his chambers. There he poured a couple of neat slugs of bourbon and said, "This has been the damndest trial I ever sat on. Drink up."

Chapter 10

OURTROOM VETERANS WILL tell you there is nothing, not even the weather, so unpredictable as a jury. And yet, to them, the astonishing thing was that the Alcatraz verdict should bear this out—that the word of hardened cons would carry more weight than the word of a warden and his top aide. A warden, to boot, with a fine civic reputation and every appearance of a humanist. And an associate warden with the mien of a parent who was merely nonpermissive.

The credibility of convicts anywhere is normally open to question, and far more so if inmates of Alcatraz. The simple fact of incarceration there—men beyond redemption—would tend to make them unbelievable. And so the grim recitals, while impressing the jury, left the cynical unmoved, except to disgust. Said a court attaché: 'They were all lying through their teeth. They always do, just to get back at the administration. You can never believe anything they say." And a former assistant in the U.S. attorney's office: "A dozen convicts will watch an inmate stabbing, but it's impossible to get a conviction. They will all swear they didn't see a thing. Perjury means nothing to them."

The public for the most part shared the common belief that imprisoned men will perjure themselves at the drop of a shiv. They have nothing to lose. And while the Trial of Alcatraz with its tales of medieval horror held a morbid fascination, the testimony, reconsidered in the cold light of day, seemed just that—tales.

San Franciscans were jolted one morning by a story in the papers. The news was a week old because, police said, the complaint had been filed "by error" in the wrong department. The lead paragraphs in the *Chronicle*'s account went:

"In a lot on Jackson Street a week ago blonde Thelma Fleming went to pick her mother a bouquet of nasturtiums.

"She came out of that lot bloody and bruised, her head lacerated, one eye closed, her face cut. Five stitches were required to close her wounds."

Miss Fleming was twenty-eight, a secretary for an insurance firm, and she weighed 115 pounds. Her assailant was John F. Gilmore, thirty-three, a husky six-foot-one, weighing 210 pounds.

It was Miss Fleming's custom each summer to pick wild flowers in the vacant lot for her mother. This Sunday, walking with her dog, she went into the lot again. Gilmore, who lived in an apartment house next door opened a window and shouted, "Get out of there or I'll kick you out!" She refused, saying she expected "gentlemanly treatment." Gilmore did not own the lot, nor had he planted the nasturtiums. A woman in an apartment on the other side of the lot yelled to Miss Fleming, "I planted those flowers. Go ahead and pick all you want."

Gilmore stormed out, began browbeating her, and Miss Fleming threw a bunch of nasturtiums in his face. And then, as she related: "I turned to see where my dog was and his fist caught me on the side of the head. I did not see the blow coming. My hair fell onto my shoulders. I was dizzy and sick."

She still refused to leave, because: "I didn't believe he had any authority but the authority of his fists."

Gilmore, who towered above her, struck again. His fist smashed into her right eye with such force the impact lifted her off her feet and snapped her jaws together so hard it chipped two front teeth. She fell backward. Shaken, half-blinded, she got to her feet, blood streaming down her right cheek. His knuckles had ripped open her face. He offered to wipe off the blood, but she turned from him and called her dog.

She said Gilmore followed her to the edge of the lot, repeating three times: "I hit you in self-defense, you know. You threw the flowers at me first."

She staggered down the street to the home of a physician, who gave her emergency treatment, then took her to a hospital. She said her eye was black for a week and she had severe headaches.

Gilmore declined to comment, on advice of counsel. His attorney told reporters: "He shoved her—it was a little shove—and she turned and fell and struck something."

Gilmore was a guard at Alcatraz.

Charged with battery, he appeared before Municipal Judge Theresa Meikle a month later. Miss Fleming requested a dismissal to protect Gilmore's federal civil service rating.

Judge Meikle turned to him: "Before I dismiss this charge, I want you to promise me you will never again raise your fists except to defend yourself."

Gilmore solemnly replied: "I promise."

"You know," the judge said, referring to his duties as an Alcatraz guard, "people may be deprived of their freedom, but they still retain personal rights. Your actions reflect something in your character that you should correct."

To his colleagues on The Rock, where he was popularly known as Big John, Gilmore's behavior came as a great surprise. "Big John was a pleasant, mild fellow," one recalled. "You know the type: the big, strong guy who is gentle as a kitten." Big John stayed on at Alcatraz for some years, then left to join the Immigration Service's Border Patrol on the Mexican border.

The Sunday he beat up blonde Thelma Fleming for picking wild flowers in the vacant lot was not quite three months after the Trial of Alcatraz.

Chapter 11

T O MOST SAN FRANCISCANS the Trial of Alcatraz was a spectacle, a Roman holiday. Those who could not squeeze into the courtroom, or even into the corridors, crowded the steps and sidewalk outside, craning for a glimpse of the notorious felons as they came and left in chained pairs, under heavy escort.

To the civic-minded the horrors depicted were a spur to seek anew the removal of this blight, as it was called, from the bay. So incensed was Paul Verdier, the jury foreman, that two days after the trial he began arranging a dinner for the city's most influential people to build the necessary pressure to speed the investigation of Alcatraz demanded by the jurors.

The *San Francisco Chronicle* commented editorially: "We do not enjoy the possibility of being suddenly invaded by a band of human tigers from Alcatraz . . . Alcatraz is both a blemish and a menace and needlessly."

Within a week telegrams went out canceling the Verdier dinner. No reason was given, not another word said about an investigation. Civic outrage subsided, and the trial became a nightmarish memory.

Why had Verdier so abruptly changed his mind? James Martin MacInnis reports: "Two immigration investigators called on Verdier and gave him something to think over if he persisted in annoying the Department of Justice. A question about his citizenship. He was born in Paris of American parents—a citizen of the United States. But he had, unknowingly of course, forfeited his citizenship by joining the French army at the outset of World War I. They could point out that serving on the jury was a criminal act—a juror must be a citizen. And they could threaten deportation proceedings. Out-and-out blackmail. The Department of Justice at work."

At the time, many doubtless wondered: had Verdier sudden misgivings about the verdict—a delayed doubt the convicts had told the truth? After all, the warden had earned a reputation as a prison reformer by cleaning up Folsom. He would naturally want an associate who felt as he did. (The associate warden is the man who runs a prison—an executive officer, a general manager.) And Associate Warden Miller, dubbed Meathead by the convicts, had stoutly denied their accusations that he was the chief practitioner of The Rock's dungeon savagery.

At a farewell affair years later, celebrating Miller's transfer to Leavenworth, Warden Johnston praised him as "a good man for bad men." Johnston had named Miller associate warden over Captain Paul J. Madigan, who had seniority. A custodial officer of that period recalls: "Johnston wanted somebody who could handle the men the way he felt they needed handling. He picked Miller, though Madigan was the senior officer, because he figured Miller was better suited for the job. Miller was a real tough bastard."

The verdict of involuntary manslaughter was tantamount to an acquittal of Henri Young; yet, all it did was to save him from San Quentin's gas chamber. The punishment inflicted was inconsistent with the sentence, certainly not what the jury had in mind. He drew three years, the maximum, to be served *after* completion of his current term. He began serving them the moment he returned to The Rock from court. He went straight into the Dark Hole, and stayed there well beyond the three years.

In that first year—by then Young had spent more than four years in solitary darkness—he again suffered the psychological effects depicted at his trial. He essayed a back-door parole. They found him lying in a pool of blood in his midnight cell, wrists ripped open by a jagged piece of eyeglass. They found him in time; sewed up the wounds, and returned him, minutely frisked, to the darkness.

Three years after that, in 1945, his days on The Rock almost came to a sudden end, with an assist from Whitey Franklin, the double-lifer.

The incident also revealed that, by the mysterious processes of prison smuggling, a man confined even behind the solid steel door of the Dark Hole, can acquire almost anything except, perhaps, a used car. Young and Franklin were escorted one morning from solitary to the yard for a rare hour of exercise. They were walking around the enclosure when Franklin plunged a knife into Young's right shoulder. Young had seen the flashing blade just in time to keep it out of his chest.

Young recovered and went back to the Hole. A few months later reporters on the federal court beat in San Francisco came upon his name again. He had managed to get a petition to the court, requesting that the prison officials be compelled to grant him an hour of light a day to study law. The petition was denied on the ground that the court could not dictate to the warden on administrative matters. (Prior to his trial, in his non-dungeon periods, Young had taken University of California Extension courses. One juror, recalling the trial, said the jury was greatly impressed by Young's ability as a student. Examination papers submitted by the defense showed an almost straight-A record.)

Henri Young could not claim any special distinction in the supra-judicial treatment accorded him, following his trial. Others have felt the knuckled fist of Alcatraz justice, after a trial by The Rock's own court. The expression, "taken before the court," in reference to an inmate charged with a criminal offense such as a stabbing, is common among the guards, but the court they speak of is the prison's Disciplinary Board. This board is composed of the associate warden and the captain of the guards. A onetime Alcatraz guard explains: "The captain presents the charges to the associate warden, who acts as a sort of judge. In a major case, such as an escape attempt, the associate usually confers with the warden." In the case of Tex Lucas, who stabbed Al Capone with a blade from the barber shears, the Department of Justice announced that the prison authorities had dealt out punishment and that it was against policy, as the *Chronicle* story reported, to "let prisoners have even the dubious freedom of leaving the island under guard for court appearances."

Prison authorities defend this policy with the argument that a convict may seek a trip to court as a means to attempt an escape, or simply as a vacation from The Rock. They point to the fact that it did happen on one occasion. An Alcatraz prisoner, escorted to court for a hearing on a petition, slugged a deputy marshal in a break attempt. The deputy slugged back, more effectively. The prisoner did get his vacation—days in court for trial on the escape try.

What astonishes lawyers is the notion of the penal authorities that the verdict of the prison board in criminal cases should supersede the verdict of a trial jury. Prisoners *acquitted* of an offense by a jury in federal court have nonetheless been punished for that offense, before and after the trial, because the prison "court" had rendered a *prior* verdict of guilt.

Jerry W. Clymore, twenty-six, Louisiana bank robber, stood jury trial in January 1961 for the nonfatal stabbing of a fellow inmate. He claimed self-defense and was acquitted.

Warden Madigan told Dale Champion, a *Chronicle* reporter: "I'm amazed at the jury's action. I just don't believe it was self-defense. Regardless of the acquittal, Clymore will go back to solitary confinement because the prison disciplinary board has already held him responsible for the stabbing."

Roland Simcox, a military prisoner, had a similar encounter with Alcatraz justice in 1957. Acquitted by a jury of a stabbing charge, he returned to solitary on a prior conviction by the prison board.

Officials have a defense for this too, a government counsel putting the case: "I'm not at all shocked. These are two quite different sovereignties. For a jury, guilt must be proved beyond a reasonable doubt. A warden is not so restricted. For him it's an administrative matter, and he must do what he feels is best for the conduct of the prison. Also, a convict may be acquitted of a stabbing on a plea of self-defense, but the fact he had a knife in his possession would be a violation of a prison rule."

Foreseeing such practices accounted in part, perhaps, for the grave misgivings voiced by penologists when the idea of Alcatraz was first broached by the Department of Justice. Their voices have been raised over the years against the philosophy of The Rock, but in vain. The notable Osborne Association of New York, which surveys impartially the nation's penal institutions, inspected Alcatraz in 1942 and urged its abandonment, after the war, as an outmoded concept. Its report said:

"Anyone who has been on Alcatraz Island when the almost ever-present fog has shut down and cut it off from the world, when the low groan of foghorns and the cry of sea gulls vie with the moaning of the wind for supremacy in macabre effects, has had an experience reminiscent of prisons of the Middle Ages. . . .

"Alcatraz stands today, not only in the United States, but throughout much of the civilized world, as the symbol of crime control through fear of severe punishment. . . . The purpose in establishing Alcatraz, publicly expressed by the Department of Justice at the time, was to strike terror into the hearts of potential offenders.

"If this type of punishment had demonstrated its efficacy in controlling and reducing crime, few would argue against its use, but leading criminologists today . . . question the efficacy as a deterrent.

"The Alcatraz Penitentiary was established during a period of public hysteria on the subject of crime, engendered in part by publicity and propaganda of the highly inflammatory type. Such hysteria and the laws and procedures which usually result from it tend to postpone rather than hasten the day when crime will be substantially reduced by an intelligent and sustained attack on the problem."

The report suggested as a "practical solution" that trouble-makers at Atlanta and Leavenworth, chief sources of tenants for The Rock, be confined in "a type of segregation unit which would be, in effect, a small but complete prison attached to and operated as an annex."

Prison people felt otherwise. Ten years after the Osborne report, Warden Swope said: "If these men were scattered out through the prison system, they could cause a great deal of difficulty, and perhaps loss of life." And Paul Madigan, who followed him as warden of Alcatraz, insisted: "We are a vital link in our prison system."

Not the men, but the officials themselves, have generated a great deal of difficulty at Alcatraz—bitter strikes, even the wholesale slashing of heel tendons, over the periodic suppression of petitions to the courts. Or an official will assume a judicial role and decide on the merit of a petition, a practice frowned upon by the courts.

Henri Young's request to study law and equip himself to seek judicial relief in a question of possible denial of Constitutional rights was not unusual. Many Rock convicts became students of the law, some even arguing their way to freedom on fine legal points. Under normal conditions, a prisoner scrawls a petition, then has it notarized by the captain of the guards. The petition is typed up and dispatched to the court. If the judge considers it proper, he will set a hearing; and if, after arguments, he rules against the petition, the prisoner has the right of appeal.

Undoubtedly the smartest lawyer The Rock ever contained was Cecil Wright, who was forty-one when he stepped off the island—for the second time—in November of 1948, a tribute to his self-acquired legal skill. He had the look and bearing of a successful barrister, dapper in a gray pin-striped suit custom-made by a convict tailor in payment for a writ. He had paid eighteen years for joining three others in a $2.43 stickup of a drugstore in Strasburg, Illinois, in 1929. He drew two terms: one year to life in the state prison at Joliet, and a fifteen-year federal rap because the pharmacy was also a post office. A model prisoner at Joliet, he was paroled in 1938. Federal authorities, waiting at the gate, hustled him on to Leavenworth. He was a model prisoner there too, but was shipped off to Alcatraz the next year because he was considered a nuisance. He had given legal advice to other inmates and the warden frankly said he "didn't like it."

During his years in prison—Joliet, Leavenworth, Alcatraz—Wright, whose law school was a cell, estimated he had prepared some six hundred writs and motions to vacate. At Alcatraz alone his legal talents had won shorter sentences for at least forty prisoners, some unable even to sign their own names. He rendered this gratuitous help on the sly, at the risk of solitary confinement.

Wright first freed himself from The Rock in 1943 by a habeas corpus writ, contending his federal sentence should not have begun until his parole from Joliet had terminated, that technically he was still an Illinois prisoner. He went to Danville, Illinois, and set out to make a new start in life. He got a job and was planning to marry. And then his state parole ran out.

Department of Justice agents bounced him back on The Rock. Dismayed, but undaunted, Wright resumed his cell law practice. His thirteenth petition paid off. Granting of this writ of habeas corpus indicated he had served those eighteen years in prison possibly without justification, for it was based on this ground: that his constitutional rights had been denied at his original trial, in 1929, because his attorney also served as counsel for three codefendants who had turned state's evidence. When he bade farewell to The Rock he told reporters he had left behind a personal library of some four hundred lawbooks: "They may help someone else to get out sometime."

At the Fort Mason dock to greet the handsome, graying ex-convict was Assistant U.S. Attorney Joseph Karesh, who had lost the legal bout before the United States Court of Appeals for the Ninth Circuit. They shook hands warmly, and Karesh later told reporters: "Wright is the world's greatest authority on habeas corpus writs. In fact, I'm damned glad to get him off that island because he's been writing writs for all the other prisoners. They're smartly done and they're a headache."

Wright told the newsmen: "They've got nothing over there but a bunch of young boys. Brutality? Sure, there's brutality. But to tell the truth none of the guards ever picked on me. If they shook my cell down, I gave them a little soft soap. Because I had a lot of papers in there relating to other men and that's good for solitary."

Not all of Wright's pupils made good. Most of their prayers to the court were distinguished chiefly for their oddities. One convict requested $1,000 a day for each of the 165 days he had done in the Dark Hole, claiming it was not a healthful place. Another sought "warmer underwear because when night falls, the fog rolls in on Alcatraz, and it gets mighty cold." He kept his cotton long johns. A prisoner contended the denial of tobacco in the isolation block was "a psychological torture even a so-called communistic system has never been accused of using in slave-labor camps." A kidnaper doing 104 years wanted the warden restrained from "the cruel and unusual treatment of unlawfully and unconstitutionally depriving petitioner of certain rights guaranteed by United States law; specifically, of food, to wit: ice cream, cake, pie."

A convict named Dorsey McMahan, apparently coached by Wright, sought a writ of mandate to compel Warden Johnston himself to pull an aching molar or have a dentist yank it, stating that the warden's refusal to do either was a "malicious and capricious denial of my constitutional rights." Caries was not the cause of the ache, he said, but a guard who "busted petitioner in the jaw in solitary and broke a jaw tooth." McMahan scribbled a postscript: "When it gets so a poor convict can't get a tooth pulled, he might as well be dead or in hell." (The need for this action was never made clear, for in those days a dentist was on duty in the prison hospital. In recent years, a San Francisco dentist has visited the prison twice weekly.)

For eleven years a Kentucky bank robber endured the strict discipline of Alcatraz without a murmur until, he claims, they went too far. They took away his Cavanaugh Method book, which teaches piano playing without a piano, and he was no longer able to play a toneless "My Ol' Kentucky Home" in his cell. His petition, demanding return of the instruction book, solemnly set forth: "Of all the suffering I have gone through in prison, the greatest blow of all was being deprived of the opportunity to educate myself in the finer points of harmony." The judge dismissed the plea with the wry comment: "Prison officials are vested with a wide discretion in the safekeeping and securing of prisoners."

Two convicts filed separate petitions with identical requests in identical words: that a guard be examined by a lunacy commission. Petitions denied, without comment.

Richard A. Numer, midway through a forty-five-year stretch for bank robbery, appeared before Federal Judge Roche in 1947 to argue his petition to compel Warden Johnston to let him take a course in English. His application had been denied when, in the space designated "Reasons for wanting this course," he wrote: "To fit myself to expose the brutality and vile conditions prevailing at Alcatraz Penitentiary." Judge Roche, intrigued by the applicant's candor in such circumstances, voiced his curiosity. Numer's reply was equally startling: "To conceal or distort the truth in this matter would be contrary to my early upbringing and repugnant to my conscience." The court, with seeming reluctance, ruled it had no jurisdiction over the prison's administration.

Such pleas may indeed be frivolous, but to the convicts they represented what they considered at the time real grievances. Warden Johnston himself spoke of the difficulty a prisoner often has in contemplating years of The Rock's monotony. An inmate who tries to whip that monotonous grind by an escape into the enchanting world of music, then finds his means of flight, his lesson book, snatched away, might well be vexed. If he can go beyond his keepers and air his problems to the court, that action itself can afford a psychological relief, a getting things off his chest. But if even that recourse is denied him, as has happened at Alcatraz over the years, it tends to widen the gap between convict and guardian, to create friction that can explode into violence.

It may be notable that Numer's astonishing petition, seeking the right to equip himself by the study of English to expose what he called the brutality and vile conditions on Alcatraz, was considered worthy of a hearing. Further, no question was raised that he was indulging in fantasies or that his brazen candor made him a proper subject for an insanity hearing instead. It might certainly have been assumed he was a bit wacky, or that if he had instances of brutality to expose they would have been the mere ravings of a convict who did not, as Warden Johnston put it, like his surroundings.

Just a month after the Trial of Alcatraz an incident occurred that dramatically portrayed another side of the custodial picture. No guard wants the convicts to like him: as keeper and captive, they are natural enemies. But that does not rule out respect, the thing a conscientious guard does desire. This incident clearly indicated Captain Madigan had such respect, to an enviable degree.

Four desperate convicts, all lifers, set a flight plan in action that had the making of a slaughter. They were Joe (Dutch) Cretzer, an instigator of the Battle of Alcatraz yet to come; Sam Shockley, a maniacal actor in that bloody drama; Arnold Kyle, Cretzer's brother-in-law and crime partner, and Lloyd Barkdoll, young bank robber from Coos Bay, Oregon. They pounced on the mat-shop foreman and dragged him, bound and gagged, into a corner. They began prying the bars of a window but were interrupted at intervals by the arrival of three other officers, among them Madigan. They too were trussed up and lugged to the corner. The convicts struggled to widen the bars. Madigan worked his gag loose, then spoke in a quiet, avuncular way: "Boys, it's just about time for the officers here to report to the Armorer and if they don't, you're going to have a flock of officers storming in with machine guns. So you might as well give yourselves up before this goes too far."

Cretzer debated a moment, said "Okay, Mr. Madigan," and nodded to the others. They untied the officers and went meekly along with the captain, to solitary.

Chapter 12

D ESPITE THE JURY'S unprecedented action in the Trial of Alcatraz—
its blast at The Rock overshadowed its actual verdict in the
case—life at the island prison went on much as it had before. There
had been no investigation of conditions at Alcatraz, as the jury had
requested in wires to Congress and the Department of Justice. And
so there had been no shakeup in personnel, the customary consequence of any publicized inquiry into sensational charges of brutality
in a prison.

World War II broke and most of the best guards at Alcatraz—
able-bodied and intelligent men, good officer-candidate material—
went off to the fighting. Replacements were recruited off the street,
for the most part rejects by the military, men without prison training.
The custodial staff sort of fell apart. In normal times, this would
have presented a serious problem, but these times were not normal.
The war spirit reached into the prison, and the convicts, imbued
with patriotism, rallied to do their part. The laundry did mountains
of wash for the military: San Francisco was a teeming port of
embarkation for the South Pacific Theater. The tailor shop turned
out tens of thousands of trousers for the Army. Convict machinists
and welders did repair work for the Navy, particularly on the buoys
for the antisubmarine nets in the bay. Many prisoners, due for parole
in a relatively short while, volunteered for the Armed Services; some,
with maritime experience, for the badly needed crews to run the
ships fast being built. Warden Johnston agreed, but Director Bennett
of the prison bureau vetoed the idea.

All this did not mean that Alcatraz had been turned into a big, happy camp where the men toiled feverishly and the guards stood around like straw bosses. It was still Alcatraz; the guards—the new ones out of fear of these "most desperate" felons, if not out of custodial training—still kept a wary eye; the convicts still dreamed of freedom, and some plotted.

Among the plotters were four who rated the description of "most desperate." They were Harold Brest, thirty-one, a handsome, cold-blooded Pennsylvania bank robber; Fred Hunter, forty-three, stoop-shouldered henchman of the Old Creepy Karpis gang of Midwestern kidnapers; James A. Boarman, twenty-four, ruthless Indiana bank bandit, and Floyd G. Hamilton, thirty-six, who once briefly wore the nation's crime crown as Public Enemy No. 1. Hamilton was a member of the Hamilton-Barrow-Parker outlaw band that roamed the Southwest in the early thirties, though not a full-fledged corporate partner. The Hamilton of the firm name was his brother, Raymond, the chieftain, who was executed after their two-year rampage came to a blazing end in an ambush by Texas lawmen in 1934 that mowed down the other partners, Clyde Barrow and his stogie-smoking, shotgun-toting moll, Bonnie Parker.

Fog shrouded The Rock on the morning of April 13, 1943, as the convicts filed down the road to the shops, and Hamilton passed the word to his coconspirators: this was the day, the day they had long waited for and put weeks of careful preparation into, and before that months of scheming. This was no rash, reckless flight planned only to the water's edge. They had managed somehow to snitch four Army uniforms from the dry-cleaning shop. Once they waded ashore near deserted Fort Point at the Presidio of San Francisco, they would don the uniforms and move freely through the city, thronged with soldiers. They had stuffed the garments into four empty five-gallon cans, which would serve a dual purpose as duffel bags and floats for the swim to the mainland. They marked the cans and scattered them in a supply stack of similar cans in the storeroom off the machine shop. They had also stashed away tools.

They were ready to go after the guard counted them into the machine shop that April morning. But the guard hung around. They scraped barnacles off net buoys and shot glances at the window: the fog was burning off, drifting by in patches. At last the guard stepped into the storeroom. They followed swiftly, dropped him with a blow on the head, bound and gagged him.

They had just picked the cans from the stack when footsteps approached on the stairs. They gathered by the door. An officer entered. They pounced, then laid him, trussed and gagged, alongside his colleague behind a large crate. They dug out the cached tools and spread the bars of a window overlooking the bay. They stripped to their long underwear. Three squirmed out onto an old catwalk used only in emergencies. The fourth struggled to push a can through. A tight squeeze, it took time. After the second can came out, Hamilton said, "Forget the others. Let's go." The fourth convict wriggled out.

The barefoot quartet, clad only in drawers, slid over the rail and down an iron post, to the rim of a cliff thirty feet above a rock-strewn shore. They began leaping, one after the other.

By now the fog had lifted and at that moment Officer Frank Johnson in the south gun tower swung his gaze off the bay. He was startled to see the white-skinned figures hurtling through the air. He fired rapid rounds as they disappeared, sounded the alarm, stood braced, rifle ready. Moments later they came into view in the water. One swam free, arms flailing. Another lay along a plank, his arms as paddles. Two held onto the floats, kicking their feet. Johnson's deadly slugs sent up tiny geysers. The flailing swimmer turned back, vanished behind the jut of the cliff. The one on the plank rolled off, swam back out of sight. One of the two still in the bay used his can-float as a shield against the raking rifle shot. The other tried, but got on the wrong side. He gave a convulsive jerk, and the can bounced aside. His head wobbled, he began to sink. The fourth escaper left his float and raced to his comrade's aid. Johnson kept peppering the surface.

The Rock bustled. Its siren wailed, its launch set out. Guards herded prisoners inside for a quick count to discover who had gone. The convicts, to distract the guards, set up a bedlam.

Out on the bay the launch pulled alongside a fugitive floating on his back, holding up a limp figure. It was Brest, with Boarman. A thin trail led out from Boarman's head and tinctured the green water crimson. Brest reached up for an outstretched hand, lost his grip on Boarman. Boarman sank, like a lead weight. They pulled Brest aboard, stark naked.

The launch cruised close to shore. Search parties headed for the water-line caves of The Rock's weather side. The tide was out, and into each cave crept a wary guard with a flashlight, covered by a rifleman at the entrance. They came upon the graying, slight-built Hunter crouched shivering behind a boulder. He had sprained his back bounding against a jagged rock in his leap to the beach and, his strength sapped by the vicious tide rips, had dragged himself into the cave.

Hunter offered no clue as to Hamilton's fate. At sundown of the second day the warden called off the search. He assumed that Hamilton had been sucked down by the strong undertow and had drowned.

Late on the third night Hamilton crawled out of the cave in which Hunter had taken refuge. The cave, like others a jumble of concrete blocks and granite boulders to halt tidal erosion, had a series of zigzag passageways negotiable only by a belly crawl, and he had wormed back to the face of a grotto. Weakened by hunger and bone-chilled by the soakings of flood tides, aching with festering cuts, he quaked all the more as he emerged into the night and a cold, misty wind off the Pacific smote him. He staggered round the point to the cove, stumbling over barnacled rocks. He clawed his way up the cliff he had plunged off, climbed the iron post to the old catwalk, squirmed through the bar-spread gap in the window, back to the prison that was now a haven.

They found him next morning, cowering behind the large crate in the storeroom. Floyd G. Hamilton bore no resemblance to the Public Enemy No. 1 who once swaggered, guns blazing, through the Southwest. He was naked except for the cotton drawers, and they were in tatters: his feet were swollen, bruised, blistered; his face and body were lacerated, and scarlet-streaked, from the jagged rocks and the keener scalpels of seashell fragments. Dried salt from the tidal spray in the cave caked his hair and eyebrows. His eyes held the terror of a trapped, wounded animal.

They fed him a bowl of soup, cleansed him under a shower. Later, as they daubed iodine on his cuts in the hospital, the erstwhile outlaw meekly told the warden: "When I got down to the water I grabbed a plank for a getaway. I got out a way and saw I couldn't make it with the plank, but was afraid to let go. When the shooting started, I did let go, made it back to shore and crawled in the cave with Hunter. I thought I'd suffocate. I was wet and cold all the time. The water came up around me when the tide came in. Last night I saw there wasn't a chance anymore. So I crawled out and back up the rocks and into the building through the same hole we got out of."

This was the second time Brest had got off The Rock, much to his regret. Acting as his own counsel, he had won a new trial and had traveled confidently back to Pittsburgh, under armed escort. He was convicted again, and his original sentence of forty-five years boosted to fifty *and* life.

Hamilton's ordeal proved no deterrent to a former associate in crime, Ted Huron Walters, thirty-year-old Arkansas bank bandit. On a foggy morning five months later he sneaked out of the laundry and over the fence. They found him hiding among the rocks of a cove. He had tested the water with a toe and found it "too damn cold."

The Rock, busy again with its own war effort, enjoyed a truce that lasted almost two years. But a quiet, model prisoner, John K. Giles, was biding his time, keeping his own counsel as he plotted an ingenious getaway that would bring about a tighter security system at the wharf: no boat or barge to cast off until the dock gang lined up in the sight of the guard in that gun tower, and the remainder of the inmate population had been counted.

Giles, a half-century old, worked on the dock detail but not as a stevedore. Too slight and sickly for heavy lifting, he swept the area and tended the century plants along the path to the long flight of steps to the crest. He was a taciturn man whose mind and eyes abundantly made up for the idleness of his tongue.

At 10:10 A.M., on July 31, 1945, the *General Coxe*, an Army boat, eased toward the dock for a scheduled stop on her way to Angel Island, then site of a military installation. As the steamer came alongside the guard lined up his gang for a count. All present. He then caught the line flung from the boat, tied her up, helped with the gang-plank, and stood aside to check the supplies as they came off. That done, the guard removed the gangplank, tossed the line to a crewman, watched her cast off, turned back to his detail. No Giles. His glance swept the dock area. No Giles. Then the path. No Giles. Under the wharf. No Giles. He hit the phone.

The warden played a hunch, phoned the Angel Island adjutant to hold the *General Coxe* and anyone without an ID card. Associate Warden Miller hurried to the dock, jumped into a speedboat and raced to Angel. The *General Coxe* had pulled in, its military passengers lined up on the wharf. As Miller walked down the line a technical sergeant, stiff at attention, eyes forward, abruptly held out his hands. Onto the wrists, as the soldiers stared in astonishment, Miller clapped a set of handcuffs. T/S Giles even had a dog tag around his neck.

The taciturn Giles, goaded, talked. He would push his broom nearby as bundles off the *Coxe* were shaken out for contraband, and he would pilfer a garment, tuck it under his jacket, switch to a hoe, cache the item behind a shrub. Eventually, he had an outfit complete with dog tag. On the morning of July 31, he transferred his stockpile, piece by piece, to the rear of a dockside warehouse. He doffed his coveralls, donned the uniform, pulled the coveralls back on, resumed his sweeping. In a pocket were a pad and pencil: he had noted that telephone company and Army Signal Corps technicians, repairing a cable, came over on the 10:10 boat. When the guard turned to tie up the *Coxe,* Giles slipped under the wharf, shucked his coveralls, boarded the lower freight deck. After the steamer pulled away Technical Sergeant Giles emerged topside and stood near the technicians, jotting calculations in his notepad.

Giles, cooped in solitary for his escapade, said he had been plotting ever since he arrived on The Rock, ten years earlier. He was given three years for the attempt, delaying by that long the resumption of a life term in Oregon, itself interrupted by an escape. He appealed, contending he should not have been tried for escape from the prison because he was not in the prison itself at the time and furthermore, he was not technically in custody because the guard was off attending to the boat. He lost the appeal but had argued it so masterfully that an appellate jurist inquired where he had studied law. Giles replied, "For the past year, in Alcatraz."

In a burst of loquacity, Giles related what had motivated his earlier flight from the Oregon State Prison: "I wrote fiction for magazines and the sources of my literary creation dimmed. I felt the need for new scenes and new faces. A sense of terrible futility came over me. So I went over the wall."

With the exception of the abortive break of the Hamilton quartet, in which Boarman slipped under the surface of the bay and stayed under, these attempts were not gory affairs, and the guards may have begun to believe that the bloodshed of Alcatraz's early days was behind them. If so they couldn't have been more wrong; a violence more terrible than anything they had yet experienced was building up in the persons of six inmates surnamed Cretzer, Coy, Hubbard, Shockley, Thompson, and Carnes.

Joseph Paul Cretzer had a round face and close-cropped hair that gave him, at thirty-five, a deceptively boyish appearance. Dutch Joe and his wife's brother, Arnold Kyle, had roamed the Far West in the late thirties as the country's No. 1 bank robbing team. Captured together, they stayed paired up through a turbulent prison-and-escape career until the Battle of The Rock. They landed at McNeil, to do twenty-five years, in 1939, at a time that Cretzer's wife, Kay, a brothel keeper in the San Francisco Bay Area, was serving a jail term on a white-slave conviction. The next year they sped through the gate at McNeil in a truck, were found three days later in the brush on the 4,000-acre island. During a recess in their trial at Tacoma for that escape, they tried another break by slugging a marshal in the corridor, a scuffle that felled the marshal with a heart attack. They drew five years for the McNeil escape, then life terms for the marshal's death. They came on to Alcatraz and in a few months tried the escape, with Shockley and Barkdoll, that Captain Madigan convinced them was foolish. They landed in solitary instead of possibly the morgue. While in the Dark Hole, Cretzer hatched a bold blast-out with Whitey Franklin, still there for the slaying of Officer Cline in the 1939 break try. It would belie Cretzer's boast, when he arrived from McNeil, that he would not end his days on The Rock.

Bernard Paul Coy, rail-thin and pint-sized, only five feet four, in March of 1937 had cockily strutted up to the cashier's cage in the

Bank of New Haven, Kentucky, with a sawed-off shotgun, made off with $2,175 and hidden in a cave along the Rolling Fork River, but not for long. Four months later he was on The Rock. He was in his middle forties.

Marvin Franklin Hubbard, forty-four, dark-haired, rather handsome, wore rimless glasses that imparted a studious look. He had come a long way from the Alabama farm of his boyhood. En route he had kidnaped a Chattanooga cop, stolen his tommy gun, two pistols, and car, and driven across a state line; later had escaped from a county jail; had been shipped to Alcatraz in 1944 after engaging in a mutiny at Atlanta.

Sam Shockley, tall, stooped, pallid, was a man of thirty-six but mentally a child of eight. He began by stealing a chicken and ended by robbing the Bank of Paoli, Oklahoma, of $947.28, and kidnaping the bank's president and the president's wife, who was also the assistant cashier. His car stalled on a country road and he fled on foot, leaving his victims behind, unharmed. He was raiding a farmhouse for food when a posse rode up. He went to Leavenworth for a week's seasoning in May of 1938 before being shipped on to Alcatraz to serve out a life term. His life would end, instead, at San Quentin, up the bay a few miles.

Miran Thompson, twenty-nine, powerfully built, had a hard, square-jawed face and coldly penetrating eyes to match his criminal record and sentences: life for the slaying of an Amarillo, Texas, lawman, plus ninety-nine years for kidnaping. He had chalked up eight escapes elsewhere before being pinned down in D Block at Alcatraz in October of 1945, only months before the battle.

Clarence Carnes, the Chocktaw Kid, an Oklahoma Indian with the temperament of a wildcat, was not yet out of his teens. He was on The Rock, at nineteen, doing life plus ninety-nine years for robbery, murder, kidnaping, various assaults and escapes. He had crowded all this into three short years, starting with the day his father brought a watermelon to him in reform school. In the watermelon was a hacksaw.

Chapter 13

I T WAS A FEW MINUTES after one thirty. The date: May 2, 1946, a
Thursday. The working prisoners had filed out to the shops, and
the drowsy quiet of a cathedral on a weekday afternoon pervaded the
huge cellhouse. The only convict moving freely about was Bernard
Paul Coy, on janitorial duty, and the swish of his soft-fibered push
broom along the waxed floor created less sound than a buzzing fly.
The Rock had deflated the braggart ego of this Kentucky bank robber:
outwardly, at least, he appeared mild, inoffensive. Beneath the surface,
violence was in ferment. Earlier in the day, as he distributed books
from the library, he had stopped at the cell of Clarence Carnes, the
teenaged, copper-hued Choctaw, and asked, "How much time you
doin'? Life?" "No," replied Carnes, "ninety-nine years." And Coy
said, "Well, I'll tell you, old man, somethin's comin' off. If you want to
go, okay, it's a cinch." Now, as he pushed the broom lazily down the
lateral corridor at the west end of the cellhouse, Coy cast an occasional
glance upward. He had an absent air, but the glances encompassed the
dark figure of Bert Burch in the gun gallery and noted the progress of
the guard's slow patrol toward D Block.

At the bars of the end cell on the top tier of inside C Block, on
Broadway, stood Joseph Paul Cretzer, his sullen eyes also on the
gallery guard. He had returned to the general population only a
week before after years in solitary, where he had plotted the thing
that was about to happen. When the guard in the gallery moved out
of his sight, Cretzer shifted his intent gaze to Coy, then to the clock
on the wall above the lieutenant's desk: twenty seconds past 1:38.

Coy, now athwart Broadway, pushed the broom casually. For days he had cased Burch, for days had timed his patrol: at 1:40 he would go through the door into the walled-off isolation section and there spend fifteen minutes. Today, the moment Burch stepped into D Block, Marvin Hubbard would leave the kitchen.

Burch, a lanky Oklahoman, approached the wooden door set in the gallery to stop drafts. He was carrying a Springfield 30.06 rifle on a shoulder strap, a holstered .45 pistol on his hip. Near the door hung a gasbilly and a long cord to lower Key 88, the key to the steel door into D Block from the cellhouse. He shoved through the draft door, saw his lunchbox on the floor, gave it a nudge with his foot, closed the door, and was gone.

Coy, slowly sweeping past C Block, circled toward a point just beyond the door to the mess hall.

At his cleanup work in the kitchen Marvin Hubbard kept a furtive eye on the wall clock. The minute hand jumped to 1:40. Hubbard leaned across the table to mop a stain, slipped a carving knife up his left sleeve, straightened, drawled to the officer on duty, "Finished, goin' back to my cell." He moved, not too briskly, up the hall and knocked on the gate.

Officer W. H. Miller, on duty in the cellhouse, stepped out of Broadway and opened it. He leaned over to frisk Hubbard, a routine with all culinary workers. Coy slugged him on the back of the head, and Hubbard's fist bore into his face. Miller, though groggy, slipped a key off his key ring and into a pocket as they dragged him to Cell 403 on the outside bank of C Block. They tied him up, took his key ring.

They released Cretzer, impatient as a caged cougar in his top-tier cell, then the nineteen-year-old Carnes. With Miller's keys they opened the door to the utility corridor of C Block, where they had stashed bar-spreading equipment stolen from the plumbing shop: two specially threaded brass pipes, a specially threaded nut, and a pair of plumber's pliers.

Coy stripped to his long underwear. He climbed onto Hubbard's shoulders, then stepped on his hands, and Hubbard hoisted him to the gun gallery twelve feet above the floor. Coy, agile as a monkey, swarmed up past a four-foot-high steel-plate shield, on up the bars, up to the roof where the bars flare out like a basket top. He set the spreader between two bars, applied the pliers. The gap widened, he squirmed through and clambered down to the upper deck of the gallery, raced down a stairway to the first level, ran to the wooden door, grabbed the gasbilly off the wall, and crouched. The convicts below kept under the gun cage, out of sight.

Tense minutes passed. Footsteps approached. Coy saw the knob turn, the door start to open. He lunged, knocked Burch off balance, pinned him against the bars. He cracked the metal gasclub against the guard's jaw. Burch brought up the rifle. Coy clutched the barrel, swung again. Burch dodged, caught the blow on the back of the head. They grappled. Burch tripped over his lunchbox, sprawled backward. The rifle clattered to the floor. Coy leaped on Burch as he hit the concrete. They struggled for the revolver in the hip holster. It bounced free, out of reach. Coy got a hammer lock on the guard, beat him on the head, then worked his fingers inside his collar and twisted it tight, tighter, choking off his breath. Burch went limp, unconscious.

Coy stripped the guard, snatched the long key cord from its wall peg and lashed him to a conduit near the floor. He dropped the pistol and its twenty rounds of ammunition to Cretzer, then Key 88, and Cretzer ran to the door to D Block. Coy passed the club down to Carnes, then the pliers, Burch's uniform, fifty rifle cartridges. He kept the rifle and passed stealthily into the isolation block.

Cecil Corwin, middle-aged, graying officer in D Block, heard unusual noises in the cellhouse, then the key in the door. He ran to jam the lock. Coy, rifle leveled, barked from the gun gallery: "Open that goddam door and be goddam quick about it!" Corwin moved away, the door swung open, in barged Cretzer, Hubbard, and Carnes.

Cretzer wanted Whitey Franklin freed, but his dark cell could be opened only when an electric switch was thrown, turning the lock to key position.

"Open that goddam switch box!" Cretzer ordered.

Corwin opened the box and started to reach in.

"Wait!" cried Carnes. "If you pull that lever, does it ring an alarm in the Armory?"

"Yes," said Corwin.

"Pass it up," said Cretzer. "We're behind schedule. Let's get out to the yard and down to the launch."

"What about them?" yelled Coy, gesturing toward the upper cells. They opened those doors by the manual control. Twelve convicts rushed out, saw Coy's rifle and Cretzer's pistol, and ran down the circular stairway shouting, "The cons have taken over, let's go!" Most of them warily stayed in D Block. Two who did not were Miran Thompson and Sam Shockley.

The mutineers put Corwin in Cell 403 with Miller and started for the yard door, to the left of the mess hall. Burch, who had come to and worked the cord loose, peered over the gallery shield, into the startled eyes of Cretzer. Cretzer whipped up the .45 and snapped two quick shots. "Lay down, you sonofabitch!" Burch ducked.

(Burch later testified he had never before been in a gunfight. "I immediately got as close to the floor as I could. Shells were ricocheting a lot. They'd whistle and sing. I couldn't see any, but I heard them zip." Why had he not used the gallery phone to alert the Armorer? "I think I had that in mind, but a couple of shots from Cretzer took that out of me—mighty quick.")

Officer Joseph Burdett, in the kitchen, saw Coy run past the mess-hall door, thought he was in a fight with another prisoner and rushed out. He landed in Cell 403. As the convicts moved out again toward the yard door, Burdett asked Carnes if he might untie Miller. "Go ahead," Carnes said. The young Choctaw unknowingly prevented a wholesale break. Burdett unbound Miller, and they hid the key to the yard, the key Miller had pocketed.

At the yard door Cretzer and Coy took turns trying keys, fumbling and cursing. Epithets filled the cellhouse as they stormed back to Cell 403. They searched Miller, then beat him pulpy. Cretzer said, "Well, that fouls it up. Frisco's far away as ever."

They held a council. Surrender? They took stock: a rifle, a revolver, a carving knife, a gasbilly, pipe pliers for a dagger. "Let's go out first-class," said Cretzer. They took positions behind B and C Blocks, commanding both the yard door and the front entrance down Broadway.

View of Alcatraz from North Point, 1865.

Alcatraz Island prison train en route from Tiburon, 1934.

Three tiers of the Alcatraz main cell block, 1934.

Alcatraz inmate George "Machine Gun" Kelly, 1933.

Chicago crime boss Al "Scarface" Capone, who spent four and a half years in Alcatraz, 1936.

Convicts James Lucas and Rufus Franklin, who failed in their escape attempt from Alcatraz, 1938.

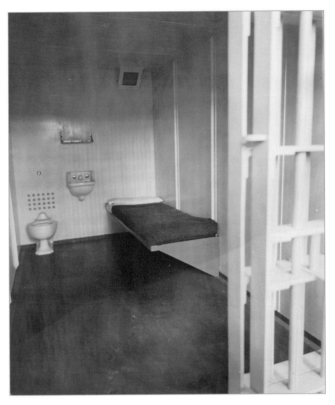

Interior of prison cell, 1941.

Solitary confinement prison cell, 1946.

Rifle grenade bursting in Alcatraz cell block during a three-day prisoner revolt in May 1946.

Alcatraz prison recreation yard, 1956.

Alcatraz prison menu, 1956.

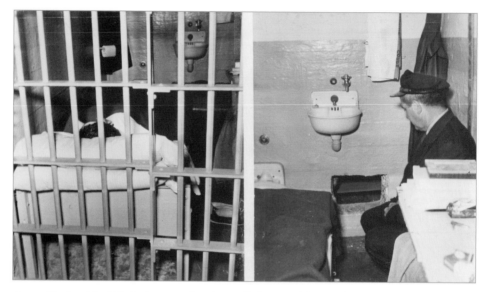

A guard looks at the hole in the vent of a prison cell dug out with a modified mess hall spoon, 1962.

Scene from the 1979 movie based on this book.

Steward Robert C. Bristow, returning from a conference, came along Broadway on his way to the kitchen. Carnes's arm shot out, encircling his neck, and the pliers threatened to close on his throat. He went quietly into Cell 403.

Guard Ernest B. Lageson, back from lunch, strolled down Broadway, was yanked off his feet, into Cell 403.

An inmate, coming up from the basement clothing room, found no guard to check him into the cellhouse. He reported this to Ed Stucker, the officer on duty below, who went to the top of the stairs and peered through the gate bars. No sign of Officer Miller. Something about the place, he couldn't tell exactly what, gave him an uneasy feeling. He went back down and phoned the Armory. The Armorer thought there might be a fight in the kitchen and dispatched Captain Henry H. Weinhold, Lieutenant Joseph H. Simpson, and two officers, Carl Sundstrom and Robert R. Baker.

Cell 403 was getting crowded. Simpson, Sundstrom, and Baker went into Cell 402. As Baker, the chief mail censor, started in, Shockley said, "You goddam mail thief," and punched him in the face. Sundstrom dropped his wallet and Cretzer snatched it up, extracted the money, and grinned. "A stickup." They made Weinhold strip before pushing him into 403. Coy donned his captain's uniform.

The missing key to the yard, their only way out, balked their grand plan to knock out the three main gun towers, storm down to the wharf, and capture the launch. Boiling with frustration, Coy strode into the mess hall with the powerful Springfield 30.06 to pick off the tower guards anyway, from windows there and in the kitchen.

It was now two thirty, and the Armorer was growing uneasy. He phoned the west gun gallery, got no response. And no word from the captain. He got on the intercom for a conference call to all posts.

Big Jim Comerford was leaning on the rail of the dock tower, watching Associate Warden Miller with a civilian paint crew below, when the call came. He went inside, listened, laid his rifle against the wall under the phone, came out again, and called down to Miller: "Trouble in the cellhouse. Better get up to the top."

He heard something explode behind him and for an instant thought his pistol had discharged. Miller shouted, "Jim, get down!"

But Comerford had already swung around and down, to grab his rifle. Coy's first shot had crashed through a window of the tower (they were later bulletproofed), on through the metal sash of the window opposite. John Barker, in a gun box on the yard wall at the prison, saw the window shatter, a moment later saw the slug splash into the calm bay. As the bullet hit the sash metal a fragment spun off, ricocheted off another sash, and embedded itself in the wood stock of Comerford's rifle.

Miller jumped into a truck and roared up the Cliffside road.

Coy's next shot went to the hill tower. The bullet hit an angle iron on the catwalk and fractured, and crippling splinters ripped into Guard Roy Best's shins. In the road tower Irving Levison had the door propped open with the wood chuck to get a bit of fresh air. After the conference call, he decided to lock the door, leaned down to pull out the chuck—and Coy's third shot crashed through, where his head had been.

The Armorer called Warden Johnston, at a late lunch. "There's some trouble in the cellhouse. I don't know what, but I think it's bad."

Johnston said, "If you think it's bad, kick on the siren." He crossed the road to the prison. Ed Miller, the associate, came staggering out of the cellhouse, gasping for breath, eyes watery, face a lampblack mask.

"Somebody's loose in there with a gun," Miller said.

"Do you know who it is?"

"I think it's Coy."

"What happened to you?"

"I heard there was trouble and ran in with a gasbilly. I thought I saw an officer, but it was Coy. He said, 'You sonofabitch, I'm going to kill you!' I raised the club. He fired twice. The gasbilly burst in my face."

Inside the cellhouse the convicts gloried in their insurrection. Carnes, the young Indian, patrolled in front of the two cells, swinging an officer's club. He said, "Never thought I'd be a cop!"

Hubbard suggested they hold the captives as hostages to barter for their freedom. Cretzer laughed. "We don't need hostages, we're not makin' any agreements. We want that goddam key!"

They hauled forth Officer Miller and again slugged him unconscious, but still no key to the yard door. They cursed and raged. Thompson now had the rifle. He swung it up and cried, "Let's shoot the sonsabitches!"

The siren blew.

Captain Weinhold said to Cretzer: "You don't have a chance. You'd be foolish to go out and get killed."

"If we're going to get killed," Cretzer said, "we'll kill you, too."

Weinhold said, "You can only die once."

Cretzer said, "Go ahead and die!"

He pulled the trigger, twice, fast. The .45 slugs ripped into the captain's stomach, and he doubled over.

Shockley cried, "Kill all the sonsabitches!"

Cretzer aimed at Corwin. The bullet hit near the left eye and Corwin crumpled, blinded by blood.

Shockley, black eyes piercing, jumped up and down. "Kill every one of the yellow-bellied bastards! We won't have any testimony against us."

Cretzer emptied the pistol into the crowded cell. A slug crashed into Miller's chest. Others dropped, played dead.

Cretzer walked to the next cell, reloading. He pumped bullets in there. Two rammed into Simpson's chest and he fell flat on the cot. Baker slumped, slugs in both legs. Sundstrom hugged the floor behind Baker.

Shockley, wildly dancing, cried, "Hey, Joe, here's a sonofabitch ain't dead yet!"

Cretzer came back, inspected the carnage in 403. Bodies lay scattered grotesquely. Burdett, wounded, sprawled across the cot, his head and an arm hanging over the side, holding his breath. Carnes looked in too and said, "They're all dead, let's go!"

Shockley pointed, "That one! He moved!"

Cretzer said, "Oh, that's Lageson. He's my friend."

Shockley said, "Friend, hell, he'll go to court and spill his guts."

Cretzer leveled the pistol at Lageson. The hammer clicked on an empty chamber.

"Take it easy, Joe," Lageson said.

Cretzer calmly removed the clip, shoved in a new one. He apologized, "Sorry, Mr. Lageson," then fired. The bullet creased Lageson's cheek and clipped his ear. He lay in the corner, still, as if dead.

In the city room of the *San Francisco Chronicle* the rewrite men were flipping coins for coffee. It was almost three thirty, and the copy was over for the first edition deadline. It had been a dull news day.

A city desk phone rang, and a reporter on the Oakland beat across the bay said, "The highway patrol on the Bay Bridge say they hear shooting over at Alcatraz. Sounds like a break. What've you heard?"

"Escape from Alcatraz!" the city editor yelled to the news editor, then to a rewrite man, "Check Alcatraz!"

An electric thrill tingled through the city room.

Another phone on the desk rang, a Marin County correspondent: "Say, we hear the sound of shots at Alcatraz. What's up?"

The rewrite man reported, "Line's busy."

"Keep on it!"

The managing editor came out. "Escape from Alcatraz?"

"Looks like it," said the city editor. "Reports of shooting over there. We're checking."

"Still busy," said the rewrite man.

"Call Washington."

A copy boy ran up with a telegram for the city editor: SERIOUS TROUBLE. CONVICT HAS MACHINE GUN IN CELLHOUSE. HAVE ISSUED RIOT CALL. PLACED ARMED GUARDS AT STRATEGIC LOCATIONS. MOST OF OUR OFFICERS ARE IMPRISONED IN CELLHOUSE. CANNOT TELL EXTENT OF INJURIES SUFFERED BY OUR OFFICERS OR AMOUNT OF DAMAGED DONE. WILL GIVE YOU INFORMATION LATER IN THE DAY WHEN WE GET CONTROL. J. A. JOHNSTON, WARDEN, ALCATRAZ.

Later in the day thirty Marines landed on The Rock, combat-ready with bayonets, grenades, trench knives. Going over they stared at a huge sign on Angel Island erected to greet troops returning from the Pacific: WELCOME HOME—WELL DONE. The Rock was reviving memories of Corregidor.

Coast Guard cutters circled the embattled island, and overhead roared military planes. The San Francisco police boat joined in, on her deck marksmen pulled off target practice at the range. In Washington, Director Bennett ordered guards flown from other prisons, then took a plane west.

Fifty children, homebound from school in San Francisco, and a score of mothers who had been shopping in town, were stranded at the Fort Mason dock. The youngsters stared intently at the besieged island, some in tears; then they played hopscotch and tag until the Red Cross bundled them off to the YMCA Hotel. On the island the clerical staff took refuge in the air-raid shelter, relic of the war; the remaining housewives, some with babies, stayed in their homes, the doors locked for the first time in years.

Word of the battle at Alcatraz spread swiftly. By nightfall spectators crowded San Francisco's hills, the Embarcadero piers, and the shoreline facing The Rock. Patrol boat searchlights crisscrossed the darkened prison. Tracer bullets drew thin red lines in the night sky and burst brilliantly against the concrete wall. An occasional flash of a grenade exploding inside the cellhouse limned briefly the tall windows. Bonfires in the yard cast a glow and silhouetted Marines standing watch on the parapet over the convicts herded out of the shops. High above, the Alcatraz light winked its warning to ships coming in from the sea.

Shortly after nine o'clock the barking rattle of small arms began and kept up for nearly an hour, the most sustained barrage of the battle. It abruptly gave way to deep rumbles, indicating new tactical maneuvers. At midnight the artillerylike booming ceased, and the conflict settled into silences punctuated by the sporadic crack of a rifle.

Late that first afternoon, Warden Johnston decided to move a task force into the west gun gallery to regain control of the cellhouse. A volley cleared the corridor in D Block, then six officers rushed the gallery. Four pushed on through the draft door. On the floor below stood Cretzer. Guard Stites, who killed Convict Limerick in the 1938 break attempt, fought a pistol duel with Cretzer. He fell. Cretzer dropped the other three. They crawled back out, were taken to a first-aid station set up in the warden's office. And there later Stites was borne, dead.

Reconnoitering, against sniper's bullets, the task force discovered the position of the hostages, and at nine o'clock the rescue operation began—the sustained drumfire heard by observers off The Rock. Machine gunners laid down a withering cover fire as guards in pairs sprinted down the C Block corridor and carried out the captive officers, one at a time. Warrant Officer C. L. Buckner, leader of the Marines' platoon, watched the operation through a bulletproof window in the visitors' room and praised the guards: "They'd make good Marines."

The toll: Officers Miller and Stites dead, thirteen wounded.

Baker, in Cell 402, reported he could hear the moans of Simpson, shot in the stomach, through the afternoon. "We didn't dare help him. The convicts kept coming back and looking in." When darkness set in, Baker, crippled by bullets, dragged himself to the basin tap and brought Simpson a cup of water.

As the searchlights played across the windows that night, Lageson stealthily scribbled the names of the mutineers on the rear concrete wall of Cell 403; Cretzer, Coy, Hubbard, Carnes, Shockley, Thompson.

Apparently the covering fire had driven the convicts into the utility corridor of C Block. Guards shot gas grenades through ventilators toward the service area, but this failed to rout the convicts. The warden assumed they had crawled into the tunnel that carries pipes and conduits beneath the cut-off, or lateral passage, midway in the block. He called a halt to the grenade bombardment and sent to the military arsenal at Benicia for demolition bombs.

Daybreak disclosed to offshore observers the intensity of the first night's battle: the prison's concrete wall deeply pitted, the cellhouse windows shattered.

Warrant Officer Buckner, who won the Silver Star and a Purple Heart for breaking a banzai charge on Guam, decided he had not come to The Rock for guard duty. He spoke to the warden and became once again a fighting Marine. He climbed to the roof, drilled three holes and dropped antitank shells from the Benicia Arsenal on the concrete top of the tunnel to flush out the rebels. Then he came back down and crouched in the pink ice plant to lob in missiles. Hurling hand grenades would be too risky: the window bars were closely spaced. He fitted an adapter to the muzzle of a carbine to blast the bars with rifle grenades. The carbine lacked power; he switched to a Garand M-1 rifle, infantry piece of World War II. He bent the bars out of shape, then rifled grenades through the gaps: a smothered concussion, and shrapnel sprayed out for fifty feet. After a spell of this, Buckner hurried again to the roof and dropped hand grenades, some tied to string to explode at varying levels. Then back to the post in the flowers. A guard now crouched on the catwalk below the grenadier's target window, and after each blast he shouted to the rebels to surrender. All morning the tireless Marine kept at it, lobbing three cases of rifle grenades past the bars, dropping 150 hand grenades through the holes in the roof.

Crowds clustered again at vantage points in San Francisco. It was a sparkling sunny day, and every foot of space that afforded a view of The Rock held a spectator, every window was a theater box. Employers reported an abrupt rise in absenteeism. A soldier from the Presidio elbowed slowly through the mob on the fishing pier at Aquatic Park with binoculars, peddling intimate glimpses of the battleground. Once a gasp went up along the curving pier as billowing smoke obscured the prison, then the throng waited in hushed horror for the flames and the screams of a holocaust. A sigh swelled up as the prison reappeared, with only the smoke of the exploding grenades issuing from the windows: a grenade, falling short, had set fire to dry grass. At times a projectile burst against the concrete in a bright yellow flash and sent vines of black smoke curling up the wall.

The patrol fleet, augmented by Navy destroyer escorts and press launches, cruised around the island. Army crash boats churned a foamy wake from Sausalito, ferrying relief guards from San Quentin and those flown in from other federal prisons. Fighter planes from a nearby military field power-dived on the prison for psychological effect. Their roar, coupled with the relentless shelling that shook the cellhouse, brought wild shrieks from the noncombatant convicts hiding in their cells under beds or behind barricades of books and pillows. A gloom of smoke and steam, hissing from broken pipes,

filled the corridors. Officer Stucker remained trapped in the basement with a group of prisoners, and up in the hospital a dentist and
an intern waited it out with the patients.

At noon the gunfire ceased. The besieged rebels had phoned
about a deal. The seventy-two-year-old warden curtly replied: "The
only possible deal is this: Throw out your weapons."

A pregnant silence prevailed through the afternoon as the mutineers considered the ultimatum. The warden took advantage of the
truce and moved the yard convicts, who had been heckling the
Marines, into A and B Blocks. He was heartened by a visit from two
distinguished military men, General Joseph W. (Vinegar Joe) Stilwell
and General Frank Merrill. General Stilwell offered army aid, but
the warden felt the rebels could not hold much longer. They had no
access to food, and the water mains had been shut off after the pipes
had burst. The Armorer told the police chief of San Francisco on the
phone: "I think we'll wind this thing up in the morning."

The truce ended late in the afternoon. A bullet zinged past a
guard's head as he crept warily by the utility corridor of C Block on
a reconnoitering mission. The single shot was the mutineers' reply to
the warden's terms: unconditional surrender. It indicated too that the
bombing had driven them from the cut-off tunnel.

As a second dusk fell over The Rock, the convict war surged
anew. Fusillades resounded almost continuously hour after hour
until, at nine o'clock, the warden ordered a cease-fire. He stationed
night watches at the utility foxhole and in the gun cages.

At 8 A.M. Saturday, the third day of the battle, six Marines moved
along the catwalk and set up a ladder at a cellhouse window. A prison
guard mounted the ladder, peered in cautiously, sighted a rifle upward
through the window, and fired a single shot. The maneuver, repeated
at window after window, drew no responsive shot. The group retired.

At 9:20 a burst of gunfire sounded in the cellhouse, a dozen
rapid reports. Then silence. At 10:40, three shots, like hacking
coughs. They were the last. The Battle of The Rock was over.

After the window reconnaissance the warden had ordered an
assault on C Block's utility corridor. At 9:20 guards opened the east
door and raked the dark interior with rifle fire. They waited. They

fired the final shots. Guard Donald H. Mowery entered, riflemen at his rear. He waded in a foot of mucky salt water, splashing over the twisted, cracked pipes. Deep in the darkness the beam of his flashlight picked up Coy, in Captain Weinhold's uniform, sitting in the muck, covering this entrance. He still held the rifle in his hands, ready to fire, but the grip was that of rigor mortis. Beyond sat Cretzer, facing the other entrance, wearing Guard Burch's coat and holster with ammunition belt. On Cretzer's lap lay the .45 pistol, his forefinger resting on the trigger, also in rigor mortis. Between them Hubbard sprawled against the rough concrete wall, the long blade of the carving knife protruding from the dark water, leaning against a knee. His body was still warm.

An irony came to light. Hubbard had petitioned for a writ of habeas corpus, claiming he had been beaten into signing a confession and submitting hospital records to show that, soon after his arrest, he was treated for a broken nose, a possible skull fracture, and multiple bruises. His petition was scheduled for a hearing in federal court on the following Monday, two days after the battle. It was dismissed on motion of Prosecutor Joseph Karesh, who said that Hubbard would have had "a fair chance" of walking off The Rock a free man.

After the last shot had been fired, a Navy demolition crew went over the battleground and gathered up eleven unexploded grenades.

Late that Saturday night Warden Johnston held an unprecedented press conference, the first time since The Rock opened, twelve years earlier, that newsmen had been invited to the island. He took the reporters on a tour of the cellhouse. It reeked of the acrid smell of battle and burst sewer lines. A night chill drifted in the paneless windows. Convicts catcalled from the tiers.

As they walked down Broadway and back past the hostage cells, the warden said: "Coy must have been planning this for a long time— he and Cretzer. They had Burch cased."

Thompson, Shockley, and Carnes were tried for the murder of the two guards. They appeared in court as if stamped out of the same press: black suits, black shoes, black ties, white shirts, white socks.

Shockley's counsel built a defense on mental deficiency. A psychiatrist testified he had hallucinations that minerals were served in his food on The Rock, that he was a walking radio station, picking up news around the prison, and that at the outset of the battle his internal radio had transmitted: "Let her go off!" The psychiatrist said the convict, with an I.Q. of 54, was not smart enough to fake insanity. Shockley was adjudged medically, but not legally, insane.

Carnes went back to The Rock with time to serve now topping Whitey Franklin's record: two life terms and ninety-nine years. Thompson and Shockley drew the supreme penalty. "Hell," said Thompson, "I'm not afraid to die. If I was, I wouldn't be in this racket." He offered his eyes to a blind person. On the morning of December 3, 1948, they sat in the twin oak chairs in San Quentin's octagonal, green-tinted gas chamber and inhaled the sweetish, almond-scented fumes.

Of the grim Battle of Alcatraz, the *San Francisco Chronicle* editorialized: "As to why this judgment goes wrong (i.e., judging odds against them), perhaps William Bolitho was right; that the adventurer is peculiarly drugged by the stuff of adventure and cannot think of failure. It may be, as Sigmund Freud had it, that there are men in subconscious search of death. . . . In any case, it was an epic drama of man bound upon a rock, and Aeschylus would have left it to the lane of universal tragedy and grandeur."

Were these men merely lusting after excitement or subconsciously wooing violent death? A less romantic view came from a nameless individual who walked into the *Chronicle*'s city room on Saturday, the final day of the battle, and talked to a top staff writer. His story:

EX-CONVICT TELLS WHY

By Robert de Roos

It is easy to forget that the convicts who died in the abortive Alcatraz Prison break had friends.

Yesterday, a former Alcatraz inmate who did his stretch of 11 years on The Rock came forward with this story, a story that is at once a thoughtful word for the dead and a bitter denunciation of the prison system he blames.

Calmly, sincerely, he criticized the harsh reality of Alcatraz Prison, a place without hope, a physical prison which is the more terrible because it is a prison of the mind. He should know. He was there from the time it became a Federal prison.

He criticized Warden James A. Johnston and James V. Bennett, director of the Federal Bureau of Prisons, as symbols of the repressive system.

This is the convict, a mail robber, talking:

"I'm out now. I've got no beef. I just want to see something done so things like this riot won't happen again.

"I know that if they treated the prisoners half civilly, they wouldn't react like vicious beasts.

"You can't coop up men and take all hope away from them.

"Warden Johnston always says the trouble with Alcatraz prisoners is that they want their freedom. That's right. They want to get out.

"They realize they are in prison.

"If they were treated better they'd still try to get out, but they wouldn't shoot innocent people in cold blood.

"A good example of this is Joe Cretzer. He was a nice young boy and I liked him. Well, he tried to get out of Alcatraz five years ago, remember?

"What did he do then? He captured four guards in the mat shop. He had knives and hammers. But he didn't use them. He didn't harm the guards.

"Now look. This time he was shooting people in cold blood, at least that's what the reports say.

"You see the way the place worked on him?

"Look, I've been pushed around over there and I yapped right back. I had my share of troubles. I've been in isolation and in the dungeon—11 days barefoot on a concrete floor, six or seven days without food—and it's tough.

"But not as tough as going without newspapers. Or only getting to see a show six or seven times a year.

"Every time we got any privileges—Johnston calls them privileges, but I say they are necessities—somebody had to suffer.

"The proof of the pudding is in the eating. Johnston's and Bennett's system doesn't work. If it worked they wouldn't be in trouble so often.

"Of course, Johnston has to defend the system. And he has to whitewash everything. He's got to make people believe he's got 300 desperadoes on his hands. Shucks, there aren't more than 50—I'll bet not 20—really hardened, desperate men in the place.

"But they won't give you a break.

"I was a seaman before I started stealing. Well, at the beginning of the war when they needed seamen so, I asked for a parole—I had three years to go—so I could go to sea.

"Johnston said he thought it was a good idea. But Bennett wouldn't have it. They had to take the last drop of blood.

"Nobody's asking them to take the guards away. Nobody's asking them to turn the place into a country club. All the guys want is some, just a little consideration.

"I never saw anyone get smacked around over there unless he was really out of order. It isn't the physical treatment, it's the mental treatment you get.

"The only thing that kept me going was the thought that I could get out some day. I had a home to come to and a trade to get back to.

"My friends say I took it pretty good. Eleven years in Alcatraz is a long, long time. I wish something could be done about that place—the little things that would count."

Two years before his violent end, Joe Cretzer gave a guard a poem penciled on a sheet of blue-lined paper; written very likely, the guard believes, with an assist from his in-law and cellhouse neighbor, Arnold Kyle. In its bitterness, it seems almost a portent of the slaughter to come. Cretzer's outpouring:

I Wonder

1. You can see at once
   As you are not a dunce
   This is written of the man;
   Not he they've broke
   With that burdensome yoke,
   In life's early span.

2. But am I to say
   In my humble way
   If another's right or wrong?
   Or am I to judge
   With never a budge
   If another is weak or strong?

3. We speak of God
   And the path He trod
   And of that righteous day;
   When in early dawn
   With a loathsome yawn
   He played with a piece of clay.

4. From it man grew
   As perhaps you knew
   And he roamed the earth at will.
   The things he built
   And the blood he spilt
   Are a small mark on the bill.

5. He was good-bad,
   He was happy-sad,
   He came down through the ages;
   Then he wrote a code
   In his own small mode
   And he built for his brothers iron cages.

6. *Sat himself on a throne*
   That he alone
   Might judge deeds of others.
   And through his greed
   And wanton need
   Created the sins of his brothers.

7. *He said with a sneer*
   I am the peer,
   And this is the rightful code;
   (Lo to the unfair judge)
   Before me you stand
   Why lend a hand
   It's you who must carry the load.

8. *He put in the mold*
   A piece of gold
   He said to himself
   This is God;
   It makes more complete
   My lordly seat
   For to it all men will nod.

9. *How long the lout*
   Could stand and shout
   Of God and noble things
   Then turn around
   To knock to the ground
   The man who laughs or sings.

10. *He looked at the brook*
    At his neighbor's nook
    Then laid a cunning plan
    To sack his home
    And break his bones
    He spared the life of no man.

11. *Is this the part*
    God had in his heart
    That man was borne to play;
    Was it His dream
    Omnipotent scheme
    As he toyed with that lump of clay?

12. *Did He really make*
    In that stupendous wake,
    A scale of right or wrong?
    Does He sit on a throne
    With never a grone
    And watch with cynical sight?

13. *Has this lowly creature*
    Mastered even the teacher
    In his flight across the sun?
    Does the Creator smirk
    At his handiwork
    Or smile and say, Well done.

Chapter 14

OVER THE YEARS EACH BREAK, or violent break attempt, had dealt a reeling blow to the security-conscious prison authorities, both at Alcatraz and in Washington, for The Rock from its inception had been a pet of the Justice Department.

The Roe-Cole escape had first set them back on their heels by shattering the myth that Alcatraz was actually escapeproof, and particularly disillusioning was the ease with which the Oklahoma badmen had slipped off the island. Officials, recovering, announced that measures were being taken to make The Rock *more* impregnable but what these measures were, beyond replacing the toolproof bars sawed by the Oklahomans, was never disclosed.

The cellhouse itself, protected by the finest gadgets science and metallurgy could offer, had always been considered secure against assault from within. Then came the dismaying break of the quintet, not merely from the cellhouse but from the innermost security of the isolation block, with a fragment of a hacksaw blade. Director Bennett, patently shaken by the penetration of this "first line of defense," set to work rebuilding the breached defenses, to make Alcatraz as "impregnable as the mind of man can conceive." This was a simple enough job: the replacement of the old, soft-iron bars in that block left over from the Army days with bars of alloyed steel, presumably toolproof.

And then came the severest jolt of all, the Battle of Alcatraz with its staggering toll of five dead and thirteen wounded. Convict cunning and patience had again breached the first line of defenses. And again the defenses were rebuilt, made even more impregnable, as much as

90 percent more, Warden Johnston said. A mesh screen of heavy, tough wire was laid over the bars of the gun galleries, making it virtually impossible for any inmate to cut and spread a way through. Even if he did, a recurrence of the big blast-out attempt was now out of the question; there would be no weapons available; the guards in the galleries, like the guards on the floor, thereafter were unarmed. As a substitute, and to retain the deterrent effect of ready gunfire, ports an inch and a half in diameter were bored in the south wall, through which guards on a catwalk outside could shove rifle or machine-gun barrels, a system of surveillance already in use for the mess hall. The ports, though covered by metal flaps, heightened the howl of the wind, which could push the flaps aside as readily as could the guards.

This matter of the assaultable gallery and guard was not the only, nor the major, flaw in the security setup. The Battle of The Rock hammered home the truth of an old saying among prison people: regularity of bowel movement may be salutary, but not for guards. Too many eyes are always casing a guard's routine to fit into an escape plot, thus making it the weakest link in the security chain. Warden Johnston, who had long before warned officers to regard every inmate as a potential escaper, now began to shore up the prison's custodial defenses. He hired many veterans, chiefly those with military-police or navy shore-patrol experience, and revised the training course.

Senior guards instructed the rookies how to frisk an inmate suspected of carrying contraband from a shop to his cell, and how to shake down a cell to uncover a hidden tool, knife, homemade gun, or even an extra pair of socks. They were warned: "Leave the cell, which is the prisoner's living room, in orderly condition so as to avoid any ill will and resentment that could be caused by a sloppy search."

The course laid particular stress on the importance of counts "to insure safe custody." Johnston said a guard must be quick and accurate "when he counts prisoners as they go back and forth from cells to yard, yard to workshops, to bathhouse, dining room, dock, outside detail, chapel service, or picture show." The new officers were taught to guard against convict tricks and to avoid distractions, a favorite inmate pastime, which could cause errors of confusion.

One significant item of custodial care, the warden related, was alertness against "the use of 'dummys' (*sic*) shaped to resemble a human form with heads or hands or hair faked to deceive the inexperienced and the careless counter."

A former guard tells of the devious ways a convict will harass an officer: "He'll stamp his feet suddenly, or stand right near you and drop a book flat on the concrete floor, just to bug you. A guard should never show nerves, but in a place like that, you hear a sudden loud report like a dropped book—well, it takes steady nerves not to jump. A con likes to stare at a new man on duty in the dining room. He dog-eyes you, you dog-eye him. It becomes a contest. The guard usually wins—he'd damn well better, or the con might consider it personal.

"Then there's what we called negative swearing. An inmate is talking to the man next him at table but he's looking right at you as he says, 'Screw you, mister,' or 'You're a no-good louse, if I ever saw one, a real sonofabitch.' Things like that, just to razz you. All you can do is ignore it, but a new officer sometimes takes it personally and tells the con to lay off. He doesn't last long. Once they know they can get his goat they don't let up, and his nerves snap. This happened even in the days when they had the rule of silence. Some of the convicts became damned good ventriloquists. They could call you a sonofabitch without moving their lips.

"We had two Negro guards, at different times, but they couldn't take it. The prisoners left the mess hall in a loose line and a convict would walk straight up to the Negro guard as if he were going to tear him apart, then suddenly pivot away from him. The guard would look up at the ceiling, tense, holding his breath. One of the Negroes stood it four days, the other quit after two. For some reason, it was the colored convicts who kept harassing them.

"But they weren't the only new guards who couldn't stand the bugging or the tension of the place. Now and then a man would report for duty at eight thirty in the morning and take the noon boat back to the city. A half day, and he'd had it."

Warden Johnston retired in 1948 and was succeeded by Edwin B. Swope, former warden of the New Mexico State Prison. He resembled

Johnston in many ways: rimless specs, gray hair, soft voice, pleasant smile, unassuming, a grandfatherly look. Summer or winter, he always wore an overcoat around the island.

Swope had been broken into the federal penal system by a spell at McNeil Island, where the prisoners learned trades in busy factories, farmed, and ran a herd of beef cattle to supply their own food. He deplored the lack of vocational opportunities and classrooms, even a prison farm, at Alcatraz. With all its complex security mechanisms, weighed against the enforced idleness outside the shops, he was unwilling to consider The Rock troubleproof. He once told a reporter, "Anything can happen."

Despite its emphasis on punishment rather than reformation, Warden Swope felt Alcatraz had its place. In 1953, after four years on the island, he said: "Science has done a great deal in certain fields, such as polio and other diseases, but not much about the human mind. They've just got to dig out some cure for these people. Until they do, Alcatraz, or some comparable prison, will be a necessity in our penal system. . . . There is always that small minority needing an Alcatraz."

(Director Bennett of the Federal Prison Bureau, in an interview that same year with Pierre Salinger, then a *San Francisco Chronicle* reporter, took inventory of the previous twenty-five years and said the American penal system had made progress "but it has been glacially slow. We just have not kept pace with what we know.")

Swope, unable to bring along from McNeil such benefits to prisoners as vocational classes and a farm to tend, did try to import changes for the custodial staff, changes that nettled the guards and lowered an already low morale. One was the removal of a stool in the gun towers, so that a guard, forced to stand during his eight-hour shift, might be more alert. The guards rebelled, and the stools were returned to the towers.

A new bureau policy in 1952 abolished wages and extra good time for the culinary workers, making kitchen duty a household chore on a rotating basis. Twenty-five inmates struck and were clapped into solitary. Swope told the press they had not exhausted their appellate rights, explaining that a convict may appear before the warden at any time to request a job assignment and, if denied, can appeal to the bureau in Washington by sealed, uncensored letter.

When the inmate culinary workers—waiters and kitchen crew—walked off the job, Swope manned the pots and pans with administrative personnel, supervised by stewards flown in from other prisons. He put guards to waiting on table. This was a severe blow to morale, as the guards felt that waiting on the convicts at meals put them in a menial position and thereby diminished the inmates' respect.

"For years," says a former guard, "the officers' morale at Alcatraz has been low and the turnover so high that we called it the West Point of the California penal system—a man took a job at Alcatraz and after a few months of training 'graduated' into a job at a California prison. Alcatraz guards get the same salary as those at Seagoville, the minimum-security institution in Texas that, compared to Alcatraz, is a gentlemen's home; or the same pay as those at some nice camp. At Alcatraz the guard puts in more time—he has to take the boat home, and if he misses one he's lost an hour. The climate's terrible. In and out of that fog and wind, he's sick oftener, and the fog presents a constant risk. The nights are eerie, inside or out. The wind starts up at 1 P.M. and blows continuously till 2 A.M., so strong it shakes the lights that stick out, like lights over billboards, around the edge of the roof to floodlight the prison walls."

Low morale may account in part for the behavior of individual guards. Some years earlier a veteran guard was showing a recruit on the night shift how to shake down the coveralls worn by the inmates at the shops. He found papers in one garment and, muttering "Contraband!" started to tear them up.

"Wait!" said the recruit. "That fellow put a lot of sweat into those papers."

"Sure did. Takes sweat to plot a break."

"Plot? They're exam papers—math."

" 'Rithmetic? You're nuts. Look: x's and y's. A code!" He ripped the papers to shreds. "That'll learn the bastard not to leave codes around."

The onetime recruit, recalling the incident, said: "The convict apparently took the papers to study during the rest periods. If the guard actually thought the algebra was a code, he should have turned the papers in for deciphering."

Guards, like other people, can be subject to human emotions. This was demonstrated the very same year, the year of the Battle of Alcatraz, that Warden Johnston set up his special course to make war-veteran rookies aware of the adverse roles of guard and inmate, and the need for unremitting vigilance. Along came the holiday season and Guard Oscar Eastin, washed by a wave of yuletide compassion for those in solitary on sauceless spaghetti while the world gathered round the wassail bowl to sing carols, played Santa Claus to the convicts in the dark cells of D Block. On Christmas Eve he clandestinely distributed gifts of sweets and tobacco, verboten at any time in isolation. To Jimmy Groves, a black, perhaps because as a military prisoner he had once been in the service himself, the guard was bountiful beyond the wackiest dreams of any Dark Hole tenant: a pack of cigarettes, two tins of snuff, a box of chocolates, and a half pint of whisky, bonded. Pity again engulfed the guard on New Year's Eve, a time to celebrate, and behind the solid steel door of his dark cell Jimmy Groves could fittingly ring in the new year: packs of cigarettes and gum, a plug of chewing tobacco, another half pint of bonded whisky.

There was some question as to just what led to the exposure of the guard's holiday largesse. Groves, a known snitcher, was reported to have squealed on his fairy godfather. Others say that the officer on the graveyard shift in those first hours of 1947 was startled to hear a quavering "Auld Lang Syne" issue from Groves's cell. Opening the vision panel, he was assailed by an aroma more common to a saloon than solitary. He found Groves reeling with the blind staggers, for once not attributable to the pitch blackness.

Eastin, a former Colorado hard-rock miner who had served with the Seabees during the war, seemed astonished at the fuss kicked up. He told newsmen upon his arrest: "I just did it out of the goodness of my heart. I wasn't the only guard who slipped stuff in to the cons. I didn't know it was against the law—just against prison regulations."

Queried about this, Warden Johnston said an investigation had not turned up any other smuggling.

Eastin pleaded guilty that fall and drew six months in the county jail for being, as he put it, "a big-hearted boob." After passing the light sentence, the federal judge remarked to reporters that Eastin was not the only one after all who had engaged in the practice. Queried again, Warden Johnston admitted that several other guards had been caught smuggling and that one had been dismissed.

Other elements besides a soft heart lead to smuggling. A guard who in an unwary moment does the slightest favor for a convict lets himself open to pressure. Says a former guard on that score: "A con is always watching for a chance to get a grip on you. That's why we had to be careful never to offer a con a cigarette, not even a light. In talking to a con you worried when something was said that brought a smile or a laugh. When that happened, I'd look around to see if some other guard saw it: he might figure there was wheeling and dealing gong on. If a con got the slightest hold on you, you were under his thumb. That's what turned McCandless from a guard into a convict."

Lee McCandless, forty-one, an Alcatraz guard, was picked off The Rock one April day in 1951, indicted for smuggling inmates' letters out and money in, and sentenced to five years. He was sent to San Quentin to serve the term rather than a federal penitentiary on the theory that he might, unwittingly, tip off custodial secrets to prisoners who might be candidates for The Rock.

The first hint of the guard's smuggling operations came when a surprise, minute shakedown of the prison turned up a dollar bill stuffed into an electrical conduit in the basement. This led to a quiet investigation because inmates at Alcatraz, where there are no commissary privileges, are not permitted to have any money, and the dollar bill obviously had been stashed there by a convict. A beneficiary of McCandless's illicit operation eventually snitched, and McCandless admitted he had smuggled in as much as $130 at one time.

Why would a convict want the money if he couldn't spend it? "To hoard, in case he managed to escape," says the ex-guard. "Then he wouldn't have to pull a robbery." Convicts, he revealed, had more ingenious hiding places than conduits. They could conceal bills of large denomination in the tubular shoelaces issued them; or with infinite patience they would remove the tobacco from a cigarette, slip in a bill, repack tobacco in the ends, then keep that cigarette well back in the pack. Guards could not possibly take the time to inspect regularly every shoelace or every cigarette in every pack.

When McCandless was caught, Warden Swope frankly told the press: "We couldn't understand why money was being smuggled in, unless it was to bribe somebody. If money is brought in, other things could be brought in too—a gun, or narcotics."

The ex-guard, at Alcatraz then, says McCandless was paying tribute. He owed his job to a convict, and for a curious reason. It points up the risk of indebtedness for a favor. McCandless, taking his physical, was given a vial for a urine specimen. He went into the men's room. A convict was mopping up. After desperate, doubtful moments, McCandless blurted: "I got to urinate in this and I can't—I mean, I'll flunk out. They'll find sugar in it." The convict volunteered. "He was hooked," says the ex-guard, "before he put on a uniform."

A rookie guard usually pulls a night job outside, on patrol or in a tower, to keep him out of the reach of crafty convicts until he gains experience. Even there he is not safe from insinuating gestures. "Guards on evening posts work a straight shift, and the culinary crew packs their lunches," says a former officer. "I used to check their lunch boxes as they moved out to their posts—to make sure some new guard wasn't getting an extra piece of pie, or maybe a steak sandwich when the others got bologna."

Warden Swope retired at the start of 1955 and Paul Madigan took over. Madigan, among the stalwarts who opened The Rock, found his career by chance: "I needed a job during the Depression and became a guard at Leavenworth. I had no idea I would like it." A stout, bald, ruddy-cheeked, genial man with glasses, Madigan chewed gum silently when not smoking a pipe. A devout Catholic, he joined the convicts at Sunday Mass in the chapel. Walking through the cellhouse or the shops, he stopped to hear out any inmate, chewing gum behind a closed mouth as he bent an ear. He became known among the convicts as "Promising Paul," but it was an amiable sobriquet; his willingness to listen, the promise to look into a matter, counted. He weighed circumstances, as an anecdote of his earlier days illustrates.

This was the era of The Rock when a convict would be slapped in the dungeon for leaving a scrap on his plate. An officer then on the staff relates the incident: "A prisoner left half a baked potato on his plate. I didn't blame him: it was burnt so bad I wouldn't have eaten it either. But rules were rules, especially in those days, and I told the prisoner I would have to report him. I took him to Lieutenant Madigan's desk, just outside the mess hall. I told Madigan he had left half a potato but explained why. Madigan said hi-ya to somebody passing by. I thought he hadn't heard and repeated the report, and he waved and nodded to somebody else. I finally got the pitch, led the prisoner away and told him to high-tail it on to his cell."

It was Madigan, a captain, who talked four desperate prisoners—Cretzer, Shockley, Kyle, and Barkdoll—out of a break attempt in 1941, when they had trussed up him and three other officers. Cretzer was later killed in the Battle of Alcatraz, and Shockley executed for his role in that mutiny.

Madigan's years at Alcatraz led him to believe in its necessity as a segregation facility. As warden, he told an interviewer: "Our primary function is to house men who have proven difficult to handle in other federal prisons—the hostile, the assaultive, the troublemakers. The men who come here have less prospect for rehabilitation than the men in the rest of our prison system."

The economics of Alcatraz seemed to bear him out; at least, insofar as any effort at rehabilitation there went. The major share of every dollar went into custodial care: 80 percent. Of the total cost per prisoner, only four cents went into education, chiefly for University of California Extension courses and books for the library.

Even so, the iron-bound regimen of the old days had been softened a little, and any prisoner who earned enough in the shops to afford it could help rehabilitate himself by the purchase of a musical instrument or art supplies. This easing-up process began in the latter years of Johnston's wardenship, continued through Swope, was expanded by Madigan.

Art first came to The Rock in the middle forties when John Paul Chase and several other convicts, encouraged by Warden Johnston, bought paints and began daubing at canvases. It received a boost in the fall of 1946 when George Harris, a San Francisco muralist, volunteered to teach a Saturday afternoon class. Three years later eleven Harris pupils had become proficient enough to enter thirty-four works—oils, watercolors, gouaches, drawings—in San Francisco's annual Open Air Art Show in Union Square. The city's Art Commission, sponsor of the festival, had strict orders not to identify the artists, but the grim Rock and all its crushing discipline could not stifle the pride of creation: each offering bore a signature, self-effacing initials or the full dignity of a name. The Alcatraz exhibit drew the biggest crowd, and on the opening day nine pictures brought the convict artists a total of $200. A bank president bought an oil by a bank robber. Alfred Frankenstein, distinguished art critic, saw no budding Rembrandts: "All one can say about the best of these artists is that he has another 192 years to spend on The Rock." But he did commend this double-century termer whose paintings, signed O.L.D., depicted mountains, valleys, and hunting scenes "in a highly eloquent if primitive style." He also cited another Harris student as particularly capable, a William Grump, who caught the somber pattern of wire as seen from the inside looking out, on a canvas entitled "How Far to the Bridge? Five Years." The work that most astonished the patrons was a portrait of Leopold Stokowski, the conductor, copied from a photograph with, as one critic put it, "all the meticulous skill that had landed the artist, a counterfeiter, in jail." Seven Rock artists, among them Chase, later offered their work at a Cancer Society benefit sale in San Francisco. Again nostalgia—a landscape bore the inscription "Sunset on the Farm"—was the dominant theme.

Harris, understandably pleased with his eager pupils, commented: "A couple, at least, would never have gotten mixed up with crime if they'd taken up art. Some will never have any trouble making a living as commercial illustrators, if they get a chance. One or two could even become fine artists if they wished." His students' paintings decorate the large, airy office of the warden.

Warden Swope in 1950 brought a new diversion to The Rock—movies, every other weekend, in the chapel upstairs over the administration offices, reached by a stairway in the cellhouse. By now the work week had been reduced to five days and the men given an extra recreation period in the yard on Saturday afternoons. On movie weekends—mostly western and musical-comedy films, now and then a war picture, but never a gangster or sexy show—half the general population attended on Saturday, the remainder on Sunday afternoon. Only prisoners in good standing—out of D Block—were granted the privilege.

In 1955, another welcome innovation came. Radio outlets were installed in the cells at the suggestion of Director Bennett. The convicts were permitted to tune in on two approved stations devoted primarily to light music. They could lie on their cots, adjust their headsets and listen until lights out at 9:30—later, for major-league night baseball broadcasts. This inevitably led to wagering, and it was common such nights to hear a bet offered, and taken up, at adjacent cell fronts: "A hundred the Giants beat the Dodgers." Not a hundred dollars, but pushups; and it became apparent on weekends in the yard who were the losers. Sometimes the bet was a hundred tailor-made cigarettes. They were now issued three packs a week.

Introduction of radio had little effect on the convicts' reading habits. They still continued to peruse books—an average of seventy-five to eighty a year—as they listened; usually, light escape literature such as western novels, but volumes on philosophy and other intellectual fare were also well thumbed. Convicts could order books, or censored magazines, from a mimeographed library catalogue. They returned a book, along with a request for a new one, by leaving it on a wheeled table as they entered the mess hall for breakfast. Books and magazines were delivered to the cells during the morning by inmates on temporary library assignment. (The library now has about 15,000 volumes.)

University of California Extension has had a contract with Alcatraz since the thirties but in the past several years, for reasons unexplained, very few Rock inmates have enrolled, or been permitted to enroll. Some attribute the decline in Extension courses, once quite popular at Alcatraz, to the competition of radio, but the drop in enrollment has been fairly recent. University officials privately wonder about this in view of the great, continued success of their program at San Quentin where inmate students have gone forth, upon parole, to pursue careers that in many cases have won them distinction.

With the easing of restrictions came a lengthening of visits convicts could enjoy with a relative or now even a close friend—almost two hours a month. (To some, this is still a punitive limitation, as a relative may have to travel thousands of miles.)

Warden Madigan inspired a new kind of bloodletting at Alcatraz. In April of 1959 fifty inmates each donated a pint of blood to the Irwin Memorial Blood Bank in San Francisco, credited to the account of the U.S. Public Health Service, whose medical staff at the Marine Hospital, San Francisco, is on call for emergencies. The blood donors enjoyed an equally rare social hour in the prison hospital, with sandwiches, coffee, lemonade, and cakes.

For some years the inmates had received a Christmas booty of six candy bars and two pounds of jawbreakers. Madigan added six cigars in 1957, two years later made another concession: any convict with two dollars in his account could buy a two-pound box of chocolates. He also created a new holiday spirit by providing special menus on Christmas and Thanksgiving, except for those in D Block.

All this did not mean that Alcatraz had been converted into a super-maximum-security country club, nor that violence had come to an end. In 1953 a score of convicts kicked up a fuss that quickly flared through the blocks. Warden Swope told the press: "It was caused by race prejudice. They demanded the right to be permitted to select their own cells. They challenged the authorities of the institution and created a disturbance," indicating that, as always, the Department of Justice won. A few whites objected to living in a cell next to, or even opposite a black, and the disturbance they created was perhaps, outside of the Battle of Alcatraz, the worst bedlam that ever shook the cellhouse walls. They shouted curses to the rafters, banged tin cups on bars, beat their iron beds on the concrete, slammed hinged table tops against steel walls. They broke up toilets and washbowls, they set fire to papers and bed sheets, they even flung flaming garments into the corridors. And in the end, the challengers of the authority of the institution, not the Department of Justice, won. Thereafter, the black convicts were segregated in the bank of D Block facing Broadway. The tiers across the way, the inside of C Block, were set aside as a quarantine section for the temporary confinement of new prisoners.

Blacks were now segregated in the dining room by the simple process of ringing out inside B Block as a group. Racial segregation was even extended to the showers: whites first on Tuesdays, blacks first on Saturdays, the order reversed each week. At the movies, the black prisoners were directed to sit in the back rows.

Nor had the prison administrators experienced the last of their headaches over court petitions. An unusual incident occurred in February 1954, this time not the suppression of a petition but the denial, by an odd means, of a convict's right to argue it in court. Prison officials had long maintained that no convict was ever sentenced to Alcatraz, nor ever paroled from there; he was "seasoned" at some other prison, later transferred back to that prison for discharge. This particular convict was booted right off The Rock.

He was Earl (Writ-a-Day) Taylor, an accountant who had been sentenced to five years in Leavenworth for tax evasion, then shipped to Alcatraz. He had no sooner settled in his cell at Alcatraz than he began firing off petitions, almost daily, thereby earning his nickname. He charged that his removal to The Rock was "a bum beef," and at length a federal judge set a hearing for 10 A.M. Wednesday, February 3. At 9:45 a guard came to Taylor's cell and said, "Get your things together, you're getting out." Taylor later told the press: "They handed me five bucks and rushed me down to the boat. I didn't want to be discharged. I had this petition for a writ of habeas corpus pending and I was supposed to be in court to argue it." Taylor said he was convinced he was liberated, without parole restrictions, as a means of "beating that court order." Prison officials declined comment.

Before that, in 1948, Warden Swope won a petition bout with Robert Stroud, the Birdman, but not before the judge offered a stinging reminder about the rights in general of men imprisoned. Stroud had petitioned the court to compel Swope to permit him to correspond with a literary agent and during one of the hearings Federal Judge George B. Harris commented, "To deprive a man of the fruits of the industry of his mind is to completely destroy that man."

Said the prosecutor: "But a criminal is civilly dead."

Retorted Judge Harris: "He may be civilly dead, but he's not buried."

Even with Warden Madigan's excellent background at Alcatraz, and his experience with these very men, the old petition grievances kept recurring. After a prolonged dry spell, a flood of legal paper rolled over to the federal court during a fortnight in June of 1960. Madigan seemed hard put to explain the sudden rash of actions. "Perhaps it's just a way of passing the time," he told reporters.

Curiosity was not confined to the reporters. E. Herbert Schepps, law clerk of Federal Judge William T. Sweigert, likewise wondering about the tide of pleas, went to Alcatraz on his own initiative to discuss the matter with Madigan. He said the warden appeared evasive regarding the previous silence of the convicts but at one point let slip a remark: "Well, we sometimes consider a petition too scandalous and send it back to the prisoner." This put the warden in the role of jurist, ruling on the merits of petitions. Schepps explained that federal judges were concerned about an individual's constitutional rights, that men in prison have access to the courts.

"Wardens usually recognize these rights, even though convict petitions may mean extra secretarial work," he said. "Many petitions may be frivolous, but what of the one with merit, the one that should be heard?" Men on Alcatraz have won their release by the time-honored habeas corpus process, by a showing they were held there unjustifiably."

In September 1960, just months after this conference between law clerk and warden, a mysterious "lay-in" strike hit Alcatraz. The entire felon population refused to budge from their cells. It lasted more than a week and came to an end after a dozen suspected leaders were lodged in solitary, where they somehow managed to get hold of razor blades and slashed their heel tendons.

Madigan said convict tailors, paid seventeen cents a garment for making Army bakers' pants, had started the trouble in a bid for higher wages but had never made any formal demand. Federal beat newsmen in San Francisco received reports, unconfirmed, that the strike and tendon cuttings were in protest against a denial of access to the courts.

This form of protest, common among chain-gang convicts in the South, broke out at Alcatraz in the fall of 1958 with a few scattered cuttings, then a batch of seven in one day, all kept secret. The first intimation to the press came after a rash of slashings that Thanksgiving. Warden Madigan said this is what happened: Razor blades were passed out in D Block around noon for the thrice-weekly shave. Three men, protesting the ban on desserts and smoking in solitary, severed their Achilles' tendons and several others "scratched" their heels. For the next three weeks they enjoyed hospital privileges of sweets and cigarettes. Thereafter, electric shavers replaced blades in the isolation block. Nevertheless, a few weeks later two more took that drastic means to get their desserts and smokes, and the warden said it was a mystery how they came by the razor blades.

Actually, the Thanksgiving Day carvings reached an appalling toll. One of the surgeons summoned from Marine Hospital says, "Yes, I recall that Thanksgiving well. A real bloody holiday. Fourteen cut their heel cords, and four of us spent the day repairing the damage."

Former inmates offer still another contradiction. Blades were not passed out in D Block three times a week. The men were permitted to shave only after a twice-weekly shower in the block's own shower room. A guard stood by as the naked convicts shaved—with a *locked* safety razor, such as those used in mental hospitals, to prevent removal of the blade.

Early in January 1959, newspapers heard of more tendon slashings, and Madigan said two convicts again had obtained razor blades in some mysterious way. This will clear up that enigma, and the riddle of the blades in subsequent cuttings: They were smuggled to the men in the dark cells by the occupants of the light cells directly above. How *these* convicts acquired them cannot now be disclosed.

To understand the smuggling maneuver, consider certain features of the cells. The upper ones had a wash basin and toilet; the lower ones neither, only a hole in the floor connected to the same outlet that served the basin and toilet above, and flushed by the guard in the corridor. Before passing down a blade, the man above talked to the man below over probably the world's most novel telephone system. He tapped a signal on the floor, and the man below bailed the water out of the hole with his paper cup (no tin cups in D Block). The man above drained the trap under the basin by removing the plug or blowing out the water, then spoke into the basin, his voice traveling down the sewer pipe to the man listening at the hole.

They could carry on a conversation in normal tones. "Sending down a blade, Stu," and Stu would reply, "Okay, Mike, let her come." Mike would drop the blade, tied to a long string, into the toilet and flush it. Stu would wait for the water to rush past, then reach in and pull out the string, untie the blade and say, "Okay, take her away." And Mike would haul up the cord for future use.

Madigan, who had withheld the names of the "three" Thanksgiving cutters, readily identified this January pair as Joseph Wagstaff, thirty, a Washington, D.C., robber doing eight years, and Homer Clinton, forty-one, the Oklahoma kidnaper-lifer known as the Green Lizard, the trade name of a hair tonic he preferred over bourbon. It seems the warden forgot two: Jack Waites and Red Stetson, a brace of bank bandits. The surgeon summoned for the suturing also missed them—they were already back in the Dark Hole. A medical technical assistant, or MTA, had looked at their wounds, remarked "Hell, they're only superficial," and sewed them up.

Waites's tendon had been cut, but not quite severe, and it kept bothering him. One day, about six weeks later, he fell down; his right ankle just gave way. His left leg, its heel cord cut in the mass Thanksgiving demonstration, was still wobbly, and he was unable to stand up. They carried him up to the hospital, and it so happened than an orthopedic surgeon was there, called over on a sacroiliac case. He inspected the scar left by the January repair job and ordered him into surgery at once. A witness recalls, "He found an inch of Jack's tendon rotted away. He spliced it together, then asked who had done that needlework. The MTA owned up to it and, man, did that orthopedist chew him out! 'This is strictly the work of a physician,' he told the MTA, 'and I don't want to ever hear you messin' around with it again.'" What happened to Red Stetson could not be ascertained.

During this latter-day period of The Rock's existence, conditions in the hospital gradually worsened, report a number of former patients. To reach the hospital, over the mess hall, an ailing convict entered the hall and turned left to a locked gate. A guard opened it, and he climbed a stairway to another gate. He pushed a button. An officer came down a long hallway and let him in. He walked down that corridor through a third gate into an infirmary starkly grim as a morgue. Fronting the duty officer's desk were three large ward cells, each with five hospital-type beds. In addition there was a doctor's office, a dentist's office, the chief MTA's office, a treatment room, a surgery, a medicine supply room, a kitchen, two isolation wards (the "bug cages" of prison argot) for mental patients, and next to these a similar ward, also with both a gate and a solid wooden door, built especially for Stroud. The kitchen, where dietary meals were once prepared, was now reserved mainly as a retreat; the doctor on his daily visits usually had coffee there with the MTA on duty.

The hospital, the pride of Warden Johnston in the old days, was then accredited and staffed by medical men. In recent years, as the treatment accorded healthy convicts improved, care for the sick declined. Instead of a medical officer in charge, the director now was a Chief Medical Technical Assistant, in charge of Assistant Medical Technical Assistants. Even so, the hospital was staffed only during the day; the duty MTA left at 8 P.M., and another came on at 7 A.M. the next morning. At night the custodial officer doubled in brass as "medical" officer in charge. A private-practice doctor took the nine o'clock boat over in the morning, rode the bus up the cliff, made a swift round of the patients, rode the bus back down, returned on the ten o'clock boat. For serious illnesses or an operation or an emergency such as a stabbing or accident, the medical staff of the Marine Hospital was on call.

Patients receive the same food as that served in the mess hall and, with the exception of dessert and tobacco, have no more privileges than convicts consigned to the Misbehavioral Treatment Unit, i.e., none. This is to encourage a faster convalescence. Patients must keep the wards clean, but if a patient asks for a bucket and brush to scrub the asphalt tile floor, or even a broom to sweep it, or a cloth to dust, he is considered well enough to return to the general population downstairs. Former inmates say the wards lacked the dustless, antiseptic aspect usually associated with a hospital.

Because of his limited time, the doctor could make only a cursory examination. One morning he stepped to the foot of a patient's bed and inquired, "What seems to be the trouble?"

"Chills and fever, doctor. Retchin' all night."

"Well, you'll stop vomiting in twenty-four hours."

The patient was then running a temperature of 104° and, as it turned out, had pneumonia.

The doctor moved over to the foot of the next bed and said to that patient, who had complained of chest pains: "I checked your X-rays. You can go back to your job. There's nothing wrong with your chest."

"Doc, them X-rays is two years old."

"Look, boy, I told you, there's nothing wrong with you," and he walked out.

Once the doctor almost missed the ten o'clock boat, as an ex-patient relates: "One day he has a con on the table—prostate trouble—and has his fingers up his behind examin' him when he happens to see the time. 'Oh, oh,' he says and yanks his hand out. 'See you tomorrow,' and he rushes out."

An ailing convict must first pass the test at the gate at the top of the stairs. Not every guard is inclined to grant admission, in the belief most convicts are malingerers. Another former patient says, "Some bulls figure like this: if you ain't bleedin', you ain't hurtin'. One night I saw the bull shove a sick con in a bug cage and tell him, 'I'm gonna give you one week to get well. If you ain't well then, I'm gonna throw you in isolation.' After a week in the bug cage he'd welcome TU.

"Another time, a con hurt his back exercisin' in the yard, liftin' weights, and they brung him up, lettin' out a yell every other step. A bull pushes him in the Birdman's old room and says, 'Okay, we can stand it as long as you can.' Then he closes the wood door to drown out the screams. Next morning the doc looks at him and says, 'Your back'll stop achin' in twenty-four hours.' Only it don't. Every time he moves wrong, he lets out a bloody scream. They figure he's a real bug and call over a head shrinker, tellin' him this con's a faker. So the head shrinker has it all doped out and he tells the con: 'What happened is, you made a bet with yourself you could lift that weight and when it fell, you lost your bet. You didn't want to lose the bet, so your mind makes up an excuse and blames it on your back, and the bet is called off. So you *think* your back hurts.' The con kept on thinkin' it was his back."

In a place where tempers and smoldering hatreds can flare into violence, the absence of a resident physician was deplored by a former inmate: "What can the MTA do? Take the con stabbed in the shower room one day—knife in his back right through the spine. A couple MTAs bring him up on a stretcher, then call a doc in Frisco. The guy has to lay on the table, waitin' for the doc to catch the next boat, the knife stickin' out of his back. Cons bleed to death waitin' for the doc."

Sometimes a convict with no ailment will make the hospital, or just as likely get his treatment, a forced feeding, in his solitary cell, as an ex-inmate relates: "These are the leaders of hunger strikes. A couple of bulls will hold a man down while the MTA runs a rubber hose in his nose and pours in milk. After a while the fellas decide it's easier to sit up and eat, and the strike ends." (This is an old prison custom. Kidnaper Harvey Bailey went on a one-man hunger strike at Leavenworth in 1934 and called it off after taking a gallon of milk a day through his nose for several days.)

There are no reports of such activities during the days when the hospital had a regular medical staff. A guard of that time relates an incident, not so much of custodial callousness as a natural human impulse: "A prisoner in an isolation ward worked loose an iron slat from the bed, wrapped it in a strip of bed sheet, then insisted on seeing the captain about a complaint. He struck the captain a sharp glancing blow that cut open his cheek. We finally subdued him by shoving his elbow down the toilet and holding the wrist over the side until it became numb. He quieted down and we took him into the treatment room for a checkup before bedding him down under a restraining sheet. One of the guards, who had the iron slat in his hand, started out, came back, took two swipes across the prisoner's rump and walked on out. We all felt better. It was a sort of tribute to the way we felt about the captain."

Olin Blackwell, the rangy, congenial rancher from Coryell County, Texas, who had spent twenty of his forty-four years with the federal penal system, was associate warden when the tendon-cutting epidemic broke out in solitary in September of 1960. Nine, among them the ringleaders of the "mysterious" lay-in strike, sliced their Achilles' tendons. A few days later five more hacked their heels. Blackwell said the first batch had used fragments of eyeglass lenses, the second tiny pieces of sharpened metal. But they were "feeble" attempts, the wounds superficial and requiring "only a couple of stitches and a piece of Band-Aid."

The grapevine hummed. All had been taken to the hospital, sutured, and their legs put in casts. Some had slashed both heels, had both legs in casts. All had been taken right back to their dark cells, and there beaten up. A former inmate says, "They hadn't used any broken eyeglasses, but sharp pieces of metal sure enough. Razor blades. Man, that shook the bulls up. Bad enough having a razor blade in TU, but blades in the Dark Hole—and after they'd switched to an electric razor. The bulls was really shook. They walloped the bejesus out of the guys, trying to find out where those razor blades come from. Nobody snitched."

Every prison has a remarkable news service, but The Rock's grapevine is undoubtedly the most amazing. Attorney Stanley Furman of Beverly Hills, who volunteered his services to Stroud, offers a dramatic illustration. In his last eight years at Alcatraz, Stroud was kept in the special ward built for him in the hospital, behind *two* doors, one solid. He had no radio, no newspapers or news magazines, censored mail, no contact with other inmates, presumably no contact with the outside world, sealed off in a little bug cage upstairs, and what he was reading at the time was 2,000 years old: Latin.

After the third jury had decreed execution, Stroud's lawyers carried a plea to the Supreme Court that he had been placed in double jeopardy because the second trial jury had recommended against the death penalty. The high court rejected the plea. On one of his visits, Furman found Stroud strangely elated. "I've got it made!" the Birdman said, and at Furman's quizzical look: "Why, the Supreme Court decision in the Green case!" The court had recently ruled such a plea valid. Furman hadn't heard.

Tendon cuttings kept occurring periodically—and kept, as usual, from the press. On an August night as late as 1961 ten cellhouse convicts, in a desperate try to reach the courts, cut their heel strings. "We were stacked in the Dark Hole like cordwood and not given any medical attention till the next day," says a participant. The Hole became their convalescent ward, and there they continued their drastic protest. A convict in an open-front cell above called on the sewer line: "I got the thing—drink some red wine," and flushed down a strip of metal off a coffee can.

Chapter 15

A T THE BEGINNING OF 1960, when Frank Lee Morris shuffled onto The Rock in leg irons, all the evidence seemed to indicate that Warden Johnston's buttoning up after the Battle of Alcatraz had made the prison truly escapeproof. Only one serious try had been made during the fourteen years since the desperate and bloody battle, and the results of that one should have discouraged even the most determined.

This attempt took place on the afternoon of September 29, 1958, and the participants were a brace of robbers, Clyde Johnson and Aaron Burgett. Johnson, forty, was serving forty years for the armed robbery with an accomplice of the North Side Branch of the First National Bank of Memphis, a job that netted $43,162 in currency and enabled him to pursue for another two months his dual personality of Clyde Milton Johnson, robber, and John Horace Alexander, bon vivant. He had first tried his hand at crime in a series of chain-store robberies in Los Angles while AWOL from the Army, forays from the barracks that earned him a discharge "other than honorable" and a prison term. In those holdups he had always used a paper bag to carry off the cash from the till and thereafter, in periods of freedom on parole or as an escapee, he had a predilection for the brown paper pokes in stickups of supermarkets, night clubs, and banks across the country. He also had a partiality for flashy cars, whisky mixed with lemon juice, and a plump blonde named Butcher Knife Billie Glaze, whose husband was in prison. The FBI admittedly found his trail hard to follow because he was quiet, well-mannered, courteous. His easygoing, casual way of handing a teller or store manager a paper bag and saying softly, "Fill this with money," invariably led the victim to laugh it off as a joke—until Johnson backed up his request with a gun. He was shot, the bullet boring just an eighth of an inch from his heart, in the FBI chase that ended his active career in 1949.

Nine years later he was on the garbage detail at Alcatraz with Aaron Burgett, twenty-eight, a rangy gunman doing twenty-six years for the $15.26 robbery of the post office at Banner, Missouri, in May 1952. Burgett was the tenth child of a Missouri cotton picker and had acquired the nickname of Wig as a boy because of long blonde curls. His father said after his capture: "I was father and mother both to him, after his ma died when he was three. He was a mighty good boy, never drank none, went to church, never got in fights, and made an honest livin' pickin' cotton till he got mixed up with a no-account woman." He went off with her to St. Louis and joined a gang, was picked up one night after the postal robbery when a state trooper stopped his car and found eight loaded guns in it. The trooper said Burgett impressed him as "a sadist who doesn't seem to have any reason for wanting to live."

Burgett's blonde hair had darkened to brown, and was crewcut, by the time he had reached Alcatraz and was picking up garbage in the residential area that September afternoon with Johnson. A heavy fog, rare in late September, had rolled in over The Rock; so thick, in fact, that Guard Harold Miller was startled to see a knife inches from his face and to hear Burgett saying, "Be good and you'll be all right." Miller was good. They roped him like a steer, tied a strip of cloth tight over his mouth, another strip over his eyes, then lugged him behind the houses and dumped him in a clump of bushes. They gathered up escape gear they had stashed away among other shrubs and made for the shore.

A half hour later the lieutenant of the guards, wondering what had become of Miller and the garbage detail, launched a search. They found him thrashing around in the bushes. The Armorer kicked on the siren. A Coast Guard patrol boat's searchlight, boring through the fog, discovered Johnson standing waist-deep in the bay, his teeth chattering like castanets. "We made a good try," he said, "but it just didn't work."

For five days, while the convicts were locked up, listening on their headsets to the World Series, searchers poked in the caves at the foot of the windward cliffs. And then Warden Madigan told the newspapers: "I'm satisfied Burgett isn't on the island. I think he's drowned. It's a tough swim, even for an expert."

On the thirteenth day after the escape, a guard came on duty at 8 A.M. in the south gun tower. He swung his binoculars around the bay in a routine scanning. He spotted a body, or a log, floating a hundred yards off the southeast tip of the island. It was Burgett. Either the tides had carried him out the Golden Gate and brought him back, or he had snagged on a rock when he went down. That was the normal time for a body to come up.

"If a body doesn't surface in the first few hours, then it takes ten days to two weeks," explained Dr. Henry W. Turkel, coroner of San Francisco. "It depends on various factors: what the individual has ingested, the bacteria in his stomach, and whether the crabs get to him. It takes gas to float to the top, and if the body is caught on rocks it will take longer, upwards of two weeks, for the bacteria to produce enough gas to set the body free and let it rise. But if the crabs puncture the stomach and release the gas, the body will never come up. That's why, in burials at sea, they always make an incision."

Burgett's body was considerably decomposed, but there was enough left of a thumb for an identifying print, and his convict number, 991, was stenciled on the belt. His body was still weighted with equipment he had painstakingly gathered, hidden away, then donned or strapped on for the swim to San Francisco. In a pocket was the thin, sharp knife he had made himself, the shiv he had stuck in Guard Miller's face. Apparently he had lost only his cap in the struggle with the tide rips. He was warmly clothed to endure the cold water, and that ironically may have been his undoing: the weighty garb, once waterlogged, probably made him sink.

He was wearing heavy shoes and an extra pair of socks, and he had pulled an extra pair of long cotton drawers over his trousers and fastened them with a safety pin. He had tied the pants legs snug around his ankles with black plastic tape to make them watertight. He had improvised a "water wing" out of the sleeve of a black plastic raincoat, which he tied to his belt. His ditty bag—a small bag convicts use to hold dominoes—was also attached to his belt, probably as a repair kit. Instead of dominoes, it held an odd collection: a coil of tape such as that binding his pants legs; a circle of string, like a key ring, holding safety pins and short pieces of wire; two small rocks. And still taped securely to the soles of his shoes were what was left of a pair of wooden fins: the part projecting beyond the toes had broken off.

Aaron Burgett was the eighteenth who had tried to get off The Rock. Five, stopped by slugs, made it to the morgue. Roe and Cole vanished. Most of the others, like Johnson, were waiting in the water or on the shore for capture—or rescue. A few, like Hamilton, came crawling back.

Johnson was hauled before the prison's own disciplinary court, convicted, and lodged in solitary.

This luckless try, long after the Battle of Alcatraz, occurred just a year and three months before Frank Morris came to The Rock. Little about Morris's appearance, that January morning when he bombarded the *Warden Johnston,* would have warned of his own purpose, and his ability to carry it out. After he did accomplish it, Associate Director Fred T. Wilkinson of the Federal Prison Bureau, who was warden at Atlanta when Morris was there and knew him well, gave a thumbnail character sketch to the Associated Press: "Morris quiet and very intelligent. He's not given to rash violence. Above all, he's a planner. The whole operation seems typical of him."

Primarily a burglar all his criminal life, Morris had, as his last offense, participated in the burglary of a bank in Louisiana. Hardly a gangster show, but a look at his record explains why he was sent to this penal stronghold: a potential escape problem. His past, from childhood, was a long blotter of breakouts. He was even an escapee the night he helped burglarize the Louisiana bank. . . .

The spring harvest was in full swing at the Louisiana State Prison at Angola, about forty-five miles northwest of Baton Rouge, on a remote 18,000-acre tract in a blend of the Mississippi, partly cultivated to sugar cane but for the greater part wild brush country dotted with patches of piney woods.

Morris, doing ten years for robbery and possession of marijuana, and a fellow inmate, William Martin, were members of a work gang cutting sugar cane and hauling it to the prison mill. About four o'clock on a drowsy afternoon in late April, 1955, they disappeared.

Warden Maurice Sigler said, "We don't know how they got away." Bloodhounds led searchers off the reservation to the shoulder of a road near the home of a black farmer, who returned that night to find the law waiting on his stoop. Yes, he had picked up two white hitchhikers and let them out at an oil refinery on the outskirts of Baton Rouge.

The fugitives spent a few months in New Orleans, cased the bank in the small town of Slidell across Lake Pontchartrain, then headed north to Kansas City where with a third partner, Earl Branci, they plotted the burglary. On Thanksgiving night they bored a hole in the rear wall of the bank, burned open two vaults, and lugged out $6,165—a heavy haul, as it was all in coins. They had a fling for a month and a half, and then the FBI walked into the motor court southwest of Baton Rouge, where they were staying with three women. Morris drew a federal term of fourteen years. . . .

That's the way it had always been: a few months *out*, a few years *in*. And now, The Rock. What lay beyond Louisiana—the first wayward step that had set him off on the long, erratic road to Alcatraz? The day he ran away from home? What kid of eleven, even younger, has not entertained that notion? No, it all began that summer morning, an hour before daybreak, when, as a boy of fourteen, he silently worked loose the catch on the window screen and hoisted himself over the sill . . . it all began with two diamond rings, a lady's wristwatch, and a fistful of money. Or so it might seem.

Perhaps it began late one night about six years before he was born. That was the night his mother, Clara, willful, hoydenish, slipped out of the home of her respectable, middle-class family and stole off to the nearest city, a child of eleven. Clara was setting a course through childhood and teens that Frank, whether by chance or a genetic trait, would duplicate.

Picked up as a runaway, the child Clara was returned to her home, only to skip off again . . . again . . . again, until she landed in a school for wayward girls. Her temperament balked at restraint, and she soon left, one night after lights out, hitching a ride to Washington, D.C. In the nation's capital, as elsewhere, a teenage girl does not roam the streets after midnight without drawing official attention. She was now approaching seventeen, and she went into a reformatory. Again she vanished, stealing a nurse's uniform and money. During this interval of freedom she gave birth to a son she christened Frank Lee Morris, bestowing on him the name of a civil engineer whom she claimed, without evidence, she had married two months earlier, but who admittedly was not the father. Thus, in a sense, Frank Morris was born in and out of wedlock. The date: September 1, 1926.

Not long afterward, out of a reasonable fear she might destroy the baby during one of her uncontrollable rages, Frank was placed in a foster home. A sturdy, happy infant, he could stand in his foster mother's lap at the age of six months.

Clara was lodged in a training school for girls and at first the reports were encouraging: "A good mixer, energetic and ambitious when she wants to be. . . . Makes a real effort to conquer her temper. . . . Does well in nursing course." Signs of a mercurial nature began to appear. She developed ear trouble, spurned treatments, became noticeably deaf. She moped for Frankie, and they placed Frankie, a year old, in the institution with her. She was happy again, and diligent, full of great plans. She begged for release, that she might work for her baby.

A Catholic orphanage agreed to employ her, and Clara, cuddling her baby, was soon walking down a corridor to a new life, the spike heels of her cherry-colored slippers clicking confidently. The agency reported: "She is bright, honest, devoted to her child, a leader among the other girls." In time the sisters discerned a strange quirk in her maternal instincts: she was deriving strength from the infant, rather than supplying it. She played with him, as a toy, and ignored the normal attention a child needs. The effect on Frankie was noticeable: he cried more in her presence than in her absence.

And then one day her quiescent temper erupted. She lit into a group of girls like a whirlwind; she emerged with a black eye, scratched face, and nerves so agitated it took three hours to calm her down. She attributed the outburst to her surroundings; she wanted to live in a real home. She went to church occasionally and believed in God, but: "God didn't mean for me to suck my thumb all day."

She was placed in a private home, to care for two small boys. She left Frankie at the orphanage, visiting him twice a week. The change was good for her son: "Frankie, a very sensitive child, has improved in health and disposition since separated from his mother."

The home Clara entered was one of culture, and her new employer reported: "She is cheerful, energetic, a great help, and we are very pleased with her." Clara had climbed another ecstatic peak, as quickly to descend it. She began to chatter incessantly—romantic, erratic tales of her husband and the magnificent home she planned to build. One day the maid discovered a silver butter knife secreted between the layers of Clara's mattress—a gift, perhaps for Frankie—but the next day it was back in the silver drawer. She left abruptly, with the parting word: "I don't want to be introduced to my friends as a servant." After that, her visits to Frankie became less frequent, but each time she vowed: "I'm going to get a good job and take Frankie and hire a woman to care for him."

This portrait of Frankie, age three, emerges: "A very pleasant, intelligent-looking child who understands all that is said, but talks very little. He is sturdy and runs about the halls, and the sisters make a great pet of him."

A little later he was placed in a foster home, and his development duly reported: "He does and says only what he chooses. He digs in the backyard and when told to come in, he screams. He is made to sit in a chair as punishment. He dominates even older children. . . . Everyone who comes to the house spoils him because he is so cute, and he is a great favorite in the home."

Two days after Christmas of 1929 Clara visited him, for the first time that year. Frankie, three years old, did not recognize her. She wore heavy makeup, spoke in a loud voice, and walked unsteadily.

She brought Frankie a present, a bag of cheap candy, and tried to force him to take it.

The foster mother intercepted the bag. "He can't have it now, it'll spoil his appetite."

"Aw, give the kid a good time," Clara said. After an awkward moment, she said, "Well, I got to hurry back and cook supper for my man," and weaved out to a car in which a man was waiting.

She returned at Easter. She was now a chorus girl at a burlesque theater, and she lived the role, cosmetically, offstage. She brought Frankie a little basket of colored candy and apologized: "I can't stay, I got a friend outside."

Frankie, at four: "A nice looking child, with a clear delicate skin and golden brown curls. Well behaved and likable. Inclined to be self-willed, but easily managed by anyone who understands him and whom he likes."

Clara paid no visits during the next two Christmas seasons, but she suddenly appeared on the day after New Year's 1932, so thin "she almost rattled." The report shed further light: "She was dressed in a long black chiffon gown, black satin high-heeled slippers, a short black coat, and no hat. Her flaming red hair was tossed by the cold wind. She was made up in real theatrical style. She still refused to tell how or where she was living." Again her post-yule gift to Frankie was a bag of cheap candy.

Late that month the foster mother suggested a place with larger grounds for Frankie, at six a bundle of energy. Furthermore, with babies in the home, she had another concern: he liked to scratch kitchen matches to hear them snap, then watch them burn to his fingertips. She reported: "While he gives the impression of being rough, he is really quite gentle and timid, and his blustering manner is only assumed."

This surface behavior got him into trouble at school, but his sub-surface gentleness got him out of it. Said his teacher: "I really don't like to reprimand him because he's such a nice boy." This conflict between inner and outer self took serious turns: he stole small change from the teacher's desk; he rifled other children's lunch boxes; he snatched an orange from a little girl, although he had a tangerine in his own lunch box.

These actions occurred after sporadic visits of Clara—visits that had the effect of visitations. Frankie had no idea of his relationship to this woman whose gaudy getup, to a sensitive child, gave her the aspect of a dressed-up witch. Her appearances left him upset, excited for hours. The school principal, unaware of all this, one day asked the foster mother for permission to spank the boy.

A rural environment was tried. His reaction was normal for a city-bred child: the big dog and the horses terrified him. After two months the new foster mother reported: "He is not at all homesick, but he's still very much afraid of the horses. He must have been told scary stories of wild animals. He is particularly afraid at night."

Frankie seemed ashamed of his fears. At three, he was proud that he had not flinched, nor cried, at the vaccination needle. Now he found another way to display his manliness; he picked up a cat and threw it with all his might into a puddle on the frosty ground.

Five days after Christmas of that year, 1932, Clara materialized again, a more garish spectacle in contrast to the simplicity of the farm folk. With her was a man, and a woman who was even more flashily attired and more cosmetically emblazoned than Clara. It was forenoon, but both women wore evening gowns, somewhat rumpled. The fresh country air began to reek of stale liquor.

Frankie, eyes dilated, pressed hard against his foster mother as Clara stumbled near, her hair, a deeper scarlet, falling about her face. She held forth an unwrapped present and said, "See what Santa Claus brought? Look, it dances!" It was a monkey on a string, and it was worn and ragged. She jerked the string, and the monkey flapped grotesquely. She dangled the monkey in Frankie's face. "Here, kid, take it!" Frankie kept his arms rigid, and the farm mother could feel the trembling of his body.

Clara held up the toy for the farm woman to inspect and grinned idiotically. "Looks kinda beat up, don't he? Got it down on Seventh Street a week ago and been playin' with it so much, not much left of him." She leaned down, and her voice became animated. "Know what else I got you for Christmas, Frankie? At the Fox Theatre? A great big bag of oranges and nuts and candy!" Then she pouted and shook her head dolefully. "It's all eaten up."

Frankie never saw his mother again.

In the summer of 1937, now back in the capital and aged eleven, Frankie fell to brooding. One day he asked his new foster mother why the other children in the house had visitors but no one ever came to see him. She explained, gently, that he had no people. Her report on the episode said: "Really, it seemed to relieve his mind and he has been lighthearted ever since. I told him it would be a fine thing for him to say a prayer for his people, who are in heaven, and he's been doing that."

Years later, Frank Morris told the FBI his parents died in 1937.

With the relief of mind, and the lightheartedness, came another reaction to the revelation he had no people. Not long afterward Frankie set out on the same course that Clara had taken at the same age.

There is a final, brief report on Clara, almost an epitaph. She was seen on an afternoon in May of 1936, on a downtown street in Washington, bareheaded, her once flaming hair henna-dull, huddled in a shabby fur coat, on a day far too warm for a fur coat, so intoxicated she walked with great deliberation.

This was the mother of Frankie, and Frankie was the boy of the delicate skin and golden brown curls that became the man now biding his time on Alcatraz, waiting to jolt The Rock out of existence.

Chapter 16

THE RIGOR OF THE ROCK had eased by the time Frank Morris reached there, but it was still Alcatraz, as an associate warden had once impressed upon an inmate who had complained that harsh punishments were dealt out even when no prison regulation had been violated.

Morris was booked into quarantine, the inside half of C Block, on Broadway, where he would remain locked up, except for trips to the mess hall and the basement shower room, until he was fully processed and put to work. (This step was skipped in the case of blacks, who went automatically into the segregated black section, the inside of B Block across Broadway from the tiers for the white transients.)

Within the cellhouse, a huge structure resembling a warehouse with tall windows and skylights, were three big blocks—A, B, C— and the isolated D Block, or Treatment Unit, and the library, behind a grated partition. With the rapid dwindling off of arch-desperadoes after the doughty G-men had brought an end to the gangster era, A Block fell into disuse and was now reserved solely for storage. This block, where the Army had its solitary confinement cells on the side facing the north windows, was used in the old days mainly as an isolation quarter, particularly in the period after the dread dungeon was abolished and while the old D Block was being modernized after the break of the Doc Barker quintet in 1939.

The other big blocks, B and C, contained a total of 336 cells in double banks of triple tiers; that is, each block had two banks, each bank three tiers, and each tier had twenty-eight cells. Along the center of each block, between the banks, ran a utility corridor, commonly known as "the tunnel," a narrow dark passage cluttered with the sewer pipes, water mains, and electrical conduits that served the cells. The solid steel doors at either end of this corridor, on all tiers, were locked, and the tunnel inaccessible to convicts. At the tier levels inside the service corridor were plank catwalks for the plumbers and electricians. (An astute guard had once suggested that these narrow walkways be replaced by floors the width—about three feet—of the corridor to prevent convicts from climbing to the top of a block and setting up a sniper's post, as they had done during the Battle of Alcatraz. If the guard's suggestion had been taken up, Morris could not have carried out his incredibly bold scheme.)

Broadway runs between the two big blocks, at one end the main entrance to the cellhouse, the dining room at the other. These blocks quarter the "general population." The library occupies half the area against the south wall, across from the outside of C Block; the other half, in the southwest corner of the house, holds D Block, variously known as the isolation quarter, the Treatment Unit, or simply TU. This small block, sealed off by concrete walls and a solid steel door, has forty-two cells in two tiers, six of them, on the bottom row, set aside as dark cells for solitary confinement, each with two doors, one grated and the other solid.

This was the physical setup of the cellhouse when Morris came. A little after four o'clock on his first afternoon there, the quiet was broken by the heavy, trooping tread of the convict workers returning from the industrial shops, through the door from the yard, between D Block and the mess hall. Like all newly arrived prisoners, he would have cased this activity. The desk of the lieutenant, next to the mess-hall entrance, was out of his range of vision, as he was in the second cell from that end, but this would not have fazed a man of his ingenuity. By holding his mirror through the bars he could have watched the process, particularly the custodial part, with a convict's habitual eye for routine and the slightest variation that could be significant.

He would have noted that the workers—as always, in manageable groups of about fifteen—upon entering passed through the high-silled frame of a movable Snitch Box like sheep into a paddock. The lieutenant beckoned a prisoner out of each batch for a spot check—a quick frisking for nonmetallic contraband that could slip by the electronic detector. The convicts climbed the circular steel stairway to their tier level and disappeared into their holes like pigeons returning to a loft—and a guard at the control box at the end of the block clanged the cell doors shut. The pattern of group arrivals varied daily, as did the pattern of their treks to the mess hall. Once all the workers were locked up, guards made a count, the lieutenant phoned the Armorer in the control center that all was well, and the tramp to dinner began, again by controllable units.

Morris, who had had only a snack in the course of his first day's processing, welcomed this break, both to eat and to case. In the early years, when silence was a strict rule, the inmates sat on one side of long tables, all facing front. Now, he noted, they faced one another across the tables. The room, large and airy and done in green and ivory, was lighted by barred windows along the north wall overlooking the bay. Fainter light entered from the south where an outside balcony ran the length of the mess hall, patrolled during meals by armed guards. A guard also sat in a gun cage midway in that wall, a barred and mesh-wired recess dimly lit to provide better vision. Morris spotted small apertures beneath the south windows—gun ports.

His roving eye caught another feature: silvery ornaments that embellished the ceiling. He might have guessed, accurately, their purpose was more functional than decorative. The pretty pendants were tear gas bombs, inspiration for the convicts' grim baptizing of the dining room as the Gas Chamber. They were deterrents to trouble in the mess hall, traditional focal point for prison riots. At the touch of a button by the sentry in the gun cage, they would explode into clouds of blinding, choking, nauseous fumes.

As he moved along the steam tables in the cafeteria-style line, Morris observed inmate cooks at huge copper kettles in the kitchen beyond. His tray held a plastic bowl, a compartmented plastic plate, metal fork and spoon—no knife, an implement issued only on the infrequent occasions when a steak or roast was served. This night's menu, the Thursday regular, offered soup du jour, now thick with the daily dumping of leftovers since Monday; Polish sausage and potatoes; bread, coffee or tea.

Something else had changed radically since the old days. Although the men had only twenty minutes to eat, they did not bolt their food, for this was a break in routine, a gap in the monotony that stamped all the days of the year with an almost unvarying sameness. But the non-ravenous devouring was not the notable change: the men did not eat all they had taken. Many, either without an appetite or lacking a relish for Polish sausage, left half their dinner. Even more striking was the obvious fact that mealtime on The Rock had truly become a diversion: around the room playful convicts chunked doughy wads of bread at one another.

A convict said with a grin, "Recreation period." And then he explained: "What can the bulls do? Put everybody in TU? It's not big enough. Club them? Shoot them? Pop those pretty gadgets on the ceiling and gas everybody? Nope, they don't want the SPCA in their hair."

At the end of the allotted time a guard glanced down both sides of the table to check the flatware, then gave the nod to a group. The meal schedule was so precisely clocked that the first unit was marching out as the last unit came in.

After dinner the convicts lined up at their cell fronts, inside, for the last stand-up count of the day. It was now 5:30, and they were sealed in for the long night, thirteen hours. They had four hours until lights out, four precious hours to use as they pleased, within the limited confines of their cubicles, separated from their neighbors by steel-plate walls.

As this was his first night on The Rock, Morris's curiosity about the security setup would have been too acute to listen to crooners on the radio headset or thumb through the library catalogue. He would have, in the manner of most newcomers, yanked the light cord and stood at the front bars, the darkened cell affording him a sharper view of the scene, like a box at the theater.

The winter night had already blacked out the skylight. The big globes overhead cast a cold glare, and the scattered lights of the occupied cells in the bank of tiers across Broadway vaguely resembled a huge bingo board. The concentration of the convicts imparted to the beehive cell blocks a strange elfin quality—captive dark elves of the caves, bent to the night's mischief. Not so strange at that, for these studiously engaged men had a distinction in common: they were known to the world outside as unredeemably evil—murderers, kidnapers, robbers, rapists, thugs.

Morris became aware of sounds. Someone playing a guitar, softly. A thin voice from the tier above: "King knight to black bishop three," and shortly a gruff response: "Queen pawn captures." Chatter with a Deep South lilt drifted up from Broadway: two blacks in conversation, sight unseen, in adjoining cells on the bottom tier across the way. Several inmates—there were at least three voices—had been talking quietly below him, but an argument was developing: the pitch was rising. Above all the confusion floated a note like the insistent moan of a muted wind instrument.

Morris studied the officer on the floor. He caught every slight movement as a guard patrolled Broadway, observed the casual way he glanced at the cells on either side, the pace of his stroll, like that of a monitor indifferently looking for cribbers during a classroom exam. The guard had good reason to feel secure in his pottering patrol: he was as safe from the reach of Morris, or any of the others, as a zookeeper from the claws of a caged lion. As the officer turned right at the corner and disappeared behind B Block, Morris glanced in his mirror at the clock on the wall above the lieutenant's desk: 6:42.

He now focused his attention on the gun gallery that ran along the west wall, at twice a man's height from the floor, accessible only from the outside. Presently that guard walked into view, his patrol also deceptively casual, like a ship's watch on a calm starry night. The guard stopped, directed a glance down the inside tiers of B Block, then the inside tiers of C Block. He sauntered on out of sight toward the Treatment Unit. Morris clocked him. His sharp eye very likely detected something surprising: the guard in the *gun* gallery was *unarmed*.

Morris cased the opposite gallery, on the east wall. It was dark. Perhaps that officer preferred the advantages of a dim post, just as Morris chose to be a spectator from the shadows of his own cell. He kept his gaze riveted on the gallery section visible between the blocks, straining for a movement. At length, a motion did attract his notice, but it was below the gunwalk: the floor guard was rounding the far end of B, into Broadway. Morris glanced at the clock in his mirror: 7:28. It had taken him roughly forty-five minutes to go around the block.

The guard in the west gunwalk passed slowly north, and Morris again studied the east gallery. Still no sign of activity. The gallery was dark apparently because it was empty. Then he caught a motion, a blur that ran upward, then streaked slanting down the mesh: a huge rat. That settled it. He could tot up his observations: the east gunwalk unmanned; the guard in the west cage unarmed; only one officer, unarmed, on the floor. It added up to an air of security that seemed audacious, and it must have given Morris a sinking sense that he would spend a large slice of his life in a cell such as this, enclosed by thick concrete, solid plates of steel, and bars that would take a stick of dynamite to spread. Once in the cellhouse, he could be certain, he was barred, bolted, buttoned up. In the work area outside? A chance, perhaps, a chance. . . .

Morris glanced ceilingward. A skylight ran along the roof, directly over Broadway, but there were no rafters to crawl along, and the skylight was beyond the touch of fingertips standing tip-toe on the cell block. Atop a cell block? Steel bars, close together, ran from the block to the ceiling. He could not even get on the top.

Abruptly the bright cells blacked out. The house lights now shed a ghostly twilight on Broadway. It was 9:30, bedtime. The curfew silenced the calls of the chess players, the laughing chatter of the black convicts, the argument downstairs. For a time the stirring of the inmates shucking off their clothes and settling down for the night filled the corridor with a sound like the swash of waves on a beach.

Without the rivalry of the voices, the moan of the muted horn grew suddenly sonorous, and Morris could distinguish it for what it was: the wind. As he lay in his bed, head to the bars, it seemed to rise to the force of a gale, howling through the cavernous cellhouse.

Soon another uproar came racketing into the cellhouse—the hoarse bellowing of foghorns, one upon another, from either end of the island. Fog had swirled in through the Golden Gate on the night wind.

A convict new to The Rock usually sleeps the sleep of exhaustion on his first night. He has heard such tales about the place, and has built up such anxiety en route, that even the shrieking wind and vibrant foghorns have no effect against the sedation of fatigue. Morris must have experienced that, and if so it would take the rise-up-and-shine blast, like that of a foghorn at his very cell door, to yank him out of his deep slumber. Six A.M. Twenty minutes till the head count; twenty minutes for personal and housekeeping chores.

Morris, informed of regulations, would wash quickly in the cold water from the single tap and brush his teeth with the powder, then get into his clothes and cinch the belt—a wooden buckle to keep the electronic eye of the Snitch Box from blinking. Make the bed, straighten up the cell, take a position at the front bars. A guard came along, gave cell and occupant a cursory survey, passed on, the first of twelve official counts of the day. Then the lieutenant's command, "Ring in outside B!" and the trek by units to breakfast began.

Upon leaving the mess hall this time, the convicts filed through the Snitch Box, rolled over from the yard door—one of the unscheduled mechanical friskings designed to discourage the pocketing of a fork or a spoon, items the prisoner sometimes purloined just for the thrill of it or possibly to be caught and sent to the Treatment Unit as a break in the monotony. The men marched back to their cells, were counted, then rung out to the shops. Morris watched them go from his quarantine cell. After the cross-country journey in an air-conditioned Pullman compartment, he was still sensitive to the mild odor of disinfectant that pervaded the prison. He would soon grow accustomed to the scent, just as he had at other institutions; just as a printer or a fish dealer or a fertilizer-plant worker becomes inured to the distinctive aroma of his trade. He stretched out on the cot for a nap.

After lunch came sick call. Ailing inmates lined up at the lieutenant's desk where a medical technical assistant—the MTA to the convicts—listened to a recital of symptoms and passed out aspirin. If the MTA, unlicensed to practice medicine, decided an illness required a more professional diagnosis, he sent the sick convict to the hospital upstairs to await a checkup next morning by the doctor on his daily, roughly half-hour visit from the city. Another cell count after sick call, then the lieutenant rang the workers out to the shops.

Early that afternoon, his second day on The Rock, Morris had a caller—the classification and parole officer, the man who assesses a newcomer's abilities and probable behavior pattern. He also receives the inmate's requests for visitors and correspondents, for approval of the prison bureau director after an FBI investigation. (Even a lawyer must obtain the director's permission to consult an inmate client.)

"After you're here three months, you will be permitted two visitors a month," he informed Morris. "Neither can be a former inmate of another prison."

"Kind of sets a limit," said Morris.

"I'd like the names now of the two people you'll want to visit you."

"Can't think of any."

"Members of your immediate family?"

"No family."

"Relatives?"

"No relatives."

The officer hastily checked a document. "Sorry. A girl? Some friend?"

"Mister, you just said I couldn't see my friends."

"How about correspondents? You can send out two letters a week, receive seven."

"Same rules?"

The officer nodded.

"Outgoing mail carries an Alcatraz postmark?"

"Of course," said the officer.

"Check me off that list, too," Morris said.

Later the associate warden dropped by, to spell out the house rules: discipline is strict, but never inhumane; good behavior begets good time, and good time means a shortened term . . . a lecture in deportment that Morris listened to with courteous interest.

During the interview the associate warden, who kept glancing with patent fascination at an item on the file sheet, finally remarked: "Morris, you're pretty smart—smarter than most. It's got you out of other places, but let me give you some friendly advice: all it'll get you here is the loss of your good time—maybe more time added. If you're as bright as it says here, you'll understand what I mean. Give us no trouble, we'll give you none. Okay?"

He reached out his hand. Morris gave him a level look, said "Okay," and shook. The associate warden left.

The item that had held such fascination was: I.Q. 133. Not a genius, 140 I.Q., but a convict of superior intelligence.

Next forenoon, Saturday, a guard came along and said, "Shower. Take your dirty socks." He moved down the tier instructing the other newcomers in the ritual of the twice-weekly shower.

The officer in the basement shower room directed each to a bin that bore his number. "Drop your socks in there. You can pick them up next shower day."

"Pick 'em up where?" asked a convict.

"Out of the bin."

"When's next shower day?"

"Tuesday, 3 P.M."

"What about our other stuff?"

"You dump that in Tuesdays, pick it up Tuesdays. Pillow case, *one* sheet, towel, three pairs of socks, underwear, shirt, pants if they need it. Saturdays, turn in the other three pairs of socks. Clear?"

"Our stuff won't get mixed up?"

"You come straight here from college? Look." The guard grabbed the inmate's towel. "See that number? Everything's got your number on, except socks, and they don't matter—they're all the same size."

"When do we shave?"

"You'll get blades tonight." The officer gestured toward the row of showers. "Get to it."

This was a movie weekend, and half the general population saw it during recreation period that Saturday afternoon, the other half on Sunday afternoon. Morris was in the Saturday matinee crowd, which gathered, as always in any mass movement of prisoners, in groups. Morris descended the spiral staircase from his tier, marched with his unit down Broadway toward the main entrance, turned right, went past the prisoners' side of the visitors' room, through a gate at the southeast corner of the cellhouse, up a stairway to the chapel, a room about 50 by 100 feet. A screen stood at one end, a projection booth at the other. A guard stood sentry at the door, and a guard in the east gun gallery, manned for the movies and chapel services, kept watch through a window from the second level of his cage. The movie was *Pork Chop Hill,* about the Korean War.

After lockup that Saturday—5 P.M. on weekends—guards passed out two razor blades to each inmate, a week's supply. Morris could now whip up a lather with the cold water in the old-fashioned mug with its round cake of soap and enjoy a shave. Conditions had indeed improved on The Rock: no guard stood over him in a suicide watch.

Sunday came to Alcatraz as early, and as abruptly, as any other day: the wake-up blast at 6 A.M. Morris climbed out of bed, remembered it was Sunday, climbed back in. He had been told that Catholics could eat after the nine o'clock Mass. Later he joined a dozen other Catholic convicts on the escorted march to the chapel, which had been transformed from a movie theater by the simple process of rolling up the screen, revealing the altar. The rows of folding chairs now served as pews, and just beyond the front row was the rail where communicants partook of the Sacrament of the Eucharist. The convicts, cheeks scrubbed and shaven, comb streaks in their hair, sat with rapt faces as the priest celebrated the ancient, solemnly beautiful liturgy. The guard near the door watched with the indifference of an usher who has seen the show innumerable times, his eye darting toward the cluster of worshipers at every movement, a genuflection or sign of the cross.

Afterward, only a few headed for the mess hall, the others returning to their cells. Morris fell in with the breakfast group, but was halted by the guard who had shepherded them to the chapel. "Back to your cell," he ordered. "I didn't see you take any of that bread up there. Regulations." Only those who received Communion and its bread, or host, which required a three-hour fast, had the privilege of breakfast after Mass. Morris, like his mother not too devout, had apparently forgotten about this reason for a belated breakfast.

Other cell doors clattered open and about the same number of inmates tramped upstairs for the nondenominational Protestant service. By now Catholic and Protestant chaplains both came over every Sunday, instead of alternate weeks.

That afternoon Morris went out to the yard for the two-hour recreation period. A few convicts loped around its borders, like boxers in training; teams played softball with a Big League intensity, but here a ball over the fence was out, not a home run. Other prisoners leaped about at handball, bumping into outfielders. Cliques stood apart, chatting. Bridge experts sat at a few card tables along the foot of the counterfeit bleachers, but a casual observer would not have guessed the same. Their cards were dominoes with playing-card markings instead of dots, the dealer shuffling them as in dominoes and each player setting up his hand on the table in front of him. The men bought the domino cards, and a ditty bag to hold them, out of shop earnings. (Prisons ban regular playing cards because they are usually made of celluloid which the convicts can grind up and use as an explosive.)

The day was clear, and the view from the top steps spectacular, but a chill wind blew off the ocean through the Golden Gate. Morris, clad only in his light prison garb, retreated to a protected spot near the cellhouse door and, out of the wind, soaked up the warm winter sun. He noted most of the prisoners wore snug peacoats and caps and made inquiry. "You got to ask for them," said a convict. "A jacket, too, to wear around the cell. Navy sends over the peacoats."

He discovered that Alcatraz had three seasons: winter, summer, and October. Only in October was the weather invariable—golden, balmy days, the sky a deep blue. Winter and summer were variable—rain, wind, or fog, on occasion a day with none of these, a day of sparkling beauty. Summer differed from winter in the absence of rain. Every afternoon , with the regularity of a railroad schedule, the trade winds whipped in through the Gate and on most days, especially in summer, they brought along a thick, wet fog. "Hell," said the convict, "summer's about the coldest time of the year here. The bulls on outside patrol wear heavy overcoats in July and August." Morris put in a request for a peacoat, cap, and jacket; also a raincoat.

On his twelfth day, Morris was assigned a household job, cleaning vegetables in the receiving room of the kitchen basement. This took him out of quarantine into a more permanent living room, as Warden Johnston once called the inmates' cells. He moved into Cell No. 138 on the bottom row of outside B Block, across from the deserted A Block.

Next door lived Allen Clayton West, a thirty-year-old native of New York City who had picked up a slight southern accent during years in Georgia and considered himself more of a Georgian than a New Yorker. He was stocky, brown-eyed, and dark-haired, with a complexion a little on the swarthy side, perhaps from exposure to the southern sun in convertibles with the top down, and in the fields of Georgia state prison farms. He had acquired many cars but never by purchase, and as a consequence had served three prison-farm terms before he finally drove one across the Georgia line, a federal rap that eventually landed him on The Rock. Here his deep tan began to fade. He was now serving ten years for car theft. Like Morris, he was addicted to tattoos and sported one on the back of each finger of both hands. Unlike Morris, he was a compulsive chatterer, and that was likely the reason that Morris did not cotton to his neighbor right off. West played an accordion, a big one with a big dark case that stood against the rear wall.

Several weeks later Morris won a sort of promotion, to library messenger in the mornings, janitor in the afternoons. On his morning rounds, delivering books and magazines to cells, he had an opportunity to observe inmate living habits. Some cells had a monastic bareness; some held a pack-rat clutter; others had a barracks look, with pinup-calendar nudes; still others resembled a college dormitory, with books on a rear shelf, homework on the table; some were studios—walls hung with originals, a partly finished landscape on the bed; a guitar or horn indicated a musician.

Eventually, he was assigned to an industrial job and on that first morning as they moved out of their cells, West said, "Got yourself a payin' job, eh? What'd you draw?"

"Brush shop."

"Glove maker myself," said West. "I'll show you the brush-shop line when we get out." In the yard he pointed to one of three painted yellow strips. "Yours. Be seein' you, boy."

Once all the workers were assembled, the lieutenant called, "Glove shop!" A guard-foreman nodded to his crew on a line, and the lieutenant made a count as they marched out a gate at the far corner. "Tailor shop!" Finally, "Brush shop!" Morris stepped through the gate of the high-walled yard, followed by a convict from the South labeled the Green Lizard. They descended a steep flight of steps in the Cliffside to a landing midway, passed through a Snitch Box, then down another flight to a road, bordered on the bay side by the cyclone fence. While they were in the yard, armed guards in the gun boxes on the wall peered down at them with a sort of languid interest. From the moment they emerged from the yard, until they reached the shop building, other eyes watched their progress from the lofty gun tower back up the road and the tower on the factory roof. The eyes of the road tower guard were not strictly on the men every moment this particular morning, for suddenly rifle fire rattled menacingly.

"Somebody make it to the water?" Morris asked.

"No siren," said the Green Lizard. "Must be a log goin' by on the tide. They take potshots at anything driftin' by, case it's a con makin' like a log. Target practice. Also a kind of a reminder to us goin' down this lonesome road, pal."

They were counted into the shop, then every half hour thereafter. Men worked at lathes fashioning the wood parts for the pushbrooms; others glued on the fibers; still others screwed in handles. Alcatraz's factories then numbered three, turning out these brooms; a variety of work gloves, plain cottons to welder's gloves; and in the tailor shop, the convicts' own gray-and-white trousers, the nickel-gray trousers for the guards' uniforms, blue dungarees for the Navy, and white pants for Army cooks and bakers and orderlies in the Veterans Administration hospitals.

The pay rate was based on group piecework, which averaged, depending on skill, from $12 to $70 a month per man for a six-and-a-half-hour day and five-day week, the highest wage going to the tailors. The prisoners could send their earnings home or buy art supplies, selected magazines, musical instruments, chess sets, domino cards, law books, and, a little later under the next warden, even knitting and crocheting needles and yarn. Shop work also earned a prisoner "good time" on a graduating scale that, at the start of the fifth year, reached a peak of five days off his sentence for every month of employment. This was in addition to the statutory ten days off for every thirty days served as a model prisoner. Attempts to escape, or infractions of rules that put a convict in the Treatment Unit, could mean the loss of good time on both scores. The fact that a convict will feign a fight in the yard or commit some minor offense to be sent to TU as a sort of vacation from routine, at a cost of good time and all privileges, seems a graphic indication of the depressing monotony.

(In this society of Rock felons, an ex-guard says, TU also represents a status symbol: a sojourn there bestows a tough-guy stature, a con who would not turn stoolie. Top status goes to the man who had made the Hole, and even that has its own strata, defined by the length of solitary confinement. Stroud, who spent more than half his life in solitary, attained a peak of inmate respect at Alcatraz. In the isolation block when he was in residence there, the other prisoners manifested their sentiments by bluntly calling to a guard, "Hey, Jones, get me a drink of water," but invariably addressing the Birdman as "Mr. Stroud.")

In the open-front cells of TU, or D Block, the cells with the grate doors, the prisoner has no radio outlet, no books, sees no movies, has no period in the yard—nothing to do except walk, lie, or sit, but he has a bed to lie on and light to walk or sit by. He does get the same food, served him by inmate orderlies off a wheeled table, as the men in the mess hall.

In the six closed-front cells, the Dark Hole, life is tougher. Warden Madigan substituted a gruel—but still no meat, nor dessert—for the bread-and-water and tasteless-spaghetti diet in solitary. "It was found," he said, "that bread and water did not encourage repentance." (On the mess-hall diet granted those in the open-front cells, he commented: "Our prison rule is fairness but no pampering.") A man in solitary has no bed, curls up on the concrete floor with a blanket. A former inmate recalls a sojourn in the Dark Hole: "The worst things were boredom, and no cigarettes to help endure the boredom, and the darkness, never knowing whether it's noon or midnight. You walk around in the darkness a while, always touching a wall so you won't bump into it. You lie down a while, maybe take a catnap. Then you just stand a while, and every once in a while you say to yourself, 'Boy, what wouldn't I give for a cigarette.' You start wanting the wackiest things, like a match; you'd like to hold a match and just watch it burn down to your fingers. Or you might wonder if the sun's coming up now, or is it going down?"

Morris lost his neighbor for an indefinite period in late summer of that year, 1960. West helped stage a fracas at a noon meal to draw the guards and give robber Joseph Wagstaff a free hand to stab an inmate at another part of the mess hall. Off to the dark cells of D Block they went.

One evening in October, as he sat at dinner, Morris saw a face grinning at him across the room, and his eyes widened in surprise. It was John Anglin, whom he had known at Atlanta before Anglin and his brother, Clarence, were transferred to Leavenworth, leaving a third brother, Al, to stick it out at Atlanta. The Anglins, three black sheep among thirteen children of a "Tobacco Road" family along the backwater of the Little Mantee in Florida, stuck up a bank in Alabama and made off with a tidy $19,000. But the FBI nabbed them in Ohio before they could settle down to a spree, and the bank got the loot back. At the time, Clarence and Al were fugitives from the Florida state prison (it was Clarence's fourth escape), and John had just wrapped up a stretch for grand larceny. For the Alabama job John drew ten years, the others fifteen each.

Clarence, assuming a prerogative of the warden, tried to ship John out of Leavenworth. He cut the top out of a big bread box and the bottom out of another. John sat in one, and Clarence set the other on top, then packed in loaves of bread. A truck was ready to haul John and other boxes out to a prison farm camp when a supervisor, apparently wondering why the helpers had struggled to hoist that particular double box onto the vehicle, grew suspicious. He pulled out a few loaves, and in no time at all the warden exercised his own prerogative and shipped John out, to The Rock.

Clarence came along in January, and the brothers occupied adjoining cells, Nos. 140 and 142, just four down the row from Morris, on the theory that, as Blackwell later explained, they might want to discuss family affairs in the evening hours. (Two other brothers lived side-by-side between Morris and the Anglins.)

The Anglins were the roughneck type, the direct opposites of the introspective Morris. John was thirty-two, of medium build with blue eyes and blonde hair; Clarence a year younger, but huskier, almost six feet. Wilkinson, who knew them too at Atlanta, said they were "more on the natively cunning side, throwbacks to the swamp country, more impulsive, more given to action than Morris."

In June of that year, 1961, Warren Madigan took over the top post at McNeil, noted for its rehabilitative work, and there his talents flowered. His associate at Alcatraz, Blackwell, became acting warden, and on November 26, 1961, was officially named keeper of The Rock. Blackwell moved Arthur M. Dollison, superintendent of the shops, into his old spot as associate, to oversee the prison and, in Blackwell's absences, to act as warden.

Warden Blackwell, a man of picturesque speech and Pickwickian bent, soon stamped Alcatraz with his own good-natured personality. Unknown to the world at large, The Rock softened, lost much of its grimness, even some of its old and unrelenting monotony. It took on, unbelievably, the aspect of a school for wayward girls. He added more variety to the games in the yard, but that wasn't what did it. He posted a new purchasing privilege: the men could buy crochet needles (four inches long, in exciting colors) and slender knitting needles (both plastic, too brittle for less delicate use), along with yarns of all hues, patterns and, an obvious complement, instruction books. In the evening hours before bedtime, the nation's most desperate and hardened criminals, at first clumsily, and then deftly, were soon crocheting doilies, pink or blue booties, and gorgeous bedspreads garnished with red-yarn rosebuds. Knitting needles flashed in fingers that once knew only triggers as the erstwhile bank robbers purled one, seldom dropped two, and skeins of yarn sped wondrously into sweaters. Blackwell did impose one stern rule: these new Rock needlemen must not cover their own beds with the spreads, nor wear the sweaters (every shade but gray), nor use the doilies as place mats at mess. They went out as gifts—booties for sister's new baby, a bedspread for Mom, a sweater for Pop. Blackwell took a fancy to some of the doilies, proudly hung them on a wall in his office.

Dollison too, as overseer, had a distinctive influence on The Rock—no startling innovations, such as Blackwell's, but a gradual change that seemed to sift down through the echelons. A more relaxed atmosphere began to exist among the custodians, no doubt partly induced by the clicking of knitting needles, a sound not normally associated with menace. And so the officer on the floor in the cellhouse rarely made a patrol in the four hours before lights-out, unless out of curiosity to see how a sweater or a bootie was taking shape. The rap of the rubber mallet on the bars in the weekend security checks abated to a languid tap, then into long silences. The cell shakedowns stirred less and less dust, finally became hasty glances. Upstairs in the hospital the MTAs and the duty officers for the most part still looked upon the sick as goldbrickers; outside, the guards at the gun ports and in the gun towers were still ready to pepper away; but inside the feeling seemed to be: the doors are locked, everything's tight, the men embroidering doilies.

The convicts were not taking over the joint by any means, but this slackening had an infectious effect. Mealtime became playtime, the mess hall abuzz with chatter, the air filled with doughy missiles as the fun-loving felons now flung wadded bread at the guards, whose only reaction was to duck and glower. In the after-lockup hours men talked to neighbors at their cell fronts in louder voices, or called to friends across the corridor or the tier above or below; convicts with banjos and guitars plucked livelier tunes, and cornetists tootled away. Beneath this clamor, the quiet ones tended to their knitting. And in Cell 138 Morris was weaving an escape plot.

One morning in the brush shop, after the guard had made a half-hour count and left, a coworker handed Morris a small flat bottle and said, "Hold it a second." He expertly filled the vial with white glue from a half-gallon jug, recorked it and slipped it back in his pocket, under the coveralls. "Just cork and glass," he said. "It'll go through the Snitch Box."

"What if you're frisked?"

"Ten days in TU. Figure the odds: about once in thirty times I'm pulled out of the line. Maybe I'm clean, so that jumps the odds sky high. Same with snitchin' from the mess."

This led to talk of the security-tight cellhouse, and the convict chuckled and said, "There's a way out if anybody had the nerve. What block you in?"

"B."

"Well, there's a shaft right over your head you can climb out of onto the roof."

He then related what was common knowledge among older prisoners. Willard Winhoven, released in 1959 after serving twelve years on The Rock for robbery, had been an inmate-electrician. In 1957 he removed a fan motor from a ventilator shaft over B Block, and no replacement was made.[1] The guard supervising the work had commented after removal of the blower: "A good way to get out."

For a moment, this revelation seemed to alter things. A daytime break under cover of a fog held the hazard, with the half-hour counts, of alerted guards swarming with rifles. That tower guard's target practice on a drifting log had had an unsettling ring. An after-dark departure had the advantage of getaway time, perhaps half a night. Fine, except the shaft was out of reach: bars ran to the ceiling, and the steel door to the top of the block was always locked.

"How do you get up there?"

The convict grinned. "Ask the bull for the key."

---

[1] Willard Winhoven related the story of the removal of the shaft motor in 1957, along with the guard's comment, to a reporter for the San Francisco *News Call Bulletin*.

Chapter 17

I F THE VENTILATOR SHAFT, an escape hatch just thirty feet above his head, had tantalized him at first, Morris doubtless put it out of mind once he had explored its possibilities. He was a plotter who picked over minutest details before acting, and there simply was no way to reach the top of the block except on a detail with a guard. At night, impossible. Only way off The Rock was still in a thick fog, outside the cellhouse.

On a fall evening in 1961, Morris sat clipping his fingernails. The clip, two inches long, had a pair of pivoting arms that lay, one upon the other, on its surface. The longer arm, with a tapered tip, swung out and doubled back to serve as a lever to snap the nail-clipping jaws. The shorter one had a file, and a pointed end to clean under nails.

Morris clipped the last nail and swung the lever back in place, pulling out the other to clean under a nail. Then, as a man in a musing moment might absently open and close a penknife, he kept swinging the file-cleaner out and in. At length, he snapped it back in place and gave the clip a little toss. As he caught it his eyes fell on the air vent below and to the right of the wash bowl. He stared, fascinated. And then, still staring, he slowly slid the cleaner out again and ran his thumb over the sharp point. He got up, scouted the corridor, then went swiftly to the rear and knelt at the vent. He picked at the concrete at the edge of the metal grille. Nothing. He picked harder . . . very hard. A few grains fell to the floor. He tried the opposite rim, a firm grip, a stiff jab. Bits came off. He chipped at the top. Miniature flakes tumbled down the black grille. He jabbed at the bottom. Tiny fragments gave way.

He stood up, trembling. A weary prospector had stumbled onto a rich lode. He knelt again, inspected the gouging. Small scars showed. He wet his thumb, gathered a thumbload of fallen particles and pressed them into the tiny gap at one side of the grille, then smoothed it out, his thumb a trowel. He did this all around, then moistened a corner of his blue handkerchief and wiped the grille and the powdery residue off the floor. He stood back. The vent looked untouched.

Then began the wrestling. It'll take time to loosen that grille, maybe a week, maybe longer. How to hide the work? Let the towel sag? West's accordion case! But West was still in solitary. He'd buy his own. What kind? Size? He couldn't say: *Oh, big enough to cover the vent.* Wait for West. Ring him in on it? He's a talker. The Anglins? Too impulsive: *Okay, what're we waitin' for? Let's go!* This called for planning.

Details, details. Once the grille came out, what? Crawl on through? Too small. How thick was that wall? How big a hole did he need to squeeze through? Could he do it alone? The hole—he'd be digging *in* the hole. No lookout. And the bull comes by. He had to ring in West, after all. The Anglins? Clarence had a real knack for breakouts. But not yet, not yet. John'd stand watch for Clarence, Clarence for John. Away they'd go. He'd wait for West—and pray he left his heels alone.

Next morning he cased the end of the cell block, the width to the utility door, the depth of a cell. He gauged the wall's thickness at maybe a foot. He cut a two-foot length of wood, reed-slender, in the shop and stuck it in his belt at the back. That night he angled it through the grille, touching the side wall until the tip slipped off the far edge. The wall was about eight inches thick. A drill? He glanced up at the light hanging in the center of the cell. Out of the question. He'd need a motor.

He checked the library catalogue and next morning left a request for a book on structural engineering. He studied up on concrete and mortar. He learned that damp concrete, if heated suddenly, tended to spall or chip out in cone-shaped flakes as the steam escaped. Enough heat might cause the concrete to crumble even if dry. But there were drawbacks here: this concrete did not seem damp; in either case, there was no means, short of a welder's torch, to apply sufficient heat.

Details, details. How big a hole—to squirm through at an angle? Shoulder width sixteen, maybe seventeen inches—he'd need an exit about ten inches high, fourteen wide. The vent was now six high, ten wide. He chipped at the concrete again. Damn tough. Take weeks. What if they shook down his cell some Saturday? And looked behind the accordion? Hell, he'd be playing it down in the basement! *This thing needs more planning.*

How to hide the hole . . . how to hide the hole . . . he climbed out of bed to go to the toilet. Those hiding places in the base—covered by paper painted white! Very simple. A sheet of paper pasted over the hole, a black grille painted on it. Paste . . . ? Glue! Snitched from the brush shop. As the con said, the odds were with him.

Paper? Over an *air* vent? Rumple sure as hell. Make a bull curious, a *rumply* metal grille. Take something stiffer than paper. Cardboard. Must be some around the shops. He'd ask one of—uh, uh, let's not go asking a lot of questions. . . . He'd make his own, by God! *Papier-mâché!* He'd made it as a kid in grade school—a Halloween mask, a Christmas crèche, something like that.

Details, details. Once he scooted, what? Christ, the screw'd find him gone on his first patrol. The siren'd let go before he got off the roof. He'll need a dummy. Up near the bars, have to be goddam life-like. Maybe switch sleeping habits? He hated his head next to a toilet, but—no good, the bull might reach in to shake the dummy's foot. There goes the siren.

For the dummy, what? Head and neck, pillow and peacoat under the covers. Where'd he get stuff for a head and neck in *this* joint? Hair was easy—bristles from the brush shop. Bristles, hell. With Clarence a barber? Maybe he'd better ring the Anglins in—*after* he got things set up. He'd need raincoats for a raft, and John works in the clothing room. That dummy. Hair, okay. The rest . . . ?"

It popped up late one night. Like raw material fed into a mill, worked over, and out comes a bright red convertible. And so simple: *He would order what he needed, through the prison's purchasing officer!*

West got out of solitary early in 1962, and Morris ordered an accordion exactly like his. It came over from the city in a couple of days, and he was set. The dining room now resembled a large cafeteria, the long tables replaced by table sets seating four, the sets in varying bright colors. Morris, West, and the Anglins shared a table. Once he had his accordion, Morris sprang his plan.

"Well," said Clarence Anglin, "what're we waitin' for? Let's go!"

"This is Alcatraz," said Morris, "not a road camp. We don't walk away from here. Starting tomorrow morning, and every morning for a while, we order all the magazines we can from the library."

"I sure fell behind on my readin' in the Hole," said West.

Morris shot him a hard, level look, and West shrugged apologetically. Before bringing him in on the plot, Morris had laid down the law: keep his speech at a minimum, lest an unwary word spill the works.

"Why magazines?" asked John Anglin.

"For cardboard," Morris said. "Cut out only the pages with ads on both sides, and close in, so they won't be missed."

"So what?" said John. "They'll think it's the censor."

"We don't want them to even *think*," said Morris. "We take no chances. Clear? No chances. Slip the pages under your mattress. I'll fill you in on each step as we go along. That way, nobody jumps the gun."

"That a crack?" asked John.

"Nope. I'm after teamwork. That's what this needs. Also a brush and paints. Who wants to become an artist?"

"Why not borrow 'em?"

"Less in on it the better," said West.

"That's right," said Morris. "We'll order our own supplies from the purchasing officer."

"Man, that's real brass," said Clarence. "Four breaks, and I never once thought of askin' 'em for tools. I'll take up painting'."

"Okay, we'll need white, pink, and black paint, and—"

"Black? A bull reaches in and pats John's crew cut and it feels bald, Jesus, man. Look, I work in the barber shop."

(Prisoners were assigned to barbering as to any other household chore: professional experience unnecessary.)

"Don't worry, you'll be filling your pockets. Get turpentine and a canvas—and slap a little paint over it, out of each tube. We'll make our own plaster for the dummies—bits of this and that, thickened up with soap, maybe a little glue."

"What about the stuff we dig out—flush it down the toilet?"

"And clog it up? We don't want any plumbers nosing around. West and I'll carry it out and scatter it on the way to the shops."

A guard came up. "What's keeping you men?"

"Sorry, sir," said Morris, and they filed out.

On Monday, after lockup, Morris gave his light cord a tug, then sat a while to accustom his eyes to the dark. No lights shone in deserted A Block across the way, and that was fine: it meant no prying eyes. The reflection from other cells in his tier bank, along with the house lights, soon turned the darkness into a twilight gloom.

Then, with West standing watch next door, he removed the accordion case and set to work. He turned his peacoat inside out, to avoid telltale dust, and laid it folded along the floor below the vent, to deaden the sound of any large fragments that might break loose. He knelt and began chipping. It was slow, tedious work. He switched to the larger blade, the one that served as lever for the clipping jaws, and found it sturdier, more effective, though there still wasn't enough of a handle for a real grip. He decided to dig just enough each night to fit in his pockets without a bulge.

After about an hour's labor he felt the gouged side of the grille, then the tiny pile of rubble on his peacoat, and estimated he had a big enough load to carry outside. He gathered a handful and placed it in a pocket, checking an impulse to pat it with his dusty hand. He was scraping up another fistful when he suddenly let it drop. He picked up a few particles and rubbed them with his fingers. *Bits of this, bits of that . . . plaster!* Some of what he had dug out, the surfacing on the concrete, was already plaster.

He sat back on the floor to consider the idea. Where would he hide it? In his ditty bag? The bag wasn't large enough to hold all the stuff he would have to scoop out to enlarge the vent to a body-size hole. *Hole . . . Perfect!* He would store it in the hole itself as he went along. He would conceal tonight's rubble in the bag.

He fell to again. He chipped close to the grille, to speed the job of loosening it and maybe leave enough bite to hold the metal frame temporarily. When his legs cramped under him, he changed position and kept on. His fingers ached gripping the small tool, and he sweat with the pace and the tension. He had no way of gauging the time and that began to worry him. He got stiffly to his feet, rubbed his legs and went up front, working his fingers to ease the ache. "What time do you think it is?"

"Must be getting close to 9:30," said West. "Better knock off."

He returned to the rear, scooped the concrete flakes off his pea-coat and put them in the ditty bag. Then he ran his fingers probingly over the coat for particles that might scatter over the floor when he picked it up. Satisfied, he gathered it up with care, as if it were a baby. He held its folds funnellike over the wash basin and gently shook the jacket, then ran a hand down to brush off the remaining dust. He turned the peacoat right side out and hung it on a peg. He moistened a piece of paper and wiped the grille softly and the floor beneath it. Then he set the accordion case back against the wall.

He stepped to the center of the cell, pulled the light cord and sur-veyed the rear wall. It appeared just as it had at lockup. Not a sign—except the basin. He ran the water and swished down the concrete dust, then washed his forearms and face. He reached for the towel, remembered his hair—it might be gray with dust. He doused his head, dried himself, and went up front.

"All's well," he said.

"Good," said West. "Must've had a workout."

"Pooped."

His hand was blistered but that was a small discomfort compared to the ache in his fingers. With so little dug out in one night, the task ahead—eight inches of concrete—looked formidable. He needed an attachment of some sort for the nailclip, to provide a handle, a better grip. Perhaps he could turn a handle for the clip on the lathe in the brush shop.

"How'd it go?" he asked the Anglins at breakfast.

"Part way down one side," said Clarence. "Sure tough digging. That clip ain't like grippin' a pick handle."

Morris, eating oatmeal mush, became aware, curiously aware, of the spoon in his hand: an institutional spoon, about the size of a household tablespoon, perhaps a trifle larger. It had a heavy handle, a nice heft. He took a grip on it: *a real nice feel.*

When he returned to his cell from the shop for the *pre*-lunch count, the magazine he had requested was there. And when he came back to his cell for the *post*-lunch count, a spoon was in his pocket. He opened his accordion case and tucked the spoon in a fold of the bellows.

That evening after lockup he sat for some time trying to figure out what, if anything, he could do with the spoon. The spoon itself was useless for digging: it took an instrument with a point to chip the concrete. He liked the handle, the feel of it in a firm grip, but there was no way to attach the nailclip to the bowl; he saw it was even ridiculous to try. And even if he could fasten it to the other end, the bowl section would make an awkward handle. He decided it would be useful in mashing the magazine pages into pulp for the cardboard, and let it go at that.

He yanked the light cord and sat down to adjust to the darkness. As he waited for the corridor light to have effect, he toyed with the clip. The lever arm suddenly came off. It startled him at first; he had forgotten this blade was removable. Abruptly, he jerked on the light and held the loose blade against the spoon handle, down near the bowl. He put the piece from the clip aside and began bending the spoon handle back and forth. He held the bowl under his shoe and tried it that way. After a great effort, he managed to break off the handle. He laid the nailclip blade against the spoon handle at the broken end. *Welded, they'd make a damn good tool.*

Fine, except for one serious drawback: there was no way to get the tool welded. The welding shop was in an isolated structure near the powerhouse on the north shore. Convicts once did welding, but no longer. *All right, why not weld it in the cell? Take a real hot flame.* Maybe snitch a soldering iron—no, it wouldn't get hot enough. Plug a pair of elements in the lightsocket, hold them close for an arc? Too risky—might blow a fuse.

Brazing . . . ? Brass required less heat than steel. *No, silver brazing!* Silver, softer, required even less heat; just a quick, intense fire. Fire, fire—those fires set off in the shops by the little drum with rubber bands that snapped match heads ablaze. A bunch of matches, properly shaped . . . But the silver—where, on Alcatraz, would he come by silver? He needed only a very small amount. Sometimes a shop guard shed his coat on a hot day—and before long a convict had a few extra cigarettes, perhaps a penlike flashlight that clipped to a breast pocket, maybe a coin or two.

Morris went up front, whispered to West, "Got a dime?"

West, startled, took a moment to reply: "What for, a cup of coffee?"

"I'm serious—an experiment."

"Wait a second." He left the front, soon returned, handed around a dime. "A panhandler in *this* place!"

"Now let me have all your matches."

"Huh? What'll I do for a light?"

"Keep a few."

West came up with three full books. "What's cookin'?"

"Something, just keep an eye peeled."

Morris laid a sheet of paper on the table and scraped the dime with the sharp points of the nailclip's curved jaws. He gleaned a tiny pile of minute specks and shavings of silver. He clipped at the edges and chewed off slightly larger particles.

He now searched his own pockets—pants, jacket, bathrobe—and collected another five matchbooks, some complete. He pulled out fifty matches, bunched them tight with a rubber band, gently tapped the top level. He then poked in the heads with infinite care to form a cone—a very precise cone, so that no heat would be dispersed by any unevenness. This was the principle of the "shaped" charge: the exploding force concentrated at a point.

Next he poured the dime scrapings onto the spoon handle, toward the broken edge, and spread the little pile with his forefinger. Glittering bits stuck to the finger, and he scraped them off onto the silver nest with the nailclip blade. He then pressed the wide end of the blade down hard on the silver. He drew four matches part way out of the bundle, to serve as legs, then centered it over the brazing materials. It seemed too low. The focus of flame had to hit the critical spot exactly right to make the silver flow and bind blade to spoon.

Try a test? He checked the matchbooks—plenty left. He set the cone by itself, struck a match but blew it out—the downflare might leave a telltale scar on the table. He removed a shoe and braced it, upside down, with books. Much better. He stood the cone on the sole and, gauging how much space the other items would occupy, touched it off. The fire came down in the right shape but flattened out. Too low. He grabbed the shoe and doused it under the cold-water tap.

West called, and he hurried up front. "What the hell you doin'? I smell burnin' leather."

"Hot foot. Just keep a sharp lookout."

Morris waved his peacoat about to clear the air. Then he fashioned another match cone with precision and extended the legs almost full length. He book-braced the shoe again, fixed the brazing pieces with extreme care, and positioned the straddling cone exactly. He lit it. The hot, massed flame, perfectly shaped, bathed the metals. He let it cool for about five minutes, then tried it gingerly. A firm brazing job.

"Just made me a damn good pick," he reported to West. "Tell you about it later. Keep a watch."

He doused the light, adjusted to the dimness, then resumed chipping at the rim of the grille. The new tool made the digging easier and faster—relatively. In time, all of them had an improvised digger.

Thursday evening, four nights after he had begun on the grille, Morris was jabbing away in the dusk at the back of his cell when he felt the pick penetrate just a little before it struck concrete. He ran his fingers around the rim of the metal frame, then sat back and inhaled deeply, letting his breath out in a soft whistle. He had finished Phase One. He rested only a moment, got back on his knees, clasped the sides of the grille and pulled gently. It failed to give. He exerted more force, with great care: he wanted as little sound as possible, as little crumbling of the edges as possible. He gradually increased the force.

The grille wouldn't budge. He stood up and shook his trousers, to avoid trailing dust or cement flakes, then went up front.

"I'm going to turn on my light a minute," he said.

"Okay," said West.

He pulled the light cord, then knelt and studied the grille. It seemed clear all around. He got the nailclip and poked the small, thin nail-cleaner blade between the grille and concrete. It went through. He pulled it along, down the side. It struck something. He took the spoon-handle pick and jabbed there. It was solid, gave a metallic sound. He probed with the smaller instrument. The obstruction was about an inch long. The blade ran free another inch or so, then met a second metal block. He began to suspect what they were: hook anchors. He slid the little blade on down, along the bottom, up the other side. There it struck two similar obstructions. The grille was welded onto four pieces of strap iron, embedded into the concrete at an angle, with hooks on the ends to keep them from pulling out: hook anchors.

He reported the setback at breakfast, and a gloom descended on the table.

"You think the grille's welded on them things?" asked Clarence.

"Sure of it," said Morris.

"How about a file?" suggested West.

"Look, man," said John, "that can't be much of a weld. Get a little old wedge in there and I bet you can knock it loose."

Morris selected a short piece of broom handle from the scrap pile at the shop and fashioned a wedge out of it on the lathe. It was fairly hard wood. Later, worrying, he took it back to the lathe when the foreman stepped out. He smoothed the other end, gave it a slight slant. He was glad of the foresight when, stepping through the Snitch Box after entering the cellhouse, he was beckoned out of line by the lieutenant for a spot frisking.

"What's the wedge for?" asked the lieutenant.

"Wedge, sir? That's a clothes peg."

"With an edge like this?" and the lieutenant ran his thumb along the sharp end.

"Hold the clothes better," said Morris. "Got the idea out of a magazine. It goes on vertical—the edge—like this," and he demonstrated.

"Well," said the lieutenant. "I'll have to try that. Let me know if it works."

"Yes, sir."

It worked. Morris slid the wedge in and hammered it cautiously with the heel of his shoe and in a moment he heard the first one crack loose, then the others. He carefully pulled the grille free, fragments of concrete thudding lightly on his peacoat. He set the grille aside and reached into the dark hole, exploring its sides with his fingers, then the far rim. He placed his fingertips at that rim and held his forearm rigid and then, using the side of his other hand as a marker, withdrew the arm. His earlier measurement with the reed-rod was correct: the wall was about eight inches thick. He replaced the grille, pushing it gently, then tested it with a light tug. It held.

"Got her loose," he reported to West.

"Great," said West. "When do I start?"

"Clarence and I had better go all the way through first. Be safer that way. Also, you and John can learn from our experience."

It was still early, so Morris turned Cell 138 into a pulp mill. He removed the blade from his safety razor and, with infinite care, cut advertisement pages out of the magazine he had borrowed from the library that day, cutting them as near to the binding as he could get to conceal the fact they had been excised. Then he got out the pages he had stashed under his mattress. He soaked them well in the basin, let the water run out, then with the spoon bowl as a pestle mashed them into a soggy mass. He heard West start whistling "Home on the Range," pushed the sodden bulk down in the basin, grabbed up the magazine, and lay back on his cot.

In a moment he heard a guard go by on patrol, and a little later he went up front, "Wonder what got into him?"

"Just out for a stroll, I guess," said West.

Morris gathered the pulp out of the basin, dumped it on the steel table top and kneaded it as though it were dough. Satisfied as to the texture, he flattened it out with his palms, then pressed it to the thickness he wanted with the sole of his heavy shoe. By rule of thumb, marking it off with the spoon, he measured an oblong a fraction of an inch larger than ten by fourteen inches, then cut it out with the razor blade. He shredded the trimmings and flushed them down the toilet. At lights-out, he slid the pulpy oblong off the table onto the magazine, then eased it onto the top wooden shelf at the rear. It was still quite soggy next morning, so he eased it back onto the magazine and under his mattress.

Each evening after lockup he brought the *papier-mâché* from its cache to speed up the drying process. By Monday night it was cardboard, ready to use. He centered the black grille on it and marked an outline with pencil. Then, with pigment and brush from Artist Clarence Anglin, he painted a facsimile. Next he positioned the cardboard over the vent and traced an outline on the wall. Working industriously, he chipped the outlined area to the depth necessary to accommodate the facsimile, achieving a snug fit. Only one flaw: it was off-color. He had forgotten to get the tube of green paint.

Clarence brought the green to lunch the next day, and that evening Morris, with cool patience, painted the grayish part of the cardboard. He stood back and appraised his handiwork: the cardboard blended in with the wall, and at a cursory glance the spurious grille looked real. He stopped to the front of the cell and studied it. *Sure as hell looks like the old one.* The old grille was in the hole behind its successor.

That next evening Morris began the excavation in depth, covering the stubs of strap iron with black friction tape. Evening after evening, seven nights a week, he chipped away. He grew anxious about the accumulation of rubble and began pushing it over the far edge, reaching through and spreading it along the alley wall. When the job was half completed, he squeezed his shoulders in and stuck his head into the utility corridor. Vents of lighted cells glimmered faintly along the dark passageway. A sudden burst of laughter startled him. It came out of the vent directly opposite, just three feet away, a black inmate chatting with his neighbor on Broadway. He would have to exercise more care. When he neared the end of the project he shoved his peacoat into the service corridor to muffle the sound of tumbling fragments. He finished at last and, restraining his excitement, passed the word to West.

Several nights later Clarence completed his exit. Then came a period when Morris and Clarence Anglin stood lookout while the others dug. In time four escape holes were ready, and the next phase got under way, with Morris and Clarence working, West and John standing watch.

Morris laid magazine and pages on the steel table, gathered concrete particles from the utility corridor and mixed up a batch of plaster with the aid of soap and white glue from the brush shop. He molded it into the shape of a head and neck, then used his fingers and the flat part of the spoon handle to sculpture the brow, sockets for eyes, the nose, mouth, chin. He tucked the head away in the hole.

In a few nights it was set and dry enough to embellish. He crawled into the utility corridor and groped his way down to Clarence's cell vent, came back with a brush and tubes of pink, white, and black paint. The white itself was too white, but by experimenting with the pink he managed to obtain a Rock pallor. He lightly brushed more touches of pink on the cheeks and ears. Then the whites of the eyes, black for the pupils. Gluing on the eyebrows, hair courtesy of barber Clarence, took pains. Even more so, the eyelashes. Then the hair, a full head, brushed back, no part. Morris was his own model, in the mirror.

The paint was wet, but he couldn't resist trying out his creation. He spread out magazine pages and arranged the dummy in bed, careful not to get paint on the sheet. Pillow and peacoat filled out the rest of the figure. He yanked off the light and walked from back to front, slowly, to study the effect. *Looks damn real.*

"Substitute's ready," he told West.

"How's it look?"

"Hate to brag, but looks like there's two of us in here."

He returned the paints and brush, then stored the dummy in the hole, on papers.

"Say, Al, I'd like to make a run to the top tomorrow night, if you don't mind holding off a day on your dummy. Clarence is still a day or so behind."

"Where you goin', to the roof?" West asked.

"Thought I'd go up and check things."

About a half hour after lockup the next night, as the cell blocks began to hum, Morris, who had been sitting with the light out to get used to the gloom, gave the signal.

"Be careful," West said.

"That's me," said Morris.

He had tied a string around the accordion case. He now moved the case back from the wall, bedded down the dummy, squirmed through into the utility corridor, then pulled the case back against the wall with the string. He was wearing socks to avoid making noticeable prints in the dust. He stood a moment to get his bearings, then shinnied up a pipe to a plumber's catwalk at the second tier. He waited here briefly. He looked up. In the glow of the house lights he could see a maze of pipes and conduits. He climbed to the third tier catwalk, then on up. He gripped the pipe with his legs and peered cautiously over the rim, inched higher, then ducked down again. The guard in the west gun gallery was visible. He waited minutes, peered again. The guard was moving toward D Block.

Morris crawled over the edge and wormed his way eastward toward the target ventilator shaft with its mesh-wire cage. He was now deep in the shadows: the unmanned east gun gallery was not lighted. He glanced back toward the west gallery and noted, with pleasurable surprise, that it was hidden from view. He stood up. Now he could see it. Standing on tiptoe, he could almost touch the ceiling with his fingertips. He noted that the shaft made a dog-leg about a foot below the ceiling. He crouched and entered the large mesh cage by a screen door. The shaft opening seemed five feet, perhaps more, above the top of the block, the dog-leg a good foot or more beyond. Morris, five feet seven and a half, stood up in the shaft, hands over his head. He could feel the bend in the shaft and that was all; he could not get a hold to pull himself up into it. He withdrew from the shaft and studied the situation. He needed Clarence to give him a boost.

He descended the thirty feet to the ground tier, wiggled back into his cell, stored the dummy, replaced the accordion case, pulled on the light, carefully brushed the dust off his trousers. He went to the front and reported, "I'm back."

"Noticed your light go on," said West. "How'd you make out?"

"Okay, to the top of the block."

"Not to the roof?"

"Can't get into the shaft without a boost."

He reported on his trip at breakfast. "We can use that mesh cage up there for a workshop to make rafts and water wings. Also more stuff."

"Make water wings?" asked John.

"They're not regular issue," West said.

"Raincoat sleeves tied at the ends," Morris explained. "Run them under your arms, over your shoulders. What I hear, they give you about 70 percent buoyancy. We'll make pontoon rafts with them too, if we can get enough raincoats."

"Just say how many," John said. "I can get 'em for you wholesale."

"Better start bringing them up. We'll need plenty."

"I'll wear one up tomorrow."

"Since it's safer for me, with a dummy, I'll run them on up to the workshop," Morris said.

Several nights later West reported disturbing news to Morris: "They got me paintin' the ceilin' from a stepladder top of our block."

"Bull up there with you?"

"Nope, but I thought sure the jig was up. But then, after he opens the door to get up there, he just says, 'Watch your step,' and stays behind."

As it happened, West worked days up there and finished the job—alone.

John Anglin wore a black plastic raincoat up from the basement after work each afternoon, passing it through the vent to Morris. The guard, coming on duty in a change of shifts, was not aware that he had not worn the coat down; but he halted Anglin once, out of curiosity—at a moment when Anglin, growing bold in his thievery, was wearing two raincoats.

"Leak down there?" the guard asked.

"No, why?" said Anglin, brazenly.

"Why?" The guard touched a sleeve. "Why this raincoat every day?"

"Gets chilly. I'm from the South, and this Rock ain't Florida climate."

"Get yourself a peacoat."

"None left, waitin' for a new batch."

The guard nodded, and Anglin walked on to his cell. Thereafter, he limited his daily pilfering to one coat.

At lunch one day Clarence reported: "Heard about flesh-colored paint today and ordered a tube. By God, they sure make things easy here."

Morris frowned. "What's on your canvas?"

"Like, what'm I paintin'? A barn, sort of."

"Well, wipe it off and start on a *portrait*. Ordering flesh paint—Christ, Clarence, use your head."

Finally, each had both access to the utility corridor and a copy of his head reposing to the ventiduct. On a Friday evening, dummies abed, Morris and Clarence made an exploratory trip to the top of the block. John and West remained behind as lookouts. John sat on his cot with a periscope stuck through the bars—a homemade affair, fashioned out of cardboard and his mirror, that let him see the length of the corridor. West had his accordion slung over his shoulder and, in the event John whistled him to signal the workers overhead, he would grind out, fortissimo, "Come Back to Sorrento."

Clarence sized up the situation in the mesh cage. Then he got down on his haunches; Morris, standing in the shaft, stepped on his shoulders, and Clarence slowly rose, boosting Morris up around the bend. But before Clarence got to his full six feet, he felt Morris stamping his shoulder, and he held there. After some minutes, at a toe-jabbing signal, Clarence withdrew and helped Morris ease out noiselessly. He sensed Morris's dejection and whispered, "Well?"

"After all that work," Morris whispered back. "Months of hard work. We're trapped, can't get out."

"The hell you say. Bars?"

"Two bars, near the top. And the shaft's got a cap on it, a rain hood."

"Okay, we'll spread the bars and knock the goddam cap off."

"Not this one. It's held by six iron uprights riveted to the shaft. They also hold a grid with crossbars, at the top of the shaft. A rat couldn't squeeze through."

At breakfast, Morris waited until he had eaten half his stack of pancakes, then broke the glum silence: "Well, I gave it some thought last night."

"Come up with anything?" asked John.

Morris nodded. "Maybe. Like Clarence said, the two bars are easy. We can use a spreader on them. Then the six rivet heads." He forked up a bite, gave them a level look. "A drill will bust 'em off. That means a motor. There's an outlet in the mesh cage, probably juice for the blower they took out. It's somethin' to think about."

It was Saturday, and that afternoon West and Morris, as teacher and pupil of the accordion, sat off to one side of the orchestra, over near a corner, in the stuffy room in the basement. Morris was fingering the keys in an achingly slow "Home, Sweet Home" when his mind gave gradual recognition to something his eyes had been staring at for a long time. It was a small fan, with cord wrapped around its base, sitting idle in the corner, almost hidden by his accordion case. He studied the big, squarish case, as wide at the top as the bottom. He remembered how the instrument fit inside, wide at the bottom but narrow at the keyboard top, with an empty space about four inches wide and five or so deep. The fan might fit—it *would* fit if he crushed it down into the keyboard. It might damage the accordion. *So what? I'm not takin' the damn thing along.* There was the risk of a check getting back into the cellhouse: all instrument cases must be opened for a guard's inspection at the gate at the top of the stairs. Lately, however, Morris had noted, this rigid routine had been relaxed by some guards to a spot check.

He leaned over to West, ran a finger along a line of the sheet music and said, "When the time's up, go talk to that bull—keep his head turned that way. Give me one minute."

West nodded and at session's end got the guard into conversation. Morris shoved the fan in with the accordion. As they passed through the gate into the cellhouse the guard beckoned to a violinist, three musicians ahead, to step out of line, then West right behind him. Morris went unconcernedly to his cell. He found the accordion slightly damaged, the fan blades bent.

After dinner, while West kept a lookout, Morris went to work on the fan. Using the small blade of the nailclip for a screwdriver, he loosened the set screw in the hub on the shaft from the motor. He then slid the hub back a fraction and picked off the fan blades. *Like pullin' wings off a bee.* He inserted a drill snitched from the shop, moved up the hub again, and reset the screw. The drill was not tightly attached to the motor shaft. He doused the light, put the dummy to bed and took the motor to the top. Clarence was waiting for him there, with a length of pipe he had found in the utility corridor, left by repairmen.

"Better let me tackle the bars," Clarence said.

"Okay." Morris grabbed a raincoat off the stack piling up in their workshop. "Better wrap this around it—deaden the sound."

Morris helped him up the shaft. In a short while he came down. "Bent one of the bars enough to squeeze past," he reported. "Now for them goddam rivets."

Morris plugged in the cord and piled an armful of raincoats over the motor. "Crawl out there, listen how it sounds."

Clarence crawled out and over toward the edge above the west gun gallery. The guard was in D Block.

Morris reached under the raincoats and switched on the motor. It made a muffled whir. He let it run for half a minute, then waited for Clarence.

When he had wormed his way back to the cage, Clarence asked, "What happened? Won't work?"

"You didn't hear it?"

"Not a sound."

"We got it made," said Morris, and in the shadowy workshop they shook hands.

Clarence boosted Morris into the shaft, to the bend, then handed up the motor. Morris crawled up past the elbow, waited for the Alcatraz light to flash. In its brief glare he saw that Clarence had prized one of the two bars inward until it almost touched its mate, leaving a wide gap. Morris hung the motor over them and slid down to the dog-leg, where Clarence reached up the raincoats. He went back up, squeezed on past the bars, then straddled them. He wrapped the motor in the raincoats and, guided by the beacon flashes, set the drill against a rivet head. He held his breath, flicked on the motor. He felt a slight quiver. Nothing else happened. He pulled the drill away. It began to whir. He shut off the motor. He tried it again on the rivet head. A quiver, silence. He pulled it away. A whir. He stopped it.

"I'll be a sonofabitch," he said under his breath.

He tried a new tactic. He held the drill almost on the rivet, started the motor, let it gather speed, set it against the metal. A dying whine, a quiver, silence. He turned it off, sat for a while with the motor on his lap, staring up at the hood capping the ventilator shaft, watching the bright flashes of the Alcatraz light. He wrapped the cord around the raincoats, bundling the motor, and slid down to the cage workshop.

Clarence was elated. "By God, you sure worked that great! I thought sure as hell, that electric drill gets bitin' into a rivet, smack against this tin shaft, jeez, we're gonna have every bull in the joint swarmin' up here. Frankie, I didn't hear a goddam thing."

"Neither did I," said Morris.

"Them raincoats. I sure gotta hand it to you, man."

"Look, Clarence, it *didn't* work."

Clarence squinted at him in the gloom. "No juice?"

"Not enough guts in the motor. Only a fractional horsepower. All it can do is spin a fan and maybe run a pencil sharpener. Put her up against metal and she goes *phhhh*."

"So what now?"

"Take some more thinking," said Morris, laying the raincoats on the stack.

"No, it don't. Six lousy little rivet heads ain't stoppin' us, by God. We'll take 'em off by hand."

Morris stowed the motor and drill behind the stack of raincoats in the dim recess of the workshop. "You know, we could use a flashlight."

"Fine, we'll borrow the bull's."

"I'll rustle up one, and lay off the wisecracks. Might come in handy up there too"—he nodded toward the shaft—"since we've got to take them off by hand. Any ideas about a tool?"

"The nailclip file."

"How long will that last on a rivet head?"

"We got four."

"Too soft."

"Banjo or guitar strings, then."

"I'll try to find us some Carborundum string."

"What the hell's that?"

"Mechanics use it on the machines in the glove shop. Cut through anything."

An inmate-mechanic produced the convict-dubbed Carborundum string—a cord impregnated with an abrasive such as raw grains of silicon carbide, aluminum oxide, or diamond powder and used for intricate repairs, such as fine grooving, on the sewing machines in the glove and tailor shops. Because of its nature, it was kept locked up and the mechanics had to request a piece when needed. Normally, the guards measured the string when issued, measured it again when returned, but lately were apt to be forgetful. Morris's friend received a two-foot length, took back one foot.

On occasion a careless guard will toss into a trash can a flashlight bulb and batteries not quite dead. A convict on a garbage detail will salvage them: held together with plastic tape, they might be useful some day. Here was a possibility for the shaft workers, but Morris obtained a handier one for their purpose—a "pen" flashlight pilfered from the breast pocket of a guard's coat.

When the conspirators returned to the task in the shaft, Morris said, "I'll start each rivet with the Carborundum, then we switch over to this," indicating a banjo string.

"Why not cut right through with that thing, if it's so all-fired good?" asked Clarence.

"This is all we've got, we'd better save it. No tellin' what we might run into beyond those rivets." Morris produced the pen-shaped flashlight. "This'll give us a pin-point light, better to work by and a lot less risky. Don't have to hold it." He stuck it between his teeth, flicked it on, then off. "Batteries are scarce, so only use it if you think you're about through a cut. We don't want a rivet head clattering down the shaft. West knows, you warn John. Okay, give me a boost, I'll get the first cut goin'."

It was a long, tedious job. Pairs alternated nights on the top of the block, and while one work away at a rivet, the other busied himself with getaway preparations. Morris noted one night that the workshop was getting cramped for space, and he took stock with the flashlight that West had put together for use there. He counted fifty-five raincoats, some still piled up, others sealed in layers for two rafts in the making, with rows of sleeves—stuffed with toilet paper and both ends tied—along the bottom; plus sets of water-wing or life-preserver sleeves tied only at one end. He checked the other items: the liquid plastic used as a sealer; the ineffectual fan motor, and an extra electric cord; part of a vacuum cleaner motor that had likewise proved useless; two electric drills; six small saw blades; a file; two short pieces of steel and an eight-inch length of scrap metal; two plywood oars he had shaped on the shop lathe. *Quite a hoard.*

There were also the two sham heads of the conspirators on watch below. When they had started the painstaking work on the rivet heads, Morris had said: "We'd better store the dummies up here nights till we're ready to take off. Some bull might go pokin' through the tunnel with a flashlight. He finds those heads, we're cooked." Thereafter, when they finished an evening's work they brought their dummies to the workshop for storage. Morris was now glad of his foresight: plumbers had started repair work in the service corridor of their block.

After taking the inventory, Morris told John: "Lay off the raincoats. Enough's enough. No need to take risks."

In spare moments, Morris perused magazines for ideas. Early in the conspiracy, he had run across a useful suggestion about resin—an item on how to make a lamp shade in a hints-for-home-crafts department in the November 1960 issue of *Popular Mechanics:* ". . . Apply to cloth and allow to harden. After that the cloth and resin hold their shape." Resin was not available in the shops, but liquid plastic was, and it served nicely to seal and stiffen the edges of the raincoats for the rafts.

Thumbing through *Sports Illustrated* for May 21, 1962, he found a fascinating section on "The Joys of Water," with a piece on boating and a pertinent page, "Signposts of Water Safety," with color illustrations of channel buoys indicating proper course and warning of navigation hazards. In the March 1962 *Popular Mechanics* he came across an article, "Your Life Preserver," reporting on tests of various types. He read with acute interest, and a wry smile, the final paragraph:

"Like insurance, lifesaving devices are hard to value. If you don't need them, they're useless, even a bother. If you do need them, they're priceless. Get the type that suits your need, then take it swimming and try it out. You might be glad you did."

One night early in June, Clarence came down the shaft into the cage workshop with excitement in his whisper: "Got the last goddam head off!" It had been almost six months since they first began chipping around the edges of the vent grilles in their cells. Morris now went up the shaft with six tiny soap balls and a paint kit. He worked each soap ball onto a decapitated rivet, shaped it to resemble a rivet head and painted it black—just in case a guard happened to peer into the shaft from the roof some day.

Next morning at table John said, "we ready to shove off?"

"Not yet," said Morris.

"Christ, man, we can't keep this up for years."

Morris gave him a hard look. "Know how many men got down to the water? Around thirty. Some got shot up, some drowned, some caught, others came back, half froze. Only two—Roe and Cole—ever got away, *if* they got away. *We want to make it.*"

"Okay," said John, "when do we go?"

Morris said, "I want to find out more about Angel Island and the channel between there and Marin. Also a point or two about our route down to the beach. I hear there's a pile of lumber, still on pallets, near the powerhouse. Maybe we can use a few boards to stiffen our rafts." He debated a moment. "This is Friday. We go a week from Monday night."

The guard stepped up. "Okay, let's go."

That night West called to Morris, "Keep a lookout, will you, Frankie? Got a little repair work to do."

"Upstairs?"

"No, just fix up the hole. Too damn big."

"Go to it," said Morris. "We don't want any hitch at this stage."

The Anglins had reported a shakedown of their cells the previous Saturday. John's bathrobe, hanging over the fake vent grille, had been moved to another peg. Clarence had found evidence of an inspection, but the large towel with the original owner's name— UNITED STATES MARINE CORPS—in block letters down the center remained draped over a low cord in front of his vest.

West had discovered no hint of a visit to his cell, but he was worried: he might be next on the list, and his cardboard kept slipping out. This was Friday evening, and he decided to play it safe. He pushed his shoes into the utility corridor and crawled through. He groped toward the west end where the plumbers were replacing a toilet pipe into an empty cell. He came upon a sack of cement and filled both shoes. He did not bother to search for a trowel; he knew they wouldn't leave tools.

He returned to his cell, emptied the shoes in the wash basin and mixed the cement. Spoon handle for trowel, he began reducing the size of the hole. He decided to do a good job while he was at it and slapped on all the cement, then pushed the cardboard onto it. What matter if it did set with the cement, he could rip it out: the next time he crawled through that hole would be the last. He wiped off the cement that had oozed around the edges, then cleaned the basin.

"All done," he told Morris.

"Do a good job?"

"Damn good, if I do say so."

Morris pored over tide charts and maps borrowed from the prison library.

On the *next* Monday the Anglins appeared moody at lunch and dinner, and shortly before nine o'clock that night, Morris heard a muffled voice at his vent. He pulled the light cord, drew back the accordion case.

It was John Anglin. "Get your head, Frank. We're goin' tonight."

"But we agreed—"

He was gone. Morris heard the faint rustling as he shinnied up the pipe. Then he heard Clarence Anglin notify West and climb the pipe. Morris went to the top. He met them coming back with their dummies and whispered, "Why the sudden rush?"

"Can't wait," said John.

"You said we got it made, let's get to hell out," said Clarence.

Returning with his dummy, Morris stopped at the bottom and listened. He heard the sound of digging, knelt and peered into West's cell. West was chipping away furiously.

"What's holding you up?" Morris asked.

"This goddam cement. Can't get the hole open again."

"Jesus, West, you're running a hell of a chance of screwing up the works. Hold off till I get in."

Morris crawled into his cell, replaced the case, hurried up front to stand watch. "Okay," he called, and West resumed his frantic digging.

The bright cell lights blinked out, plunging the block into a brief blackness before the overhead lights filled the steel-and-concrete corridor with a stark sort of gloaming. It became even duskier as the guard in the west gunwalk went off duty and his wall cage darkened. The sudden gloom seemed to sharpen the racket of chatter in the cellhouse. It would be a half hour before the inmates settled down for the night, like roosting fowl.

Morris gave the cell a swift final survey: the personal effects on the shelves, the garments on the pegs, the shoes beside the bed, the dummy lying there so lifelike, even without the peacoat. He was taking it, after all. He squirmed out, tugged the accordion case to the wall with the string.

The Anglin brothers brushed by without a word. Clarence started up.

"Wait for me!" came a muffled, anguished cry.

John dropped to his knees and muttered angrily, "Christ sake, West, can that racket! You're gonna bollix things!" He started up.

Morris knelt at West's exit hole. "Snap it up, man! But wait till the bull goes by before you get your dummy. See you on top."

Morris climbed the pipe, rubbed smooth by trouser legs. West's digging echoed dully, ominously, in the dark tunnel. He hesitated on the third-tier catwalk to listen: no sound of digging, nor of West coming up. Here the gloom was less dense, and the jumble of pipes, some carrying salt water to the toilets, had a marine decay, like that of a tramp ship about to be scrapped. A dark lump on the catwalk stirred: a rat watching. At the top, with the guard off the gun gallery, he walked boldly, and silently in this socks, to the mesh cage. The Anglins were waiting, water wings like stoles around their necks. At their feet were rolled-up rafts and oars. They spoke in whispers.

"We need both rafts?" asked Clarence.

"Hell, no," said John.

"I'll lead the way," said Morris. "Be careful you don't bang a knee goin' up. Once outside, no talkin'. Voices carry at night. All set?"

"Let's go," said John.

Clarence, with a boost from John, followed Morris into the shaft and lay in the crook until Morris could clear the exit. John slid an oar into a folded raft and reached it up to Clarence. He stayed in the cage; at a signal he would grasp his brother's ankles and as Clarence hoisted himself to the bars—one bent inward—he would haul John into the shaft.

Morris, astraddle the bars above Clarence's head, deftly picked off the spurious soap bolt heads and, to dispose of them, thumbed them hard against the shaft wall. One after another, he eased the six flat iron uprights free, careful not to dislodge the rivets. He brought his feet up onto the double bars, then raised himself until his head touched the crossbarred grid. He pushed on upward slowly, into the dazzling flashes of the Alcatraz light towering above the southeast corner of the prison. A cold wind was blowing off the ocean. He kept easing upward, gently, and the contraption—the grid, the rainhood, the six supports—came out of the shaft. He leaned over to lay it aside, a gust of wind snatched it, and it clattered to the roof. He checked an impulse to scramble out, ducked back into the shaft. A muttered curse rose from the Anglin below him. All three held still, straining for the sound of pursuit, waiting for the siren to kick, on. Nothing happened. Only the hubbub of convicts still settling down for the night, mingled with the wind whistling shrilly through other ventilators, came to them. Morris felt this racket had absorbed the clatter on the roof. Still . . .

The officer on the floor, making his first patrol of the night, was walking along the outside of B Block, pat the cells with the bedded-down dummies, when he heard an unusual noise. He looked up, cocking his head. He hurried back to the lieutenant's desk.

"Just heard a funny noise, up there," he said.

"The roof?" asked the lieutenant, instantly alert.

"No, sounded more like it came from the hospital."

The lieutenant went up to the hospital, returned shortly. "All quiet up there," he said. "Somebody must've knocked over a bucket."

Up in the shaft Clarence Anglin jabbed at Morris's foot and called in a hoarse whisper, "Get goin'!"

Morris eased himself out of the shaft, which rose a foot or so above the roof. He turned, and a beacon flash blinded him. He shut his eyes tight for a moment, then, shielding his face with an arm, peered into the shaft. Clarence clambered to the bars and reached up the raft roll. Morris took the roll and, bent low, ran a half-dozen steps and crouched beside a raised skylight.

As he waited for the others, Morris studied the weather. One moment the night was black; the next, incandescent. The Alcatraz light did not rotate; it flashed every five seconds, each flash lasting three-tenths of a second. Morris knew their chances of being spotted by the lighthouse keeper were remote; it was unlikely he was even up there. Danger lay to the north and south: the two main gun towers. On the roof they were visible to the guard in the north tower—unless they kept low. Descending the far wall of the mess hall—and a vent pipe from the kitchen was their only means of descent—they would be in clear view of the guard in the south tower. *Clear* view? Over-hanging lights floodlit that wall like day.

He observed the sky again. A high fog raced overhead, no more than a hundred yards. In the intermittent beacon flashes he could see the wind snatch a handful of cottony mist off the bottom and fling it along. A few more hours and the fog, pulled down into the airstream funneling through the Gate, would shroud The Rock—and obscure the kitchen wall. But these were precious hours, a head start.

Clarence climbed out of the shaft and crept to the shielding skylight. In a moment John's head crept up, and he fell in behind Clarence. Morris, hugging the skylight, dragging the raft roll, crawled to the edge of the cellhouse roof. He slipped over onto the roof of the mess hall and crept along a fire wall. He waited in the shadowy far corner for the others, moving like salamanders. He led the crawlers toward the silhouette of the kitchen vent, protruding above the roof about midway along this side. He stopped at the pipe, and the others pulled up behind. They now faced their greatest peril, the fifty-foot descent in the glare of the floodlight from the lamps projecting from the edge of the roof.

Morris, lying against the fire wall, tied the raft to his belt at the left side. Face averted to cut the risk of reflection, he moved over the rim as slowly as a slug, kept to the side away from the tower and slid down the pipe with the same even movement, as less likely to catch an eye than jerkiness. He touched ground, slid onto his knees, then down sideways in a gentle continuing motion. He crawled on his stomach into the shadows at the end of the building. He lay back and watched the others descend as he had.

Morris led the way, still crawling, across a short open space to the cyclone fence. They were now in the range of the north gun tower but at a distance that diminished the glare of its searchlight. Morris scaled the fence, picked his way over the barbed wire and let himself down. The Anglins clambered after him. They kept at his heels as he skirted a terrace and the high water tower, then slanted down a cliff covered with ice plant. He suddenly froze, and they froze behind them. Then all three dropped, burying their faces in the flowers.

A guard came along the road ten feet below them. His footsteps receded in the direction of the shops. They scuttled across the road, into the shadow of the powerhouse. They were out of sight of the gun towers, and the patrol had gone by, their last worry erased. They ran down a slope to the shore of a cove. Off west the amber lights of the Golden Gate Bridge glistened under the fog.

"Made it," said Morris, breathing deep. The cold wind felt good. He untied the raft. "Let's get a few boards."

"Hell with boards," said John. "Let's shove off."

"They'll stiffen the raft. Some stacks of lumber up the road a short ways. Unloaded the other day, still on pallets."

"I'll go along," said Clarence. He drew a dark object from his jacket and handed it to John. "Hold this."

"What's that?" asked Morris.

"Some pictures and things. Let's get them boards."

They went back up the incline, a shallow ravine between the steeper heads of the cove, and returned shortly with four boards. They inserted them in the raft. Then they put the finishing touch on the improvised life preservers. They pulled each sleeve open-ended and rapidly through the air to inflate it, tied that end to the other to for a ring, then slid the ring on like a bandoleer—several to each shoulder.

"Where the hell's the other oar?" asked Morris.

"Christ," said John, "I forgot it."

"Never mind, let's shove."

They carried the raft to the surf, climbed on, and pushed off onto the dark, wind-roughened waters. They soon blended into the night, and the slapping swish of the paddle faded toward the black mass of Angel Island, a mile and a half away. . . .

West chipped madly at the cement he had spooned onto his escape hatch, sealing himself in more effectively than the original concrete had. He estimated the times of the patrol and took breaks, climbing into bed, to let the guard pass by. It was after midnight when he made it to the corridor, up to the top, into the workshop. He found an unfinished pontoon, a plywood paddle, three "sleeve" life preservers, his own fake head staring up at him. He peered up into the dark shaft, felt a chill draft, shivered. He stared out across the top of the block. The only sound was the moan of the wind. For a moment he felt terrible alone. Then he grew panicky. *Hell with the dummy.* He dragged over the raft, folded it several times, knelt on it, then raised himself into the shaft and desperately clawed his way on up, past the dog-leg, over the crossbars. He emerged into the blinding flash of the beacon—and a sudden, screeching clamor.

He froze for a terrified instant, then ducked back in. He slid down the shaft, crawled out of the mesh cage, over the edge, down the pipe, into his cell, on into bed, exhausted, knowing that, for him at least, the jig was up. . . .

West's head bobbing out of the ventilator shaft had frightened seagulls roosting nearby. They took off shrieking, alarming gulls all along the parapet. Soon the sky rang with the raucous *awrk-awrks* of gulls wheeling above the roof.

The guard in the south tower wondered about the commotion and called the Armorer, who dispatched guards. They searched the ground behind the prison and reported, "Not a thing—must've been a rat that scared them." By now the gulls had settled down again, and nothing further disturbed the night.

Maybe

DID THEY MAKE IT? Maybe. . . .

Fog and tide are the meshes that most often entrap Alcatraz escapers. They can flounder in a dense fog, all sense of direction lost; and a swift current can carry them through the Golden Gate, out to sea. On that score, luck was with the Morris trio. At the time of the departure, the fog was high, visibility good; and during that night of June 11, 1962, the ebb tide at its peak ran only 2.2 knots, about two and a half miles an hour.

As usual, the escape generated a feverish hunt, by air, sea, land. Soldiers from the Presidio of San Francisco, carbines in hand, combed every foot of Angel Island, turned up no clue. For weeks every burglary and robbery in Northern California was carefully checked out, but none traced to the fugitives, who would need food and a change of clothing.

On Wednesday, the day after the break was discovered, the trio's prison-made oar was found bobbing two hundred yards off Alcatraz, toward Marin county. On Thursday afternoon a debris boat with a scoop net, employed by the Army Corps of Engineers to clear the bay of objects hazardous to navigation, was chugging past Angel Island when a load was dumped on the afterdeck. A crewman picked a black plastic bag out of the dripping mass—actually, two bags, one within the other, for better waterproofing, both improvised out of the same polyethylene material of the raincoats. In the inner bag, still dry, were about sixty photographs, mostly snapshots of the family-album type, including fifteen of an attractive brunette; also, a list of names and addresses; also, a receipt for a $10 money order, cashed by the mail clerk at Alcatraz and made out to Clarence Anglin.

This seemed proof positive to prison authorities that the escaped convicts had drowned. Their theory appeared to be bolstered by the muscle-cramping coldness of the water, *if* the fugitives' raft capsized and dumped them in the bay. The average June temperature of the water around Alcatraz, and between Alcatraz and Angel Island, is fifty-five degrees.

To others, a factor supporting a contrary view—that the convicts made it—seemed equally compelling; if all three went down, the odds were that at least one body would come up. None had. A dramatic boost to speculation that they got away came in mid-December when an escaper actually swam to the San Francisco shore.

At any rate, nine months after their flight the fate of the trio remained an enigma.

Why?

FROM THE DAY IT SWALLOWED up its first gangsters Alcatraz has had a reputation, fostered by the Department of Justice, as America's most dread prison. The very name, Alcatraz, has become a synonym for a Devil's Island, a penal rock harboring the worst criminal element, often chained to the wall of a dark, dripping dungeon, with only unseen rats for companions. A sort of Ile d'If incarnate. And to this day, a quarter of a century after the G-men ended the gangster era, that myth has endured as a fact.

In the early years, Associate Warden Miller made it clear to a prisoner: "Alcatraz is not a penitentiary. Alcatraz is Alcatraz." Years later Warden Swope said: "There is always that small minority needing an Alcatraz." And after him Warden Madigan said: "The men who come here have less prospect for rehabilitation than the men in the rest of our prison system." The refrain kept up into the 1960s with the lament by Warden Blackwell on the difficulty of finding convict house servants because if they could be trusted to act as trusties, "they don't belong on the island." In such ways was the myth of Alcatraz nurtured.

Why? To hold as a Damoclean gasbilly over federal prisoners elsewhere: be good, or you go to Alcatraz. The myth also helped justify the extravagant cost of The Rock's upkeep.

Has Alcatraz really housed only the "incorrigible incorrigibles"—only those with long terms that make them potential escape problems—only the troublemakers who stir unrest? Earl Taylor was an accountant serving *five* years for tax evasion, and he was given five dollars and an on-the-spot, unconditional release straight off The Rock, fifteen minutes before he was due in court to argue his petition for a writ of habeas corpus. Allen Clayton West, who cemented himself in, was serving ten years for car theft. In 1962 a man was doing time at Alcatraz for stealing a pig—a federal rap because he stole it on an Indian Reservation. Another Rock felon's offense: theft of two cases of cigarettes from a boxcar in Oklahoma. A military prisoner landed on The Rock for assault and a $1.50 robbery. To Alcatraz went another military prisoner who never stole anything, whose only offense was that he had gone AWOL; he gave himself up, later escaped, was sent to Leavenworth.

Why did such mild offenders, and many others, make Alcatraz? Were they assaultive, troublesome, escape-minded? Take the case of the AWOL soldier. He was at Leavenworth when the inmates went on a hunger strike in 1958. The Sword of Alcatraz broke it up. The warden had the Immigration Service bring up a twin-engined Border Patrol plane from the Mexican border. Then guards went to random cells: "Pack up, you're leaving." Within the hour, twenty-eight convicts, among them the AWOL young man, were flying to Alcatraz.

An isolated instance? Apparently wardens—chiefly at the maximum-security prisons of Leavenworth and Atlanta—have for years used Alcatraz as a convenient whip, and used it indiscriminately. Stan Brown, North Dakota mail robber who was in the first "shipment" from Leavenworth, served seven years and upon his release in 1941 said: "Only about fifty of the 300 prisoners rate Alcatraz. You take the thirty-seven hunger strikers they ran in recently from Leavenworth. Most of those boys were in for crimes like car stealing or something like that. Alcatraz isn't built for those boys. It was made for the big shots like Machine Gun Kelly, Karpis, Cretzer, Bailey, Capone—guys like me. I rate Alcatraz." And he waxed prophetic: "Alcatraz is a punishment prison. I think in the next few years you'll see lots of trouble on Alcatraz. When a man's on The Rock all he thinks about, day and night, is how to get off. The thing that seems impossible to you looks possible to him."[1]

Alcatraz has even served vindictive purposes. Bryan Conway gave his own case as one example in his *Saturday Evening Post* article. Conway, while a soldier at a post in Alabama, had killed a sergeant,

---

[1] Stan Brown was interviewed by Stanton Delaplane, Pulitzer Prize–winning reporter, later a syndicated columnist.

claimed self-defense and was freed by the civilian authorities for lack of evidence; was later rearrested by federal agents, convicted, sentenced to eighteen years. At Atlanta Conway said he refused to testify "as the Government wanted me to testify" in an inmate stabbing case that ended in an acquittal. Soon thereafter he was packed off, and not until the train was well away from Atlanta did he learn from his guard escort where he was headed. He asked, "What have I done to be sent to Alcatraz? My prison record is good," and the guard replied, "You are certified as an incorrigible." Yet the incorrigible Conway was released the very next year, 1937, with six years off for good behavior.

Conway also related that at Atlanta in October 1936 "when the authorities feared a mutiny, they confined eighteen men, shipping them all to Alcatraz on mere suspicion." Not all were incorrigibles: "I knew, personally, men whose only brush with the law was the single offense which sent them to Alcatraz." He told of the shipment of fourteen from Leavenworth in the summer of 1936, among them three first-offender Kentucky moonshiners who had not paid their internal revenue tax. These batches came from Atlanta and Leavenworth only two years after Alcatraz was created as a super-lockup.

Floyd Wilson was a thirty-three-year-old jobless carpenter with five children who set out from his Washington, D.C., home in the winter of 1947 with a gun to get $17 to buy a ton of coal "so my kids won't freeze to death." He tried to hold up a chain-store manager, sitting in a car in front of the store with $10,000 in a paper bag on the seat; killed the manager, fled in panic, without the money. Wilson, with no prior record, went home and waited for the police, said he had not intended to kill. He drew life, went to Atlanta, then to Alcatraz in what Warden Madigan called a "routine transfer because of his long sentence and the possibility of an escape problem." So . . . ? So he was put to work on the dock gang and one summer afternoon in 1956 he slipped away under cover of smoke from a trash fire, was found twelve hours later walking along the shore, shivering. Madigan said Wilson, who helped unload a cargo from barges, did not fill a role comparable to that of a jail trusty. "We have no trusties here," the warden said. "For jobs such as that, we try to select men who are less of a security risk."

The incident prompted this letter-to-the-editor comment by a San Franciscan, H. T. Reid:

"The temporary disappearance of Floyd Wilson at Alcatraz thoroughly explodes two carefully nurtured myths about that awful place.

"The Bureau of Prisons has long claimed Alcatraz is maintained for the 'nation's most desperate and hardened criminals.' The bureau equally contends that Alcatraz is not 'a permanent exile,' that prisoners by a 'convincing record of good behavior' can 'earn their way out . . . to some institution of less strict regimen and discipline.' . . .

"His (Wilson's) behavior qualified him for work on the dock gang, where he has worked for several years. What became of his opportunity to transfer to some place not so hopeless?

"Manifest abuse by high authorities of such a maximum-security prison, as well as its crushing effect on the human beings subjected to it, cry out for the abolition of Alcatraz as part of the federal prison system."

Not all Alcatraz inmates are federal prisoners. Felons are boarded there by states that find the federal penal system a handy weapon with which to threaten their own troublemakers. Among these boarders is John Duncan, apparently not considered by the trial judge as a dangerous criminal because he drew only a two-to-four-year term in the Maine State Prison in 1955 for burglary. But the next year he joined six others in an attempt to escape, and Maine farmed him out to the Federal Government.

Director Bennett of the Federal Prison Bureau has himself admitted men are sent to Alcatraz for reasons other than safer keeping. His treatment of Robert Stroud, described by the Birdman's attorney as purely vindictive, is a case in point. The first attempt to put Stroud on The Rock in the early days was called off after bird lovers raised an indignant storm. He was rousted out one midnight in 1942, taken summarily from his birds and research laboratory at Leavenworth, and quietly hustled off to Alcatraz while the country was busy with World War II. Bennett later told a reporter that Stroud was shipped off to Alcatraz "because he was a nuisance, not because he was a men-ace,"[2] then added, "We do it all the time." It was done in the case of Cecil Wright, the self-made legal expert, a model prisoner at Leaven-worth but sent to Alcatraz for making himself a nuisance by offering advice to others on writs.

For years most of the inmates at dread Alcatraz have been short-termers, and often first-offenders, whose crimes, had they occurred under state rather than federal jurisdiction, would in all likelihood have meant probation with a county-jail term. Sometimes the differ-ence of a few feet, or a few miles, can mean the difference between a jail and Alcatraz. The crime may happen on a sidewalk in front of a post office, keeping you under local jurisdiction; if it happens on the post office steps, it's federal, and you might land on The Rock as one of those picked by lot. If you steal a car in San Francisco and drive it to Los Angeles and get picked up, it might mean a year in jail, if a first offense, or perhaps several years at San Quentin. If you drive the stolen car to Reno, less than half the distance, it's across a state line, a federal rap, and. . . .

To many penologists, the crime of Alcatraz is that it inflicts on such young men, by their very presence on The Rock, a punishment far beyond the penalty intended by the statute. The worldwide infamy of Alcatraz tends to stigmatize them ever after as hardened criminals, to brand them with a new-type Scarlet Letter—A for Alca-traz. Even the old practice of never sentencing a man directly to Alcatraz nor paroling him from there, using way stations such as Leavenworth and Atlanta instead, although not always strictly adhered to in former days, has lapsed greatly in recent years. This can add to the young ex-convict's difficulty of adjustment if, in fill-ing out an application for a job, he honestly sets down his last place of employment as "Glove Shop, Alcatraz."

Life in a prison of punishment only, such as Alcatraz, was pur-portedly depicted by an anonymous convict in a prison manual a few years ago:

---

[2] Bennett's "nuisance" comment on Stroud was quoted by Paul O'Neil, *Life* staff writer, in "Prodigious Intellect in Solitary," *Life*, April 11, 1960.

"Maybe you have asked yourself how can a man of even ordinary intelligence put up with this kind of life day in, day out, week after week, month after month, year after year. You might wonder whence do I draw sufficient courage to endure it.

"To begin with, these words seem written in fire on the walls of my cell, 'Nothing can be worth this!' No one knows what it is like to suffer from the intellectual atrophy, the pernicious mental scurvy that comes of long privation of all the things that make life real, because even the analogy of thirst cannot possibly give you an inkling of what it is like to be tortured by the absence of everything that makes life worth living.

"A prisoner cannot keep from being haunted by a vision of life as it used to be when it was real and lovely. At such times I pay with a sense of overwhelming melancholy my tribute to life as it once was."

How did Alcatraz fail? The Rock did tame some of those gangsters who, with felons of lesser criminal stature, launched the place. By the time Warden Madigan left in 1961 for the top post at McNeil, he said: "None of the original prisoners is still here. The old gang is gone." Some served their time and walked away from the Fort Mason dock free men; others made headway toward self-rehabilitation and were rewarded by a transfer, although there is no reason to doubt that these men, such as Chase with his interest in art, could have done the same at any old prison. Many of the old gang left The Rock in straitjackets, deranged by the "exquisite torture of routine"; others left in the coroner's basket. Roe and Cole first revealed that Alcatraz was not the escapeproof bastille the Bureau of Prisons had proclaimed it to be; then came the bureau-jolting riots and breaks, each followed by frantic efforts to make it, as Bennett said, "impregnable." But with all the efforts, and the redoubled efforts after the Battle of Alcatraz, it never did become really impregnable. Morris and his coplotters proved that. And Morris was up against the tightest "impregnability" in the history of The Rock: the toolproof cell and window bars, the Chinese-puzzle security of the main entrance into the cellhouse, the other electronic locking and frisking devices, the mesh screen over the gun galleries, the gun ports for armed guards on the outside catwalks, all foolproof systems that supposedly added up to absolute inescapability.

How, then, did Alcatraz fail again? Actually, as in most of those earlier, murderous affairs, the culpable factor was the human element. During his six-year regime as warden at Alcatraz, Madigan cracked numerous cellhouse conspiracies in the hatching stage. He once told curious newsmen why: "The search out here is continuous. We check some of the cells every day, as a matter of routine. The men in here keep their heads working every minute, trying to think of something, of some way out. . . ." Madigan knew the value of alertness: he came up through the ranks, guard to warden.

Guards who had served under Wardens Johnston and Swope recalled similar vigilance. One described the graveyard shift, midnight to 8 A.M.: "I made the rounds every twenty to forty minutes. You had to stay alert—the lieutenant kept his eye on you. Some prisoners slept head at the front; others, bothered by the cellhouse lights, with their feet at the bars. It was important to know their sleeping habits: you could tell that was Pete in there by the position or the snore. Often I'd make a round and peer in a cell and think, 'Hmmm, George hasn't moved.' I'd look for a sign of breathing, or I'd reach in and tug the blanket to make him stir."

"What did you suspect—a dummy?"

He nodded.

"Any other security measures?"

"Weekly checks. Every Saturday, when the prisoners were out in the yard, we'd check the bars on the windows and cells, and shake down the cells."

"Then this last escape [of the Morris trio] should not have occurred?"

He considered a moment, said quietly, "No, never."

"Incompetence?"

He smiled. "They were at it every night for months."

What about the suspension of two guards?

"Scapegoats. The blame goes higher. Dollison, the associate warden, was moved into that spot from an executive post, manager of the industrial shops. Not coming up through the custodial ranks, he lacked the sense of urgency, of constant alertness, you need up there. If the man at the top is relaxed, the men under him become lax, all down the line. It's only natural."

Warden Blackwell and Bennett's associate, Wilkinson, who flew out from Washington after the Morris-engineered break, had a different, and rather astounding, theory. They invited newsmen over for an official explanation of the escape—why three convicts could dig their way out of impregnable Alcatraz with spoons. (Newsmen were never told of the nailclip attachment, and their request to see the spoons was denied.)

"Alcatraz is old," Wilkinson explained. "It's in a debilitated condition."

Blackwell concurred: "The concrete wasn't crumbling, but there was some erosion in it. It could be ground down with the spoons." He had an admiring word for the trio's artistic talents: "The dummies sure looked lifelike. The faces wee painted flesh color."

Dollison on the morning of the escape admitted the convicts had been "at it a long time—at least, six months," and Blackwell, rushing back from vacation, agreed: "With spoons it takes more time than if you had a jackhammer. It could have taken months." Still, the warden insisted there was no custodial lapse. He said the guards made hourly bed checks through the night and periodic shakedowns of the prison, although he could not recall, offhand, when the escaped convicts' cells had last been checked.

Wilkinson said, a bit wistfully: "Morris and the Anglins would not have got out on Monday night if they had been shifted to new cells on Sunday. All that time they had spent in preparation for escape would have been wiped out."

Blackwell said: "You must remember, the officer is making the count at night in a very subdued light. It has to be subdued so the inmates can sleep." (Convicts often read till past midnight by the cellhouse light.)

As for the ventilator hood clattering to the roof, he said: "The prison is full of noise at night and we investigate every sound. If the wind blows over a bucket and it sounds like a bucket, we still investigate."

Newsmen were not allowed in the cellhouse ("There's a certain amount of unrest in there") and photographers could shoot, no closer than eight feet, only a cot with a dummy set up in the visitors' room. The warden distributed color shots of the cells with the escape holes.

"Any other convicts in on the plot?" asked Charles Raudebaugh, a *Chronicle* reporter.

"We're still checking," said the warden.

"Anybody chicken out?"

"No one chickened out."

Back at his office, Raudebaugh studied the color photos. His sharp eye detected a *fourth* cell with a gaping hole, with a notation on the back of that photo: "Cell of A. C. West." Raudebaugh phoned the warden. "What's the first name of Convict West?"

"Why?"

"I have a photo of his cell with a hole."

"Oh," said the warden, "I shouldn't have given that out. I'd prefer you didn't use it."

The *Chronicle* felt obliged to—the other papers had it. West's role might never have come to light had it not been for the warden's blunder and Raudebaugh's alertness.

A few days later reporters on the federal beat in San Francisco were invited to the island and given a look at the cells. They inquired about the deterioration, and Blackwell said, "I've had structural engineers say that concrete doesn't deteriorate. All I know is what I see." A reporter picked at the concrete with his fingers, then remarked on its solidity, that it did not crumble to the touch and that digging through it with a spoon must have taken some doing. Blackwell said, "Spooning out sounds like they worked their way through ice cream. This isn't ice cream."

Before returning to Washington, Wilkinson announced that his investigation had disclosed "no indication of willful negligence." Three days later the guards on duty during the two shifts the night of the escape were quietly suspended for twenty days without pay.

Reporters heard about this weeks afterward and queried Blackwell. He said: "The officers were suspended for failing to make an accurate inmate count. Their failure jeopardized the security of the prison." Who were the guards? "That's a personnel problem, not a public matter," he said. "You don't want to blackball them, do you?"

Five months after the break, Bennett announced the appointment of Dollison as associate warden of the maximum-security institution at Seagoville, Texas. He commended Dollison, some thought a bit ambiguously: "His performance over the years has been of the highest quality. I am anxious for him to take a new job."

By coincidence, the *last* escape from Alcatraz—on December 16, 1962—occurred exactly 25 years to the day after Roe and Cole effected the *first*. That is, it will stand as the last escape if the prison command manages somehow to persuade the plotters to hold off a little while, until The Rock can be closed down. After the December break Blackwell commented wryly, "Apparently we weren't phasing out fast enough."

The most significant aspect of that escape, neatly interring forever the Alcatraz myth, was the feat of a convict in reaching the mainland, the first known victory over the tides by a fleeing felon. The affair also produced a full quota of blunders and cover-up attempts that took on the features of a sexless French farce.

The escapers were two long-term bank robbers: John Paul Scott, thirty-five, of Kentucky, and Darl Lee Parker, thirty-one, of Ohio. December 16 was a Sunday, and they slipped away into the dark, drizzly, foggy night after the five-thirty count. As culinary workers, they had not yet been locked up. They were missed at five-forty-seven, and a half hour later the prison launch found Parker shivering on Little Alcatraz, a rock cluster one hundred yards west. At seven-forty teenagers phoned the military police at the Presidio of San Francisco that they had come upon a "body"—it was Scott—at Fort Point, just inside the Golden Gate, almost three miles from Alcatraz.

Inexplicably, the prison waited about an hour before alerting the Coast Guard. San Francisco police were notified eight minutes *after* Scott was found on the mainland. For the next hour squad cars and patrolmen prowled the shoreline for a fugitive already in custody. Reporters finally informed police that Scott had been captured.

Blackwell, pressed, reluctantly and sparsely sketched the escape: they had cut a window bar in a storage room below the kitchen, had scaled a barbed-wire fence and gone down to the water along the route taken by the Morris trio.

Scott, semi-conscious, body temperature down to 94°, was soon revived at the Presidio's Letterman General Hospital and returned to Alcatraz. He had worn an improvised Mae West: inflated surgical gloves stuffed into the sleeves of a jacket tied around his waist. (Said Blackwell the next day: "I thought it would be pretty difficult to get those gloves, but apparently it wasn't too difficult.") Before he was silenced at the Presidio, Scott, either as a jest or to confound the prison authorities, said he had severed the toolproof bar with ordinary string, moistened and rubbed with a kitchen cleanser to serve as an abrasive.

Bennett flew out from Washington, investigated the break, then held a press conference in a seldom-used bankruptcy courtroom in San Francisco, the largest and most clamorous ever experienced on the federal beat. Poised, suavely smiling, he announced at the outset: "I've read all of the newspaper accounts of the escape. They are substantially right in all major aspects. Of course, there are certain minor details that you didn't know about." He patently intended a brief conference and several times started to rise, but was pinned down by questions. And then he made a slip—a remark about "going over the roof." The newsmen bored in, pried out the truth, bits at a time, like prying gold flakes out of quartz. Most queries drew a repeated response: "I don't know; maybe the warden knows." The warden stood mutely by, chain-smoking cigarettes. The bits pried loose added up to:

Scott worked alone in the storage room "under constant supervision." Another convict had started the cutting more than a year earlier, had passed the secret on to Scott when he was transferred elsewhere. Bars throughout the prison are "regularly" checked for soundness. Yet the sawing was never detected? Well, Scott "went when he did" because those bars were due to be checked and, though camouflaged by paint after each sawing stint, he feared his work "would be detected." (Bennett neglected to explain how Scott could be aware that the bars, so long safe from a guard's rubber mallet, were now due for a check.)

Had Scott, as the convict said, actually cut through a 1½-inch-thick steel bar with string and a sink cleanser? Well, some of the sawing may have been done that way "but not all of it." (Indeed, not. A metal expert says a convict working at it full eight-hour shifts would require about 75 years, give or take a decade; five tons of string, and perhaps 10,000 cans of cleanser to do the job.) Scott presumably used banjo strings and a saw fashioned out of a spatula by notching its edge (found in a drainpipe in the room). He removed both a 14-inch length of bar and a section of horizontal flat bar; and to do the cutting, a few minutes at a time while the guard was out of the room, he had to climb onto a table and on up the cross-bars to his project, 15 feet above the floor. Then he had to cut out a small steel-framed window.

After crawling out, Scott and Parker went to the north side of the cellhouse, shinnied up a drainpipe, crossed the roof to a blind spot (out of sight of the road tower), then descended. By another pipe? Oh, no, they'd brought along a 50-foot extension cord ripped from a waxing machine, to slide down. This route—*not* the Morris route— gave them access to an area without a cyclone fence. They hurried right by the gun tower, on down to the shore.

Reporter Rich Jordan of the *San Francisco Examiner* wrote of the news conference in the bankruptcy court: "Bennett, after a huddle with Blackwell, girded himself for an explanation to the press. Unfortunately, after almost 90 minutes of backing and filling and half-answered questions, the assembly press went away with the idea that Bennett was not sure exactly what happened, either. . . .

"Bennett, who obviously had not been briefed as well as he would have liked, had no explanation for the two-hour delay in notifying police and the Presidio, why a guard tower covering the escape route was unmanned, how presumably closely supervised convicts could saw away at a bar for, by his own admission, a year, or how they could have stolen surgical gloves."

Nonetheless, as he had so staunchly done after every escape and riot over the years, Bennett voiced "great confidence" in the warden and custodial staff. And, as he had announced after each escape over the years, he announced that the security setup would be tightened to make Alcatraz, uh, escapeproof. He remained unshaken in his belief that, though Alcatraz as an island prison had outlived its usefulness because of its "crumbling condition," Alcatraz as a penal concept was "the greatest deterrent against crime."

Several months after the Morris-plotted break, Attorney General Robert F. Kennedy came to San Francisco, and he too held a huge news conference. A reporter broached a subject that had long nettled newsmen, although no editor had ever thought to seek a remedy: "Sir, the Department of Justice apparently has competent people out here but why, when anything happens at Alcatraz, are they voiceless? At such times, why is it necessary for newspapers to go to the trouble and expense day after day of calling Washington to check out tips or other information? Have you, Sir, any proposals for correcting this problem?"

The young attorney general grinned. "Call collect."

Alcatraz, as a scientific stir secure against escape, had clearly failed. And as a place of punishment, not reformation? Again, failure. Joe Cretzer's second escape try, for example, had a cold-blooded brutality that his first lacked, five years earlier, when he docilely submitted to the advice of a trussed-up captain. As a fearsome threat to keep others in line? John K. Giles voiced a thought on this principle when the judge lengthened his term by three years for his escape attempt. The judge expressed a hope the added years would act as a deterrent to others, and Giles politely dissented: "I speak as an expert, Your Honor, and I know if you gave me a life term it wouldn't deter any escapers." He qualified as an expert: he had spent thirty of his fifty years behind bars, was a fugitive when picked up on a federal rap.

This experiment in penology, as Warden Johnston phrased it, also carried a high price tag. The cost as of June 1962, Bennett told Wallace Tower of *The New York Times,* was running $13.79 a day to keep a prisoner on Alcatraz, compared to a daily average of $5.37 in other federal prisons. Estimates on the upkeep of Alcatraz in the past have run even higher. In 1953 Senator William Langer, North Dakota Republican who had long favored abandonment of The Rock, told the Senate that Alcatraz convicts could be boarded cheaper at the Waldorf-Astoria. He said the island prison was then costing approximately $5,000,000 a year to operate and "on my last inspection trip, it had only 150 inmates." This would average $33,333.33 a year per prisoner, or slightly more than $91 a day.

Why did Alcatraz fail? Despite certain shortcomings, the men who ran it were for the most part conscientious. Former guards and convicts alike attest to Warden Madigan's decent instincts. Warden Johnston, who set up this penal lab, was known as a humanitarian for his work in ridding Folsom Prison of its medieval barbarities. Yet his own creation soon took on the aspect of medieval cruelty, refined in the mental torment of routine, raw in the physical brutality of the dungeon. Patently, it was the system itself that was its own under-mining agent.

At the very beginning, when the Department of Justice first dis-closed it had such a thing as Alcatraz in mind, responsible penologists spoke out in protests that proved prophetic. Commissioner William J. Ellis of New Jersey saw "grave danger . . . of cruelties and repressive measures." Commissioner Walter N. Thayer, Jr., of New York felt that "prison officials should be able to handle dangerous criminals by segregation within their own walls." Dr. A. Warren Stearns, Commis-sioner of Massachusetts, warned: "The history of the world if bespat-tered with stories of wretchedness and misery resulting from such concepts of the care of the criminal."

Four years after the laboratory of Alcatraz began turning out men in straitjackets, a writer, Anthony M. Turano, gave this appraisal: "France, following a recent report to the Chamber of Deputies urging that the infamous isolation system in Guiana be abolished as 'a noto-rious failure, inefficient from a penal point of view,' and a blot 'on the good name of France,' has stopped exporting its criminals to Devil's Island and vicinity.

"Nevertheless . . . the same discredited theories of criminology were pronounced valid in America. A medieval code of 'punishment and not reformation' was put in force; and the agents of justice proceeded to exemplify the general proposition that civilized society should stoop to the level of its lowest rat. . . . It is not easy to perceive the sociological wisdom of transforming convicted scoundrels into raving maniacs. Their summary execution would reflect more humanity and official dignity than the maintenance of a costly suite of torture chambers."[3]

(France stopped sending prisoners to Devil's Island in 1938, and the Free French Government abolished the penal colonies in French Guiana during World War II.)

In the 1950s, when the Bureau of Prisons sought funds from Congress for a substitute Alcatraz inland, two of the nation's top penologists, Harry Elmer Barnes and Negley K. Teeters, branding Alcatraz as the ultimate in "dead-end penology," wrote: "There were many misgivings among prison men about the advisability of creating such a bleak maximum-security facility. Their protests went unheeded and through the years the Federal Bureau of Prisons has been obliged to maintain it although its excessive expense as well as its basic philosophy of correctional treatment have never been justified. Alcatraz is a monument to the thesis that some criminals cannot be reformed and should be repressed and disciplined by absolute inflexibility. But today not even the Federal Bureau defends Alcatraz. Yet it contends that a new and more modern maximum-security plant is the answer to those relatively few inmates that defy discipline and order. All of our states must handle this type of criminal without the benefit of new construction especially designed for the 'rotten apples out of the barrel,' as Director James V. Bennett calls them. Alcatraz is no longer justifiable, but to erect a super-maximum-security prison in its place is highly debatable."[4]

---

[3] Anthony M. Turano described "America's Torture-Chamber" in the old *American Mercury*, September, 1938.

[4] The quote by Barnes and Teeters is from their *New Horizons in Criminology*, considered a bible in the field (Englewood Cliffs, N.J.: Prentice-Hall, Inc., 1959,

The bankrupt penal notion that gave rise to Alcatraz exacted a tragic toll over the years: the guards and convicts slain in revolts against its rigors, or efforts to escape them; the suicides, the self-mutilations, the men driven insane. Some of these horrors became known long after they occurred, in tips to newspapers; and this situation suggests that many others remain grim secrets of The Rock. For Alcatraz, a symbol of the Dark Ages, always operated on the theory that it was a principality unto itself, behind a veil thicker than the fogs that swirl through the Golden Gate. Even escapes, which San Francisco newspapers often learn about through their police-beat reporters, might not become known if the prison did not feel impelled to enlist the aid of the Coast Guard or the police. There's an inherent danger in such an operation: a government agency can conveniently cover up its incompetence, its mistakes; even, in the case of a prison, its brutalities. Ernest Besig, director of the American Civil Liberties Union of Northern California, comments: "When government officials operate in secrecy—when they do not have to account for their actions—they become immune to criticism. This is an invitation to mismanagement."

Why has Alcatraz stood so long? For years responsible critics and San Francisco civic groups have chipped at it, but The Rock held firm. Did the power structure of the Justice Department or public apathy preserve it? Both, very likely. The department let the storms blow over, and the average San Franciscan took a grim sort of pride in this marvel that every out-of-towner wished first of all to see. Blame must also be shared by the San Francisco news media and the news services for their willingness to accept only handouts regarding Alcatraz, and the secrecy, the no-comments, the half-truths, even the outright lies. A factor too was the bureau's view—a potent budgetary weapon—that Alcatraz was a "vital link," or in the words of Warden Swope: "There is always that small minority needing an Alcatraz."

To many, Bennett's adherence to this outdated philosophy has seemed a paradox. In recent years he has favored abandonment of

---

Third Edition). Bennett's views were set forth in *The Annals of The American Academy of Political and Social Science,* Volume 339, January, 1962.

the place—not of Alcatraz, the symbol, but of Alcatraz, the island—on the practical ground that it is "an administrative monstrosity." Yet, with the exception of this link in the San Francisco Bay, he created during his quarter-century tenure as head of the bureau a federal penal system that is considered a model. His own views, expressed in 1962, might well be taken as an indictment of Alcatraz: "What a society does with its convicted law-breakers reflects in large measure the philosophical underpinnings of its criminal law. In the United States, as in most other Western countries, the old doctrine that the purpose of the criminal law is to exact from the criminal a retributive suffering proportionate to the heinousness of the offense, if not completely discarded, has been fairly successfully dissipated. In its place, the administration of criminal justice has been searching for a more rational approach to the disposition of the convicted offender in an effort to combine the principles of deterrence and public protection with the objective of restoring the offender to a more self-sustaining status in the community."

Ironically, after all the decades of tumult over Alcatraz, the men who doomed The Rock were a burglar and a pair of sibling bank robbers. For soon after Morris and the Anglins crawled out—and the bureau's discovery why their feat was possible: the place was falling apart—Attorney General Kennedy announced that Alcatraz would be "phased out" during 1963. (The Department later set the closing date at July.) Theirs, then, became a farewell to The Rock with a wry double-entendre.

Kennedy, who in all his trips to San Francisco never visited the island (unless secretly), takes an economic view of Alcatraz. Discussing its abandonment, he said: "It would be a saving to the taxpayers because it's so much more expensive to feed prisoners there than at any other federal prison."

Later, Bennett said Alcatraz could start winding up its turbulent career as The Rock after completion of an Alcatraz Inland—a new, $10,000,000 maximum-security prison near Marion, Illinois, in a wildlife refuge in the southern tip of that state—in the spring of 1963. However, the phasing out of Alcatraz began quietly in the fall of 1962 as convicts were moved out in driblets. Warden Blackwell said they were being transferred to Leavenworth, Atlanta, Terre Haute, "and other prisons." This seemingly was a tacit admission that Alcatraz had, after all, harbored men of lesser criminal stature than the "nation's most hardened." Terre Haute is a medium-security prison.

The Veil

RESEARCHING THIS BOOK was in some ways more difficult than the trio's escape. They, at least, got through the thick concrete of The Rock. The stone wall of bureaucracy proved impenetrable.

At the outset, when I mentioned the project on the phone, Mr. Bennett, director of the Justice Department's Bureau of Prisons, said: "Fine, that's a dramatic story. Let us know when you're ready; we'll be glad to help."

With this encouragement, when ready I contacted Edwin A. Guthman, public-information director for the Justice Department. At his request, I wrote a letter detailing the scope of the book and my needs, among them a visit to Alcatraz to absorb atmosphere and interview guards and the convict West. There was no response. More phone calls; another letter. Still no response. I flew to Washington to plead my case.

Mr. Guthman said, "Bennett isn't very anxious to have you publish this book." But why, in view of his offer to help? "He's changed his mind." That meant no cooperation? "That's right. No cooperation."

A session with Mr. Bennett substantiated this. He could not permit a talk with West even for a background fill-in on the plot, and as for the guards: "I can't let you talk to guards and take up their time and waste taxpayers' money." Reminded of his offer to help, he said: "Oh, I thought you meant a mystery thriller!"

Mr. Bennett said he was not aware that West had spilled details of the plot, a fact already reported in the press. I saw his associate, Mr. Wilkinson, who said: "Yes, I talked to West, but he told me nothing I didn't already know." Oh . . . ?

It took ten weeks to get to Alcatraz. Warden Blackwell said he would show me "a little bit of the place." He was a man of his word.

There was no parting of the veil. I learned that on Saturday nights at the Officers' Club they hold square dances, but—What was Morris's job? "I have no idea." What did the Anglins do? "I have no idea."

Several former prosecutors said the West report should be available if no prosecution was planned, and they felt that was remote because of the difficulty of getting a jury to convict the man who didn't get away. Letters-to-the-editor sentiment was reflected in a *San Francisco Chronicle* editorial: "A large body of public sympathy (wearing a shamed face and expressing itself apologetically) has discovered itself in their behalf ever since they turned up missing in the steel-barred cells of the concrete cell block of the maximum-security prison on escapeproof Alcatraz. . . . If Morris and the brothers Anglin have in fact gotten away with it and stultified all the art, science and penological abracadabra that went into making Alcatraz 'escapeproof,' we offer them a silent cheer for having at last destroyed the myth of its inviolability."

A session with Cecil Poole, U.S. attorney in San Francisco, was encouraging. He also felt prosecution of West would be a wasted effort and suggested a call in two weeks. I happened to mention the segregation of black convicts, and he said: "I'm going to break that up!"

The call back brought an instant response: "I can't let you see that West report!"

"But you said prosecu—"

"I have six years to prosecute. That report's staying in the vault. Anyway, it belongs to the FBI, not me."

"What about the segregation at Alcatraz?"

"Look, I don't want any publicity on that. I'm going to handle it quietly, within the department."

It was quite clear by now that the department was a closed corporation.

By a long-established principle, the FBI never discusses a case in which it is engaged. One cannot quarrel with this policy, because it is based on the fact that the FBI is an investigative body. J. Edgar Hoover, FBI director, holds the position that information gathered by his agents should be evaluated by the judiciary.

However, the Bureau of Prisons is not an investigative body. It keeps men in detention, and the public is entitled to know in what manner. The bureau, either by design or delusion, mistakes its role for that of national security. Even so, at Alcatraz the secrecy has always been tighter than the security.

From quite a few confidential sources came the pertinent facts of the escape—the jobs Morris and the Anglins held, so convenient for their purposes; the tools and how they did, or could, acquire them; the hours they worked on the plot, and their methods; even to the fan motor that, after all the trouble of getting it up there, was shy a fraction or two of horsepower; the long, tedious task of removing the rivet heads of hand tools, and the professional burglar's caution that substituted painted-soap rivet heads in such an out-of-the-way spot.

All these, and more, were facts of the Morris plot. As it turned out, they provided not only a structural basis for that escape chapter but in addition a conclusion far more inescapable than Alcatraz: the veil of secrecy hid nothing mysterious, only incompetence.

J. Campbell Bruce
Berkeley, California
November 1962

Epilogue

THE ROCK IS ten years gone.

The escaped trio, eleven. And no more a maybe. Morris, the quiet loner, could slip into obscurity and stay there. Not the Anglins. Born braggarts, they could hardly be expected to sit forever on *that* feat. Silence seems evidence their cleaned bones lie beyond the Golden Gate, down among the whiter bones of Roe and Cole, first off The Rock.

On that present tense: the book was written in 1962. Alcatraz still had a family neighborhood, and some lad a paper route; guards still kept a wary eye in the gun towers; convicts still lived the long hours plotting; the warden still gave newsmen only the time of day, if asked. In a *New York Herald Tribune* review, John K. Hutchens took note of that tense, and the obvious reason, saying it imparted "the immediacy of the historical present tense." By then that's what it had become. (Publication date was announced for April 5, 1963. Two weeks earlier the last felons filed off Alcatraz, in handcuffs only, while television cameras rolled. And next day The Rock was a thing of the past.)

Now it can be told: how those convicts in D Block (see page 138) came by the razor blades to send down by the sewer-pipe dumb-waiter to the tendon cutters in the dark cells. Mr. Bennett, head of the Justice Department's Bureau of Prisons, had said in 1962 he could not shut down The Rock until he had a secure place to store the men—and the super-superbastille in Southern Illinois was far from ready. (It was completed in 1964.) That being so (presumably), *Escape from Alcatraz* would appear well before The Rock went out of business. My informant had my assurance the book would not reveal the secret of the smuggled blades, for disclosure would obviously halt the traffic—and deprive others of the opportunity to slice their heels. But the unkindest cut of all would be dealt the dealer in used blades, readily identifiable by the method of delivery. Within minutes after the warden's eye landed on the page, the smuggler would land in the Dark Hole—a candidate for his own, and now unobtainable, contraband.

How was it done? Quite slyly. With the easing of the D Block regimen went reading privileges for the men in the gate-front cells. The inmate on library duty made deliveries there—except to those in solitary. That meant close scrutiny—even closer after the cuttings began. The guard in D Block inspected the cart's contents, then tagged along. He could testify under oath, without perjury, that he saw only books or magazines passed through. Yet there was something else. A wink. It went with a book at a certain cell. And the bibliophile within, once they had moved on, opened the volume wide and shook well—and out of its spine fell a piece of blade. (One thin blade, broken lengthwise and the halves snapped in two, could supply four dark cells.)

The empty island was turned over to the General Services Administration for disposal as surplus property. John Hart, a big amiable man who had been a guard for fifteen years, and his wife Marie stayed on as caretakers. Their four children grew up on Alcatraz, and two daughters were married there. The Harts continued to get the *San Francisco Chronicle* every morning—dropped at their door (or thereabouts) by a helicopter on a commuter-hour traffic check for a radio station. They retired after the Indian invasion in the fall of 1969.

These were not the first Indians to scoff at the ancient myth that evil spirits dwelled on the island. In March of 1964 five Sioux, doubtless believing the evil dwellers had departed two years earlier, landed and staked a claim under an 1868 treaty giving their tribe the right to claim federal property "not used for specific purpose." This was not a seizure. They offered $5.64 for Alcatraz—47 cents an acre, the same price the Federal Government had agreed to pay California Indians for lands seized by the whites after the Gold Rush. The GSA ignored the claim, and they went away.

During the Sioux stay two men (white) planted a marker on the shore, then filed a placer mining claim to the island, calling it the

Embarrassing Mine. The Sioux said: "Let them remember General Custer." They remembered. But they had a day of limelight, for only $2.80, the filing fee.

The second invasion was in greater force (several hundred braves); of longer duration (a year and a half), and far more successful: it focused national attention on the plight of the Indian, who did hold rightful claim to the title of American Original. The GSA let time and hardship handle the situation. The Indians left a year later. They did spare the government the expense of wrecking many of the buildings, but some felt they might have spared the warden's big house on the cliff's edge across the road from the prison. A spectacular midnight blaze left it a charred shell, and destroyed the nearby living quarters of the Coast Guard lightkeepers. (An automatic light was later installed.)

Closing the problem island created a new problem: what to do with it? In the American bureaucratic tradition, studies were launched, even a $20,000 one to fix its worth. (Its worth: $2,178,000—$178,000 for the twelve acres, $2 million for the buildings. This was in 1964, when the place was still intact.) A President's Alcatraz Study Commission called for suggestions, and was almost blown away by the hurricane. Just about every use conceivable (and inconceivable) was proposed, except the one thing it finally became: part of a park.

Among the more notable proposals: a Statue of Liberty West; an anchor for a bridge to the north; a pleasure park after Copenhagen's Tivoli Gardens; a gambling casino; a cathedral; a college; an observatory; a round Parthenon, fifty feet high, with shops and restaurants in a wing-like roof; a refuge for seagulls (from the school children of Bird City, Kansas, pop. 678); a Sin City (no minors ashore); give it back to the pelicans (the pelicans weren't interested); a "nudist metropolis"; let tourists be "a convict for a day," for a fee (a Walt Disney thought); a 364-foot tower, Apollon, honoring the space program; an 800-foot parabolic arch of stainless steel, honoring the peoples of the world; a great globe of the world, 250 feet in diameter, circled by an olive wreath and resting on a pedestal of highrise buildings (by Buckminster Fuller of the geodesic dome); a vast hotel shaped like a horseshoe;

a vaster hotel and convention center accommodating 12,000 people; a shopping center. And the inevitable wag: "I think it'd make a good federal prison."

The Commission recommended a monument to commemorate the founding of the United Nations in San Francisco, which would serve "untold generations as an ennobling inspiration . . ." (They would raze the prison, though not as one person proposed; gradually, by the falling water of a jet roaring 500 feet above the fog.)

The studies, in the American bureaucratic tradition, went into the archives. Left to brood in its summer fogs, this isle of infamy, this American Devil's Island held ever greater fascination for sightseers, feeding dimes into binoculars at Fisherman's Wharf and up on Telegraph Hill. Then, last year, Congress created the 36,000-acre Golden Gate National Recreation Area—its smallest playground.

When Alcatraz was a pet project of the Department of Justice, people were threatened with machine-gun fire if they came too near. Now the National Park Service is in charge, and they can take a walking tour of the island, then a gawking tour of the silent cellhouse— even step into a cell of the Dark Hole, pull the steel door shut, and feel the skin prickle in the blackness.

J.C.B.
Berkeley
September 1973